Political Economy of Watershed Management

Political Economy of Watershed Management

Policies, Institutions, Implementation and Livelihoods

V. Ratna Reddy
M. Gopinath Reddy
John Soussan

Centre for Economic and Social Studies, Hyderabad

RAWAT PUBLICATIONS
Jaipur • New Delhi • Bangalore • Hyderabad • Guwahati

ISBN 81-316-0264-8

First Published, 2010

Published by
Prem Rawat for **Rawat Publications**
Satyam Apts, Sector 3, Jawahar Nagar, Jaipur 302 004 (India)
Phone: 0141 265 1748 / 7006 Fax: 0141 265 1748
E-mail: info@rawatbooks.com
Website: www.rawatbooks.com

New Delhi Office
4858/24, Ansari Road, Daryaganj, New Delhi 110 002
Phone: 011 2326 3290

Also at *Bangalore, Hyderabad* and *Guwahati*

Typeset by M & M Pre Press Consultants, Thiruvanthapuram
Printed at Chaman Enterprises, New Delhi

Contents

Foreword

Over the decades watershed development in India has been transformed from a purely soil and water conservation technology to a comprehensive programme for promoting sustainable rural livelihoods. Watershed development programme is among the flagship programmes for rural development in India. More than US$4 billion were spent on this programme by the central government alone since the beginning of the 8th Plan (1992). These allocations are being doubled during the 11th Plan period with enhanced per hectare investments. The complex nature of watershed development and management calls for a comprehensive understanding of the conditions under which watershed technology becomes economically viable, socially acceptable and ecologically sustainable in the long- run.

During the 1990s, watershed guidelines provided a definite design for participatory approach and livelihoods dimensions have been introduced to address the concerns of the landless in the new millennium. Several watershed-based programmes have taken shape following the new guidelines under the administrative control of Ministry of Rural Development, Government of India. States like Andhra Pradesh have been in the forefront in introducing innovative approaches like watershed-plus and incorporating rural livelihoods into the programme.

How far the policy guidelines have helped the implementation in general to improve the outcomes of watershed development programmes?

This book is among the most comprehensive studies that attempted to assess the impact of watershed development programme after its transformation into a participatory and livelihood oriented rural development programme. The important issues in this regard include the status of implementation of the programme, linkages between watershed development and crop production, impact of watershed on the livelihoods of the local communities, distribution of benefits from the watershed development to various sections of the community, sustainability of the benefits, role of project implementing agencies (PIAs), sustainability of the programme, etc. In order to include all these dimensions the book covers a wider canvas for generalizations in the policy context. The analysis is based on data collected from number of watersheds spread across different regions of Andhra Pradesh. Watersheds implemented by different project implementing agencies (GO and NGO) are chosen in order to examine the dichotomy between NGO and non-NGO implementation.

The book looks at the watershed development programme in a historical perspective and covers a number of important aspects. At the policy level, the authors identify some of the lacune like property rights issues and the linkages between property rights and collective action. Equity and property rights in natural resources are crucial for sustaining livelihoods in rainfed and resource poor regions. Failure to recognise the problems of inequity, especially in water, is fatal to the understanding the process of watershed management. The water and livelihood linkages are stronger in rainfed regions. Equity aspects are also important from the collective action point of view. In this context, access to water by the poor can only be guaranteed if property rights in groundwater are clearly defined.

The book emphasises that the approach towards watershed development programmes continues to be supply sided or target oriented to the neglect of demand side. The focus is mainly on extensive coverage by a number of watersheds rather than concentrating on exploiting the full potential of the technology, which requires an intensive approach. As a result, the long-run sustainability of the programme is at stake. Despite the emphasis on participatory process and building up social capital in the guidelines, only cursory attention is paid to this aspect. It is argued that the DPAP scheme is generally weakening and subverting the Panchayat structure - by creating parallel ad hoc and temporary village institutions (that are not statutory), which are receiving much more funds than the village Panchayat. They are actually extending the line agencies and their authority structure at the village level, rather than handing over authority to the Panchayats. It is clear that the political dimension is casting a long shadow over the potential developmental benefits. This ostensibly technical resource improvement programme is being opportunistically used to a greater or lesser extent in different locations by the prevailing political interests to promote the co-dependency and co-option of the village through financial patronage to particular political factions. Even some NGOs are getting co-opted and are sometimes resistant to the idea of strengthened village Panchayats, which might disrupt the cosy co-dependence they have established with villages on the basis of cash-based activities. Many of the shortcomings of the DPAP implementation in Andhra Pradesh reflect the political economy of power alliances both within the village and the various government structures.

The authors identify the livelihood impacts of watershed development programme using the sustainable rural livelihoods framework. The analysis brings out that WSM is necessary but not sufficient to sustain rural livelihoods in a wider context. But, WSM holds the potential for enhanced livelihood security even in the given geo-climatic conditions where it cannot bring direct irrigation benefits on a large scale. Moreover, distribution of these benefits is not egalitarian given the distorted agrarian structure and factor markets. Even the spillover or externality benefits like employment are extremely limited in the absence of significant improvement in irrigation. At the same time WSM is necessary in these fragile regions in order to strengthen the ecological base such as soil quality, water resources (including tanks), grazing lands, wastelands, etc.

In this context, WSM should not be viewed merely as a programme for income and employment generation for all sections of the population. In order to realise the full potential of watershed technology, pro-poor programmes that complement the benefits of WSM need to be introduced. These programmes include: horticultural and dairy development that would benefit from the improved resource conditions like *in situ* moisture, grazing lands, water bodies, etc. Households, in fact, seem to prefer these activities in the context of an improved resource base. Though some of these activities were already introduced in some cases, their success is dependent on infrastructure (transport, storage, markets, etc.) and credit (institutional finance) support systems apart from a policy environment that is propitious for institutional (collective systems, self-help groups, etc) evolution and development. In the absence of an integrated view on resources-infrastructure-institutions-livelihoods, these programmes may not fulfil the objective of sustainable rural livelihoods. Even the success of non-farm activities like petty business, services, etc., (often seen as an alternative to rural development) critically hinges upon the overall improvements in the rural livelihoods (effective demand).

The authors conclude that watersheds development will have a range of impacts, but these are not equally effective in terms of equity (with the better-off benefiting more) or sustainable livelihoods development.

The institutional framework presented in this book stresses the importance of policy and political environments for institutional innovation and sustainability, even though not focused on how these policy changes could be brought about. This framework distinguishes CPR situations with differential institutional capabilities and thus facilitates better targeting of policies. Assessment of institutional capabilities has to be made an important input for policy formulation. Political economy aspects along with cost-benefit aspects are of prime importance for institutional innovation and change. While costs and benefits determine the potential for institutional innovation, the actual creation of institutional arrangements is critically linked with political economy aspects. Creation of policy environment for institutional arrangements is more important than direct imposition of institutions. There is a greater need to recognise the role of external forces, like NGOs, as catalytic factors promoting institutional arrangements through leadership from within the community. The policy environment should facilitate their role. The grassroots level success and effectiveness of development policy largely depends on the synergy between the government and NGOs.

1 June 2009 **C.H. Hanumantha Rao**

Centre for Economic and Social Studies
Hyderabad

Preface

It is now well established fact that the Watershed Development Programme (WSP) is one of the important strategies in the dryland and fragile regions for promoting pro poor rural livelihoods. Unlike conventional strategies such as soil, land and water conservation, which were piecemeal and ad hoc approaches, Watershed Development Programme in its present form (post-1994 guidelines) is more holistic and address both area specific and people specific needs. It is this approach that makes WSP as unique in the dryland context. In this book an attempt has been made to understand WSP and its dynamics in transforming resource base of the dryland regions and its impact on livelihood conditions of the communities both directly and indirectly.

The empirical base for this research comes from our extensive research in various parts of Andhra Pradesh for the past seven years. Andhra Pradesh, as the first state to integrate and adopt sustainable rural livelihoods in WSD under the Andhra Pradesh Rural Livelihoods Programme, provides the background for assessing the rural livelihoods in the WSD context. Intensive fieldwork was carried out in fifteen villages spread over five districts located in Coastal, Rayalaseema and Telangana regions of Andhra Pradesh. Besides, visits to number of watershed villages in various mandals across the sample districts were used for the purpose of validation and cross checking our findings in the sample villages where we have conducted the intensive study.

The book is culmination of the three research projects related to WSP carried out by the authors in collaboration with research institutions and Government of Andhra Pradesh. In this context mention may be made to the study "Livelihoods Based Watershed Development: A Policy Action Research" undertaken in collaboration with the University of Leeds, UK (financially supported from DFID, UK) and APRLP (Andhra Pradesh Rural Livelihoods Programme of the Government of AP) followed by the phase two study supported by DFID, UK through The Stockholm Environment Institute, UK. Dr. Oliver Springate of the University of East Anglia and Y. V. Malla Reddy of RDT owe our deep gratitudes for their significant contributions in the development of this book. We are also thankful to DFID, UK and the APRLP, Hyderabad, India for providing financial support for these studies. Our special thanks are due to Mr. S. P. Tucker, CEO, APRLP for providing the flatform for 'Policy, Action-Research Interphase'.

Number of people have contributed in the process of bringing the book in its present form. Prof. Ch. Hanumantha Rao, former Chairman and Founder Member of CESS has provided critical comments and suggestions at various stages of our work. We express our gratitude for his constructive support and also for writing 'Foreward' to the book. We are grateful to Prof. S. Mahendra Dev, ex-Director of CESS and Prof. Manoj Panda, present Director of CESS for their support in bringing out this book. We also thank our colleagues Prof. S. Galab, and Dr. M. Srinivasa Reddy, Prof. V. N. Reddy for their critical inputs at various stages of our work. Mr. Sanjit Rout and Mr. Madhusudhan Bandi, research scholars have gone through the earlier drafts and making necessary corrections in the proofs. Without their generous help and hardwork, the book would not have reached the present shape. We gratefully acknowledge their help. The authors would also like to thank Mr. B. Sreedhar for his efficient typing of numerous drafts of the manuscript.

Earlier versions of the chapters in the book were published, sometimes in a different form, in various academic journals. These include *Development and Change, Economic and Political Weekly, Indian Journal of Agricultural Economics*, etc. Their rigorous review process has helped refining the analysis and arguments and we are thankful to them. Similarly, some of the chapters were presented in various seminars in India and abroad and benefited from the discussions.

The financial assistance provided by Jamsetji Tata Trust (JSTT) under RULNR – CESS Research Programme made this book possible and we gratefully acknowledge this gesture from the JSTT.

CESS library and Mr. Vijaya Kumar, Librarian provided good resource material that was helpful in the completion of the book. We owe our sincere thanks to them.

1

Introduction

Efficient and sustainable use of natural resources is *sine qua non* for economic development, especially in the resource-poor countries. More so in the agriculturally dominant economies like India where more than 50 percent of the cropped area is dependent on rainfall without any alternative irrigation facilities. Rainfed agriculture has been the victim of long neglect on the policy front. This neglect is mainly due to the concentration of public resources in the well-endowed regions for meeting the country's food requirements through irrigation development and green revolution technologies, which are complementary. Rainfed regions, which account for more than 50 percent of the cultivable land and 40 percent of the population, house a large share of the poor, food insecure and vulnerable populations in the country. Moreover, as productivity growth in the more favoured green revolution areas is already showing signs of slowing down or stagnation (Pingali and Rosegrant, 2001), future growth in agricultural production and food security is likely to depend on improving the productivity in the semi-arid and arid rainfed areas. There is also some evidence indicating that marginal returns to investments would be substantially higher in these regions when compared to the irrigated regions where potentials for productivity growth have been exploited through the green revolution technologies (Fan and Hazell, 2000).

While the policy bias, resulting in intensive agricultural practices, has paid off in terms of meeting the country's food demands in the short run, it proved to be unsustainable economically as well as environmentally in the long run. This, coupled with the limited scope for expanding irrigation (through traditional methods of damming the rivers), has prompted the policy shift towards rainfed land agriculture. Though recent policies failed to address the problems of irrigated agriculture through improving the allocative efficiency of crucial inputs like water, concerted efforts are being made towards improving the conditions of the rainfed farming. For, development of these regions, in terms of enhancing the crop yields, holds the key for future food security. Besides, these regions are increasingly being confronted with environmental problems such as wind and soil erosion. In fact, it is feared that the intensity of resource degradation is reaching irreversible levels in some of these regions. Promotion of appropriate technologies and development strategies in these regions would result in multiple benefits, such as (i) ensuring food security, (ii) enhancing the viability of farming, and (iii) restoring the ecological balance. In fact, about 15 percent of India's 329 million hectares of geographical area is already degraded (Reddy, 2000).

In recognition of the socio-economic and environmental benefits, India has one of the largest micro-watershed development (WSD) programmes in the world. An amount above Rs. 2,300 crores (US $ 600 million) is being spent annually through various projects supported by the government, NGOs and bilateral funds (Table 1.1). These allocations are expected to be doubled (crossing Rs. 1,000 crore or US$1 billion) during the 11th Five-Year Plan period with enhanced per hectare investments.[1] A 'watershed' is a topographically delineated area

Table 1.1 *Area Treated and Investment in Watershed Programmes in India*

Programmes	*Up to end of 8th Plan*		*During 9th Plan*		*During 10th Plan till March 2005*		*Total (till March 2005)*	
	Area (mha)	*Investment* (Rs. crore)	*Area* (mha)	*Investment* (Rs. crore)	*Area* (mha)	*Investment* (Rs. crore)	*Area* (mha)	*Investment* (Rs. crore)
I. Ministry ofAgriculture								
(a) National Watershed Development Project for Rainfed Areas (NWDPRA)	4.22	967.93	2.77	911.01	0.96	519.82	7.95	2398.76
(b) River Valley Project (RVP) and Flood-Prone Regions (FPR)	3.89	819.95	1.60	696.26	0.60	377.91	6.09	1894.12
(c) Watershed Development Project in Shifting Cultivation Areas (WSDSCA)	0.07	93.73	0.15	82.01	0.06	60.61	0.28	236.35
(d) Alkali Soils	0.48	62.29			0.08	20.25	0.56	82.54
(e) Externally Aided Project (EAP)	1.00	646.00	0.50	1425.01	0.86	2685.25	2.36	4756.26
Sub-Total	9.66	2589.90	5.02	3114.29	2.56	3663.84	17.24	9368.03
II. Department of Land Resources (MoRD)								
(a) Drought Prone Areas Programme (DPAP)	6.86	1109.95	4.49	668.26	3.78	845.19	15.13	2623.40

Table 1.1 (*contd.*)

Table 1.1 (*contd.*)

Programmes	*Up to end of 8th Plan*		*During 9th Plan*		*During 10th Plan till March 2005*		*Total (till March 2005)*	
	Area (mha)	*Investment* (Rs. crore)	*Area* (mha)	*Investment* (Rs. crore)	*Area* (mha)	*Investment* (Rs. crore)	*Area* (mha)	*Investment* (Rs. crore)
(b) Desert Development Programme (DDP)	0.85	722.79	2.48	519.80	2.38	615.19	5.71	1857.78
(c) Integrated Watershed Development Programme (IWDP)	0.28	216.16	3.58	943.88	2.46	1001.77	6.32	2161.81
(d) Externally Aided Project (EAP)			0.14	18.39	0.22	194.28	0.36	212.67
Sub-Total	7.99	2048.90	10.69	2150.33	8.84	2656.43	27.52	6855.66
III. Ministry of Environmental & Forests (MoEF)								
(a) Integrated Afforestation & Eco-Development Projects Scheme(IAEPS)	0.30	203.12	0.12	141.54	0.40	469.07	0.82	813.73
Grand Total	17.95	4841.92	15.83	5406.16	11.80	6789.34	45.58	17037.42

Source: MoRD (2006).

that is drained by a stream system. It is a hydrologic unit that has been described and used both as a physico-biological unit and as a socio-economic and socio-political unit for planning and implementing resource management activities. Watershed development is a land-based technology that would help conserve and improve *in situ* soil moisture, check soil erosion and improved water resources, especially groundwater in the rainfed regions. Watershed simply means improving the management of a watershed or rainfall catchments area, for instance, by building contour bunds, water harvesting structures (check-dams), field *bunds* (raised edges), etc. It facilitates higher land productivity through improved overall ecological conditions such as moisture and water availability for agriculture. It deals with adoption of watershed technologies in specific watersheds.

Though the terms 'watershed development' and 'watershed management' are often treated as synonyms, we prefer to distinguish watershed development from watershed management. While the former could be treated as purely technical, the later is broader as it concerns with both technical as well as non-technical aspects of resource management. The concept of watershed development involves planning the development of a resource region. Resource region incorporates the private property as well as common property regimes and therefore the conflicts in resource sharing and use are quite natural without proper property rights, social and institutional frameworks. The approach of watershed management ought to be holistic and integrated involving hydrological, biophysical and sociological systems. Often adoption of watershed technologies requires collective or cooperative strategies among individual households and communities as watersheds cover large areas of private and public lands. People's participation, thus, is recognised as a key factor in effective implementation of the watershed development programme. Hence, managing people for effective adoption of technology comes under the purview of watershed management and forms the core of this book.

In recent years participatory watershed management has become a central focus for rural development in India leading to massive injections of resources. Participatory watershed management is a complex issue, embracing the technical complexities of the resource itself, socio-economic complexities of the different livelihoods of local households and of political complexities regarding the collective action necessary for effective and equitable planning, implementation, maintenance and benefit sharing. For instance, the complexities of the resource stem from groundwater being by its nature a common pool resource, yet used as a private resource complementing private agricultural production. Improving the groundwater resource availability, through measures such as check-dams or through improving other common pool resources such as forests, has a differentiated impact on private production, dependent on the local hydrology, the pattern of land ownership and the extraction practices.

Collective action is a prerequisite if local priorities are to be served by the watershed management activities, and so adds the third dimension of complexity to the mix. Collective action is valuable to obtain local community inputs into planning the interventions and for supporting implementation, maintenance, and regulating the equitable distribution of benefits. In fact, collective action is critical for successful implementation and sustainable management of watersheds in the medium and long runs. Watersheds transcend households, communities and even villages, and so their sustainable development is critically linked with both inter-household and inter-village cooperation. Collective action is also a prerequisite for integrating the sustainable livelihoods approach with watershed development. Participatory watershed management is certainly found to be more effective when compared to the watersheds where people's participation is either passive or absent. A widely held and endorsed view is that people's participation is more widespread in the watersheds implemented and managed by non-governmental organisations (NGOs). But such instances are small in scale, and can only be expanded by repeating the same slow, costly, in-depth techniques (Farrington and Lobo, 1997; Knox, Swallow and Johnson, 2001). Maintaining the intensiveness of inputs required has become the main bottleneck for scaling up of the programme across India. Ad-hoc scaling up in a targeted fashion is neither effective nor sustainable. On the other hand, one is not sure whether the criticality of NGOs in successful implementation of watersheds can be generalised.

Another aspect that is observed to be important for effective people's participation in watershed management is the equitable access to and rights in resources. Property rights over natural resources are fundamental in shaping the livelihoods of rural poor. Rural poor are often found to possess the weakest property rights, such as secure rights over land, water, trees, livestock, fish, genetic resources, etc. On the other hand, it is argued that most of the poor find themselves in poverty not due to the absence of property rights, but due to their inability to assert or change them through collective action. In most of the cases the existing property rights that are embedded in political economy systems are biased against poor. Hence, collective action or social mobilisation is an important channel for asserting the rights of the poor. Collective action to alleviate poverty may be seen as a desperate effort by the extremely marginalised members of the society to secure for themselves what the wider political economy system has failed to provide for them (Bromley, 2004). Collective action could lead to poverty alleviation not only through asserting or changing rights over natural resources like land, water, etc., but also through asserting their right to information, share in the developmental programmes, etc.

Though, there is consensus regarding the role and importance of property rights and collective action in poverty alleviation, their importance, effectiveness and relative strengths in varying resource, socio-economic and political situations is less understood. Besides, there is no clarity regarding the linkages or synergy between property rights and collective action. These two are often treated as mutually exclusive, rather than mutually inclusive or complementary. How necessary and sufficient the conditions of property rights and collective action in poverty alleviation? Can either of them or both of them ameliorate poverty? If so, under what socio-economic and political situations?

These complexities are further compounded where the participatory approach addresses livelihood issues of all the rural households. While watershed development relies on the application of land-based technologies and directly helps those dependent on agriculture for their livelihoods, sustainable rural livelihoods (SRL) approach focuses on both the landed and landless poor. While watershed development is viewed as a viable technological option for improving agricultural production in rainfed and drought prone regions, the SRL approach has a more complementary aim of poverty alleviation and eradication. There is a need to integrate these two approaches in the drought-prone regions rather than treating them independently. The challenge lies in promoting sustainable livelihoods through watershed management. The policy process to support this must be dynamic and flexible, especially in the initial stages. There is as yet a lack of clarity on how to integrate SRL approach with the watershed management approach. Of late, there have been concerted efforts to integrate the SRL approach into policy making,[2] and although the SRL approach has become popular only in recent years, operationalising it in practice has so far proved difficult (Shankland, 2000). Keeping these complexities in view, this book concerns with the processes of watershed development and management at various levels and impacts.

Focal Issues

The overriding challenge for achieving SRL through participatory watershed management is firstly to identify successful models and secondly to find means for effective scaling up through appropriate policy design, tuned to the specific demands of the community. Associated with this second point is the need also to enhance the potential of the implementing agencies. The complex nature of watershed management calls for a comprehensive understanding of the conditions under which watershed development is economically and technology viable, ecologically sustainable, and socially equitable and acceptable in the long run. Hitherto the literature on watershed management has concentrated mainly on the technical and economic aspects of the programme. Though most studies make a cursory statement at the end that people's participation is essential for sustainable watershed development/management, few authors have attempted to analyse the process of collective action, either theoretically or empirically. As a result, people's participation in watershed management has remained poorly conceptualised even in policy formulations, and in consequence adoption and success rates have been low.

The new watershed guidelines known as the 'Hanumantha Rao Guidelines' released in 1995 provide a definite design for a participatory approach. The people-centred approach of the new guidelines brings it closer to the SRL approach and hence makes integration of both approaches possible (Turton, 2000; Baumann, 2000). A number of watershed-based programmes have been promoted following the new guidelines under the administrative control of Ministry of Rural Development, Government of India. While the physical action of watershed development (e.g., building check-dams and so on) is associated with technical issues, participatory watershed management (deciding where to build and how to maintain structures) demands engaging in subjective 'process-oriented' approaches to social mobilisation and intergroup planning and negotiation. This cannot be treated simply as a technical problem (as some agencies have found to their cost). While the technological success of watershed development is well established, the reorientation required by implementing agencies towards the philosophy of participation in watershed management is proving to be the main bottleneck for the widespread success of the programme.

Watersheds have been studied from various perspectives, such as economic efficiency of water use and investments, flood run-off, soil erosion, sedimentation, groundwater recharge, socio-political dimensions (Dixon, 1992). Understanding the interactions between land, water and people is equally important in studying watersheds. Given the nature of the technology, watershed management involves working across large areas covering numerous households and even villages for its adoption. Hence, technology adoption and success critically hinges upon inter-village as well as intra-village cooperation. In other words, collective participation and action is a critical ingredient for watershed management. This throws up a wide range of issues, such as social organisation and property rights that need a careful scrutiny in order to sustain the programme. The issue of property rights arises when dealing with the treatment of common lands.

In order to ensure equitable distribution of benefits from improved natural resource base or common pool resources, there needs to be effective property rights regime and regulatory structures. This has so far proved difficult because in practice access to common resurces is open and free for all in majority of the cases. This is unlike the situation in countries, such as South Africa, where landowners do not have automatic property rights to commons, such as sub-surface water. Although legislations have recently been introduced in a number of states to check overexploitation of groundwater, there remains no restriction on how much of the common property sub-surface water is 'privatised' through pumping onto private land. The only effective control is electricity power restriction, but this can be circumvented through using diesel power. On the other hand, many states have resorted to providing free power to farmers for the sake of political gains.

Social organisation, its equitability and sustainability, links to questions of allocation of property rights and the distribution of benefits across different sections of the community. Whether property rights are clearly defined and equitably distributed is more important rather than who has the rights individuals or groups. Unless property rights are defined clearly and equitably, it is difficult to ensure sustainable resource management even under community or participatory management. Allocation of rights and distribution of costs and benefits are the most important among the rules and regulations in managing the commons. These distributional aspects are important and affect the monitoring costs to a large extent. If solved to the satisfaction of all socio-economic communities in the group, they would reduce the costs of monitoring. For, free rider attitudes are more prevalent under institutional arrangements where costs and benefits are distributed unequally across households. Those who are on the other extreme (deriving least benefits) tend to assert their use rights inappropriately, such as encroaching. That is, when people view an established system as inequitable according to established social standards, they have incentives to undermine it (Hanna, 1996). For instance, grazing restrictions go against the interests of herders while they benefit the landholders (Reddy, 2000; Turton, 2000). On the contrary, small and marginal farmers tend to benefit from restrictions on groundwater exploitation while large farmers loose (Reddy, 2000). Such contradictions often result in non-cooperative behaviour among communities and hence need to be addressed in order to sustain collective action.

Sustainable watershed management calls for participation of the whole community, which requires sharing of costs and benefits in a fairly equitable manner. Participatory watershed management implies a fundamental concern for ensuring equity in benefits. While the new guidelines emphasise the involvement of all sections of the community, watershed development by itself does not guarantee the distribution of benefit flows across the communities. For, watershed is a land-based technology and hence most of the benefits accrue to landed – particularly those best placed to pump the increased groundwater – likely to be those who have land in the valley, rather than the ridge. Though landless households are expected to benefit to some extent through labour opportunities and so on, the type and magnitude of benefits accruing them are poorly understood.

Since the watershed (officially limited to 500 hectares by the guidelines) does not usually cover the entire village lands, this inevitably leaves a section of dissatisfied households. Unless benefits accruing to this section of the community are substantial in economic terms, it is unlikely that they will participate or evince any interest in the programme. In the absence of such benefits, their apathy towards the programme might jeopardise the sustainability of the programme.

Sustainable Rural Livelihoods Framework[3]

SRL approaches have recently been popularised by international development agencies and donors as an analytical tool to facilitate poverty alleviation interventions. The recasting of the household as the central focus for analysis helps prioritise interventions, which serve their developmental priorities. The analysis of livelihoods has its roots in peasant studies of Chayanov, and later evolved through farming system studies of the 1960s, farm management studies and a wide range of micro-economic studies over the last thirty years. The linked notions of access to resources, income opportunities and access qualifications were developed in the 1980s, and quantitatively modelled as an iterative decision-making model (Blaikie et al., 1979, 1985, 1994). Sen's seminal work on entitlements (1982) and later on functioning and capabilities (1985) added conceptual power to these earlier versions.

Contemporary modelling of livelihood processes has been marked by a convergence of various approaches. Carney et al. (1999) demonstrate the similarity of four of the leading institutional proponents of the livelihoods approach. They all rely on a core set of concepts very similar to the access, access qualification and income opportunity models of the 1980s. But they also incorporate substantial new material. Some emphasise the importance of security of basic needs (CARE in Carney, 1999), whilst DFID focus on the drawing down and use of five different types of capital.

There are many different definitions of livelihoods. Carney (1998) presents one based on the work of Robert Chambers and Gordon Conway (1992):

> A livelihood comprises the capabilities, assets (including both material and social resources) and activities required for a means of living. A livelihood is sustainable when it can cope with and recover from stresses and shocks and maintain or enhance its capabilities and assets both now and in the future, while not undermining the natural resource base.

In the aptly titled 'Adaptable Livelihoods', Davies (1996) provides a detailed understanding of the dynamics of the livelihoods of the poor in relation to food, as they respond to highly variable conditions (natural and human) that confront them. Davies' conceptual framework is based on five key ideas, which can also be expanded to broader issues of sustainable livelihoods: (i) *Livelihood systems* and security within them, encompassing a broader range of factors than household food systems and security to explain how and why producers pursue particular mixes of strategies to confront food insecurity. (ii) *Entitlements* to explain different sources of food and the range of calls on them within households and livelihood systems. (iii) *Vulnerability* to explain the nature and intensity of food and livelihood insecurity. (iv) *Resilience and sensitivity*, useful in analysing changes in levels and intensity of vulnerability to food insecurity within different livelihood systems. (v) *Livelihood system diversity* to account for variation in the nature and intensity of vulnerability, depending on different ways in which people acquire access to food.

Whilst developed for the analysis of food security issues in the Sahel, these concepts have generic applicability and are useful in livelihood analyses. Davies goes on to emphasise, in the context of food security, the need to pay particular attention to the micro-level analysis of the household. This characterises livelihood approaches as a whole: they are focused on the household as the basic unit of analysis and build from that starting point to integrate the household into other levels within and beyond the local community. The development of a livelihood approach is presented with the same challenges and opportunities as it seeks to create both a coherent conceptual framework and practical tools that will empower the poor to control their own lives. The approach represents an attempt to introduce some joined up thinking into development through stimulating more profound analysis and a more holistic approach to both understanding what we are trying to achieve and how we are to achieve it. This is focused on trying to understand what are the keys to improving the control of poor households over critical decisions and key assets, including through reducing the effects of factors that make their livelihoods vulnerable to disruption.

This does not mean that the analysis should be restricted in any sense to the household level: indeed, one of the potential powers of a livelihood approach is that it is capable of linking, in a systematic and analytical way, different levels from the local to the global (Scoones, 1998; Soussan, 2000). Defining what needs to be done where and when is challenging: not everything can, or indeed should, be done at once, but the priorities set and choices made need to be based on a conceptual approach that is both rigorous and accessible. The decision-making process through which these choices are made and realised also needs to be transparent, legitimate and effective, and be made through institutions that share these characteristics. This in turn means that the analysis must be able to encompass and, ultimately, influence institutional structures and processes that, as the link between levels, are the principal channel that external interventions to the dynamics of livelihoods development.

Rennie and Singh (1996) provide an outline of an SRL approach for field project development. They stress that this should not be an esoteric exercise, but an analytically powerful contribution to policy for improving the position of the poor. They argue that: "Livelihoods is a more tangible concept than 'development', easier to discuss, observe, describe and even quantify" (Rennie and Singh, 1996: 16). They stress the importance of going beyond livelihoods at a conceptual level to identify robust research and implementation methodologies for field projects. This is considered an essential step, and in many ways perhaps the most challenging. If the linkage between livelihood processes and policy is not made, both conceptually and in practice, then, the exercise will indeed become another esoteric exercise. They go on to argue that:

> Predominantly, the poor of the world depend directly on natural resources, through cultivation, herding, collecting or hunting for their livelihoods. Therefore, for the livelihoods to be sustainable, the natural resources must be sustained (Rennie and Singh, 1996: 16).

Although not universal, this contention is undoubtedly true for many of the rural poor. Addressing the role of natural resources is therefore critical for any livelihood model. Watershed-centred approach of achieving sustainable livelihoods and poverty alleviation is rather logical in this context. This study will pay particular attention to the issue of the sustainability and the access of the poor to natural capital, as it is a key area in both the lives of the poor and active policy development in rainfed regions.

This aspect of livelihoods cannot be seen in isolation, however, as access to and the use of natural capital is linked to other aspects of the livelihoods of the poor. Many policies and programmes concerning natural resources do not make these links, focusing on the management of the resources to the exclusion of other issues (much the same is true for policies concerned with other livelihood assets such as education or credit). The analysis of any one of these issues consequently needs to retain a focus on the scope of the policy, as it exists whilst at the same time making sure that this analysis is placed in a context that allows the links to other aspects of livelihoods to be made. Achieving this balance is one of the central goals of the model adopted here. It looks at the basic dynamics of livelihoods, something that is inevitably complex given the array of the factors that influence livelihood choices. Within this complexity, however, is a simple core set of contentions and relationships. These are summarised here and are further elaborated in the explanation of the model.

People draw on a set of *capital assets* as a basis for their livelihoods. Carney (1998) identifies five capitals, namely, human, natural, financial, physical and social. These are defined as:

- *Human capital:* Skills, knowledge, ability to labour and good health and physical capabilities important for pursuing livelihoods. At the formal level these include health, education, training, etc.
- *Natural capital:* Natural resource stocks like soil, water, air, genetic resources, etc. and environmental services such as hydrological cycle, pollution sinks, etc., which form the basis for deriving livelihoods.
- *Financial capital:* The capital base like cash, credit/debit, savings and other economic assets including basic infrastructure and production equipment and technologies, which are essential for pursuing livelihoods.
- *Physical capital:* The basic and common infrastructure such as roads, connectivity and other physical assests owned at the community level.
- *Social capital:* Social resources, such as networks, social claims, social relations, affiliations, associations, etc., which help people to overcome risks, uncertainities, shocks and vulnerabilities, and livelihood pursuits that require coordinated actions.

Of late, *political capital* is also gaining exclusive importance (Baumann, 2000) while here social capital is inclusive of political capital. The capitals available to individual households reflect their ability to gain access to systems (the resource base, the financial system, society) through which these are produced. As such, we can identify the *access profile* of households that defines their ability to gain access to capital assets.

Livelihoods are built from a series of choices over the use of these assets. This decision-making process can be seen as a *livelihood strategy*, and although it is a continuous process there are always key decision-making points, sometimes regular and seasonal, and sometimes occasional and unexpected. Others are reactive (selling livestock during a drought), some have a 'constitutional' character (who is involved in which decisions) whilst others are major, structural decisions that can re-define the whole nature of the livelihood (moving to the city or setting up a business).

Based on the choices made, members of the household will undertake a series of *livelihood activities,* such as growing a crop, fishing in a lake, working for someone else or making pots. Some activities may be dominant, but it is rare for a household to rely exclusively on one source of livelihood and most combine complex sets of activities. These activities are intuitively the most familiar dimension of livelihoods to people and have been the focus of many development efforts in the past. It is essential that they should be clearly represented in any analysis of livelihoods.

These activities will generate 'income' for the household: goods, services and cash. This is then allocated in four main directions: re-circulated as *inputs* into livelihood activities; *social payment*: taxes, interest on loans; *invested* to maintain or enhance the livelihood assets; or *consumed*: food, housing, clothes and all the other goods and services that contribute to the material quality of life of the household.

Many *local and external factors* that influence livelihoods include markets, the physical environment and the social and political environment. These features are themselves inherently dynamic and livelihoods are *vulnerable* to the shocks (sudden changes of state) and trends in these factors. The impact of these external shocks and trends will vary from household to household. Some are more sensitive to their influence, while others are better able to absorb their impact or respond to the opportunities they may offer. The character of these external forces represents the *vulnerability context* within which the livelihood systems of different households develop, whilst the ability of households to cope is their *resilience* in the light of these vulnerabilities.

The Livelihood Model

The goal of the model presented here (Figure 1.1) is to provide a clear conceptual framework for tracing the interconnections between the different aspects of people's livelihoods and the factors that influence them. Recognising and understanding the dynamics of the livelihoods process is fundamental for any analysis of the factors such as security, vulnerability, resilience and sensitivity identified above. These all relate to processes of change to the conditions in which people's livelihoods operate and the response of livelihoods to these changes. The structure of people's livelihoods (and in particular the strength and diversity of their livelihood assets) varies greatly, as do the effects of external influences upon them. The key objective of the model is to provide a structure for understanding these dynamics and diversity.

Livelihoods are complex. This may seem obvious, but it gives the lie to the assumption that less developed implies 'simple'. Indeed, many rural livelihoods in the South are far more complicated than in industrialised countries where one main income stream from formal employment, with fixed working hours and a known level of remuneration, is more the norm. It also has policy implications and suggests that pro-poor policy initiatives cannot be expected to have impacts that are predictable and easily aggregated across a diverse range of households and

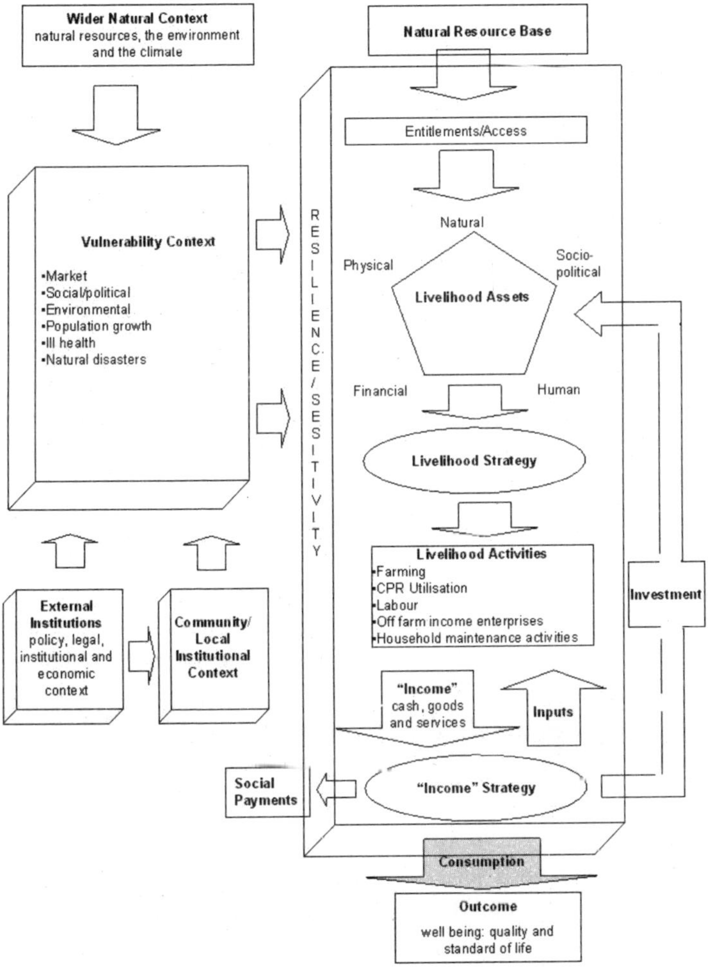

Figure 1.1 The Livelihoods Model

strategies. There is an increasing recognition that the livelihoods of people (and especially households) in the developing world are based around a wide range of activities: people are not just farmers, or labourers, or factory workers, or fisherfolk. Most families base their livelihoods around complex strategies that seek to maximise the use of the bundle of resources accessible to them: "rural families increasingly come to resemble miniature highly diversified conglomerates" (Cain and McNicoll, 1988; quoted in Ellis, 1998).

As stated earlier, livelihoods are also influenced by a wide range of external forces, both within and outside the locality in which a household lives, which are beyond the control of the family. These include the social, economic, political, legal, environmental and institutional dynamics of their local area, the wider region, their country and, increasingly, the world as a whole. We live in an era of increasing globalisation. All, including people living in the remotest parts of the developing world, experience its effects. These external factors are critical in defining the basic structure and the operation of livelihood systems. For example, land tenure laws are crucial in determining entitlements, and in consequence access to land for cultivation, which in turn is a critical determinant of the overall structure of livelihoods in rural areas, whilst prices and price variability is critical (for some crops) in determining what will be grown on that land in any particular season.

These external forces are themselves not static. It is their dynamics, the processes of change in the wider economic, social and natural environment, which create the conditions in which livelihoods change. It was noted above that these changes could be long-term trends (e.g., changing attitudes to gender roles in a society or the gradual decline in groundwater stocks in a lake) or sudden shocks (e.g., the impact of a war, a drought or a collapse of market prices for a key crop). Taken together, the threat of external shocks and trends directly affects the decision-making environment and the outcomes of livelihoods, and provides the *vulnerability context*. Of course, not all of the many different factors that need to be considered have an impact at any one time, and indeed the influence of some can be marginal at best most of the time. What is essential is that any analysis of livelihoods processes takes them into account in a systematic manner.

In general, the more affluent and asset-rich a household is, the more options it possesses in the face of shocks, and therefore, the more resilient it is to disruption in its livelihoods base. Indeed, in a livelihood context, this statement may seem tautologous in that vulnerability is both a condition of and a determinant of poverty. However, in a dynamic context, this is not so. The 'ratchet effect' (Spitz, 1979 cited in Sousson, J. et al., 2000) is a particular dynamic of the reproduction of poverty, in which the impoverishing impacts of shocks on the already vulnerable lessen their ability to plan for and withstand further shocks. Attention will be directed to strategies of the poor to avoid or palliate these shocks both *ex ante* as risk minimisation strategies, and *ex post* as survival, or coping strategies.

Rennie and Singh (1996) also identify the responses of such threats as either adaptive strategies (where a household consciously adopts a process of change in response to long-term trends) or coping strategies (short-term responses to immediate shocks and stresses). In these, the household will seek to deploy their different assets to best effect within their often-limited range of choices. This set of choices is again conditioned by the wider context within which they live, and in particular by the extent to which they can control the key decisions that affect their lives. This is (or should be) why participation is widely advocated. This idea of people making conscious choices through deliberate strategies is fundamental to the approach to livelihoods analysis presented here. It is integrated into the model at two stages: as a *livelihood strategy*, where a set of decisions are made on how to best employ the assets available; and as an *income strategy*, where choices are made over the use of the products (cash, goods and services) generated by the livelihood activities adopted.

These basic concepts can be traced through the flows shown in Figure 1. The figure is based on a core sub-model, the right hand side of the model, which represents the livelihood dynamics of a household. This sub-model starts with the *entitlements* and *access* they possess to the resource base in their locality. These in turn define the *natural capital* available to the household. This natural capital is one form of *livelihood asset*, represented by the pentagon, which can be deployed by the household in their livelihoods. When combined with the others (financial capital, social capital, physical capital and human capital), these capital assets represent the capabilities and assets, the 'factors of production' that the household can deploy to make a living. The 'entitlements' box is consequently part of the *access profile* of the household. Similar access factors can be identified for each of the other capitals, for example, the network of social and institutional relationships that a household possesses and the identity of the household in relation to factors such as caste, religion, clan or other determinants of social structure are defining in terms of explaining the social capital that they possess. One key aspect of any livelihood approach is to understand how the access profile, and consequently the assets available, change over time, and in particular how increases or reductions in their values affects the livelihoods of the household.

Taken together, these livelihood assets represent a potential, a set of possibilities for the household to secure a livelihood but they do not automatically define that livelihood, for the extent to which their potential is realised, will depend upon the way that they are used. This is reflected in a set of decisions on what assets to utilise when, decisions that together constitute the *livelihood strategy* of the household. There are always difficult choices to be made here, for example, what use of the assets will provide the best returns? What risks are involved in particular decisions? Which and what quantity of assets should be held in reserve for the future? These and many other questions have to be considered in the livelihood strategy and this strategy is at the heart of a livelihood analysis.

The choices made in the strategy will in turn define the *livelihood activities* of the household: which activities are undertaken by whom and when. Land, labour, material inputs, social networks and all other capital assets available are used in different combinations to grow crops, raise livestock, gather common property resources, earn wages, make things, trade, provide services and all other multitude of different activities that the different members of the household engage in. These together are their livelihood – the things that people do on a day-to-day basis to make a living. In some cases, there are one or two dominant activities, such as farming, fishing or making pots, but for many households the pattern of livelihood activities is varied and no one activity dominates. Whatever the relative importance of the set of activities, however, the basis for understanding livelihoods is that all need to be included in the analysis.

Households thus earn 'income' (in cash, or kind), which becomes part of the household budget. This income is in turn allocated through a second key set of decisions called the *income strategy*. Income can be allocated to savings or investments, which enhance the value of the assets to pay for inputs (fertilisers, raw materials, labour) that go into production, to repaying loans or social payments (such as taxes) or, finally, to consumption that is part of the *outcome*, that is, the total set of goods and services that constitute the material fabric of people's lives. Obviously, the greater the income, the more that is left after other obligations are met (inputs and social payments) for either consumption (meeting the needs of today) or investment (increasing the ability to meet needs tomorrow). Of course, other factors contribute to quality of life, well-being or however one wants to define the goal to which we all strive. This includes the social context within which one lives, a sense of freedom and security and many other non-material factors.

This core of the model reflects the internal dynamics of the process of gaining a livelihood on the part of individuals and the households to which they belong, but it is clear that this process does not operate in isolation from a wide range of influences that condition the flows through the livelihood, the choices available at any stage and the overall outcomes of the livelihood. The first of these is the *local community*: the social groupings, networks and institutions within which the individual household is enmeshed.

The social and institutional structures of local communities are locality specific, but reflect differing combinations of place (the locality or neighbourhood) and people (kin, religious, ethnic, occupational grouping or other social and economic characteristics) where an individual household lives.

The second conditioning factor is the *external institutional context*, the legal, political, social, economic and institutional environment: those factors, in other words, that link people and places into regional, national and global systems. This includes the nature and operation of government (which can have both direct effects, such as through agricultural subsidies or health services, and indirect impacts, such as through policy and macro-economic frameworks and political climates), the structure and strength of civil society (those non-state institutions and organisations that also regulate social and economic processes), the operation of markets, and so on.

The *wider natural environment* is also extremely important in the functioning of livelihoods. This can be through the character and variability of production conditions: the level and timing of rainfall, resource flows within an ecosystem, and its resilience in the face of management strategies, which can cause resource degradation. It can also reflect extreme events such as cyclones, earthquakes or droughts.

These in many ways define the characteristics of the different parts of the livelihood model. For example, entitlements and access to common property resources (CPRs) in a watershed to gather products such as firewood and fodder can reflect both the legal and policy frameworks (which define who owns the CPRs and what form of external regulation exists) and local customs and traditions concerning who can gather what. This in turn defines a part of the 'natural' capital in the 'livelihood assets' pentagon. Similarly, both external monetary policies and financial institutions and local moneylenders define the availability and cost of credit, which is crucial in both determining how much income goes to repay past loans and what credit is available for investments and inputs into production.

These external factors are 'filtered' through the *vulnerability context* that has already been referred to. The vulnerability context describes trends and variability in those factors that affect livelihood processes, and in particular that can materially disrupt different aspects of livelihoods. This can be specific: for example, climate change will directly affect the long-term characteristics of the resource base, with other consequences compounding through the system from there, whilst a devastating cyclone or drought will have massive immediate impacts and can cause structural change to the characteristics of a household's livelihood processes. The nature of vulnerabilities can also vary, depending on form or timing. For example, a sudden collapse in market prices for a dominant commercial crop can affect the assets available by making key assets of land and agricultural implements less valuable. It can affect the livelihood activity through leading to a decision to plant something different or it can affect income if the price collapse happens after planting. Most vulnerabilities are not different to the local and external contexts described above (climate, markets); rather, they reflect the dynamics and specific forms that those contexts take.

Finally, the point that these forces affect different households differently has already been made. Some are more sensitive to the effects of the vulnerability context, others more resilient. This can be represented as resilience 'filter', through which the flows of influence from the vulnerability context pass to define the specific impact of external forces on the livelihood system of particular households. The resilience of a household can be higher across the board: for example, secure access to credit or good financial reserves are important in relation to most forms of vulnerability or it can be specific to particular vulnerabilities: owning higher land can be an advantage if there is a flood, but a disadvantage if there is a drought or in relation to erosion.

This model allows one to 'map' the consequences of specific changes, including changes brought about through external interventions intended to improve people's lives. For example, a dominant approach to natural resources management in recent years has been participatory mobilisation to create community-based institutions to manage CPRs as well as private resources. Initiatives such as watershed development or joint forest management in India, typify this approach. The points of intervention and impact of such programmes can be 'mapped' on the livelihood model – something that will be a core objective of this book.

The Contemporary Context

This book is an attempt to assess the impact of the watershed development programme under the new guidelines (the 1994–95 Hanumantha Rao Guidelines) in Andhra Pradesh, on rural livelihoods. In the process, the study takes comprehensive look at various aspects of watershed development and management. These aspects include the policy environment, institutional evolution, implementation modalities and the impacts. The overarching issues in this regard are the linkages between watershed development and rural livelihoods, the nature of impact of watershed development and distribution of benefits on the livelihoods of different sections of the community, sustainability of the benefits, and so on. The specific objectives of the study include:

- Understanding the process of watershed policy and implementation at the micro and meso levels.
- Assessing the livelihood impact of the watershed development across the different socio-economic groups of the community, including both the direct beneficiary as well as the non-beneficiary households.
- Examining the sustenance of watershed development and management in the medium and long runs.
- Indicating possible policy interventions (issues) for sustainable rural livelihoods through sustainable watershed management.

The complex nature of watershed development and management calls for a comprehensive understanding of the conditions under which watershed technology becomes economically unviable, socially (un)acceptable and ecologically unsustainable in the long run. Hitherto, the literature on watershed management concentrated more on the techno-economic aspects of the programme. People's participation in watershed management was confined only to a casual reference even in policy formulations and as a consequence demonstrated moderate success till mid-1990s.

The new watershed guidelines, brought out in 1994, provide for a definite design for participatory approach. Several watershed-based programmes have taken shape following the new guidelines under the administrative control of the Ministry of Rural Development, Government of India. Prior to the new guidelines, the success of watershed development was often attributed to active people's participation. In this context, several studies observed that the performance of the NGO-implemented watersheds is much better compared to the government-implemented ones, for NGOs ensure active people's participation (Farrington and Lobo, 1999). What is the outcome of the policy changes stemming from this concern at the ground level? A pertinent question indeed: has the programme given emphasis on people's participation? The performance of the programme hinges on how seriously people's participation is accomplished while implementing the programme. The question crops up here, is there an overall improvement in people's participation and the performance of the programme consequent upon the new guidelines? Better participation across the board means improvement in the performance of government-implemented watersheds as well. The hypothesis that needs to be tested is whether there is an overall improvement in the performance of the programme, including the government-implemented watersheds following the guidelines or is the performance still dependent on good NGOs. In other words, how far the policy guidelines have helped the implementation in general—to better the outcome?

While the new guidelines emphasise the involvement of all sections of the community,[4] the accrual of benefits from the watershed to all sections of the community need to be appraised at the ground level. This assumes importance, as the watershed development does not guarantee equal distribution of benefit flows across the community. Watershed being a land-based technology, most of the benefits naturally accrue to landed. Often watershed (500 ha) does not cover the entire village lands and this leaves a section of households dissatisfied. Though landless farmers are also expected to benefit from the improvements to CPRs, type and magnitude of benefits accruing to landless households needs to be studied. Unless the benefits accruing to this section of the community are substantial in economic terms, it is unlikely that they will participate or evince any interest in the programme. In the absence of such benefits, their apathy towards the programme might jeopardise the sustainability of the programme.

Given this backdrop, the present study is an attempt to assess the impact of watershed development programme under the new guidelines in a wider context. The context pertains to regions as well as implementing agencies. The important issues in this regard include the status of implementation of the programme, linkages between watershed development and crop production and other related resources, nature of impact of watershed on the productivity and employment of different sections of the community, distribution of benefits from the watershed development to various sections of the community, sustainability of the benefits, etc. As observed in some of the recent studies, impact of watershed development, in terms of groundwater recharge, cropping pattern changes, etc., seems to be impressive as compared to the earlier programmes (Rao, 2000). But, issues pertaining to distribution of benefits, role of project implementing agencies (PIAs), sustainability of the programme, etc., are still to be assessed in a systematic manner. For this purpose, we have chosen a wider canvas for generalisations in the policy context. The analysis is based on data collected from a number of watersheds spread across different regions of Andhra Pradesh. Watersheds implemented by different PIAs (GOs and NGOs) are chosen in order to examine the dichotomy between NGO and non-NGO implementation. The details of sample watersheds and their profiles are discussed in details in the respective chapters.

About the Book

This book is organised in nine chapters that discuss in sequence the policy, institutions, implementation and livelihoods. The existing literature on watershed programmes is overloaded with evaluation of economic and ecological benefits. Though every study suggested that collective action and people's participation were necessary for sustainable watershed management, it remained as a more cursory note at the end of each study. Despite this, collective action and people's participation had never been central to the implementation of watershed development programmes till the mid-1990s. Further, for a long time, the theoretical frame for collective action was stuck at the famous 'group size syndrome'. Andhra Pradesh (AP) provides a best ground for assessing the impacts of participatory watershed management in the country. AP is in the forefront in regard to implementation of watershed development programme. It has initiated about 11,000 watersheds under the new guidelines since 1995. The programmes of dryland development in AP have undergone a major change since 1995–96 with the introduction of new watershed guidelines (Chapter 2). The historical and contemporary context of watershed development in India, a detailed review of watershed management, which covers socio-economic impacts as well as participatory aspects along with the empirical setting, provides the necessary background for the study.

A critical evolution of past and proposed watershed policies at the national level as well as in AP in the light of experience pertaining to watershed management argues that the comparison of the three guidelines does not really indicate any major deviations in content and spirit of the programme (Chapter 3). The analysis of the policy process concludes with a number of policy recommendations that are intended to contribute to the existing dynamic debate on the future of this and related policies in AP and elsewhere. That there is a strong policy debate on water management and watershed development in AP is reflected in the priority given to this issue by the state. However, it is argued that the policy commitments are not translated into actions, as the implementation of these programmes deserve much more attention. This chapter compares the two recent guidelines with the proposed guidelines in an attempt to assess the merits and rationale for a new set of guidelines, examines the likely contribution of the proposed guidelines towards improving the implementation of the programme in the light of the past experience and highlights the missing aspects in the proposed initiatives.

Institutions are the key to the success of watershed management. The theoretical underpinning of institutions in watershed management and the importance of collective action and property rights in sustainable management of watersheds need not be overemphasised (Chapter 4). How far the existing models in AP, with specific focus on the approaches of the government, and one of the important NGOs, namely, Accion Fraterna, that has its own watershed development programme as well as institutional model, address the important issues of collective action and property rights. It is argued that the existing institutional models, though prioritise participation and collective action, also neglect the importance of property rights in achieving collective action. The emphasis is more on capacity building and providing short-term incentive/disincentive structures. The government models include the decentralised approaches and the Andhra Pradesh Rural Livelihoods Model (APRLP).

Effective implementation of the technological components ultimately determines the benefit flows in the watershed programme. While it is observed that AP adheres to the guidelines, its overambitious extensive approach has raised questions on the sustainability of the programme. It also failed to recognise the importance of decentralisation and involving the Panchayati Raj Institutions (PRIs) in the implementation of the programme. In fact, AP has treated participatory institutions as substitutes for democratic institutions (Chapter 5). A detailed account of the implementation procedures and the organisational structure for implementing the programme set out in the guidelines vis-a-vis the adoption of these guidelines at the policy level in AP is critical for effective implementation of the programme. The observations from the field highlight the lacunae in the implementation of the programme.

The sustainable rural livelihood framework adopts the five capitals, viz., natural, physical, financial, human and social frame, for impact assessment. The analysis clearly brings out that despite being the model watersheds, in none of the sample watersheds, the programme has a significant impact on all the capitals (Chapter 6). Besides, livelihood sustenance is linked to the resilience/sensitivity of the livelihood assets to changes in climatic conditions rather than assets *per se*. For, some assets are more resilient/less sensitive than others. From the sustainable rural livelihoods point of view, none of the sample watersheds meets the strong sustainability criteria, though one of them comes close. This indicates that participatory watershed management in its present form, is a necessary condition but not a sufficient condition to sustain rural livelihoods. But, watershed management holds the potential for enhanced livelihood security even in the given geo-climatic conditions where watershed cannot bring direct irrigation benefits on a large scale. Moreover, distribution of these benefits is not egalitarian given the distorted agrarian structure and factor markets. Even, the spillover or externality benefits like employment are extremely limited in the absence of significant improvement in irrigation benefits. At the same time, watershed management is necessary in these fragile regions in order to strengthen the ecological base, such as soil quality, water resources (including tanks), grazing lands, wastelands, etc. In this context, watershed management should not be viewed as a programme for income and employment generation for all sections of the population.

A comparative analysis of eight watersheds, spread over three districts, implemented by NGOs and government line departments, is used to test the hypothesis: the performance of NGO-implemented watersheds is better when compared to the ones implemented by the government agencies. It is observed that the performance of eight sample watersheds varied in their impact on economic and ecological factors. This may be attributed to agro-climatic conditions, and the institutional arrangements of watershed implementation. Watershed implementation process differs across implementing agencies though they follow almost identical guidelines. Though the performance of the NGO-implemented watersheds is better in general, this hypothesis does not hold true in all the cases (Chapter 7). Performance of the PIA and the watershed is critically linked to the existing social and human capital at the village level. This indicates that good PIA is necessary but not a sufficient condition for the better performance of the programme. For, some of the PIAs – GO or NGO – could not implement the guidelines due to political interference or lack of cooperation from the local communities. On the other hand, watersheds implemented by government line departments have better performance indicators.

Collective action is a prerequisite for sustainable watershed management. The theoretical and empirical character of collective action in watershed management stresses the importance of policy and political environments for institutional innovation and sustainability. It distinguishes CPR situations with differential institutional capabilities and thus facilitates better targeting of policies. Assessment of institutional capabilities has to be made an important input for policy formulation. Political economy aspects, along with cost-benefit aspects, are of prime importance for institutional innovation and change. While costs and benefits determine the potential for institutional innovation, the actual creation of institutional arrangements is critically linked with political economy aspects. Creation of policy environment for institutional arrangements is more important and sustainable than direct imposition of institutions. Policy changes (or environment) need to be matched with the contemporary political environment. There is a greater need to recognise the role of external forces, like NGOs, as catalytic factors promoting institutional arrangements through providing leadership and promoting leadership from within the community. The policy environment should be conducive to facilitate their role. The grassroots level success and effectiveness of development policy largely depends on the synergy between the government and NGOs (Chapter 8).

Chapter 9 exposes the deeper political and economic interests that operate at the cutting edge level is critical for moving towards effective and sustainable watershed management. In this context, it is argued that the parallel institutional structures, created specifically to facilitate better delivery by operating in a political manner, have not lived up to their promise. These institutions have not only been political in the broad sense of becoming another site of contestation among organised village factions, they have also become implicated in conflicts between political parties. In a majority of the cases, parallel institutions are plagued with political conflicts and dominated by economic interests. Given the magnitude of the resources available in the programme, these institutional arrangements are becoming breeding grounds for village contractors and encouraging the conversion of politicians into contractors and vice versa. Even the officials are working as part-time contractors. All this takes place at the cost of equitable development delivery due to the absence of any transparency and accountability at the village level.

The relationship between the constitutional and democratic PRIs and the parallel institutions is not formal. But, there are informal relationships. These are determined by the dynamics of power equations at the village level. Conflict situations seem to arise when political interests outweigh economic interests. Nexus or compromise situations arise in the event when economic interests outweigh political interests. Destructive conflict situations are often typically characterised by the combination of social and economic powers, i.e., concentration of economic assets in the hands of socially dominant castes. For, the creation of parallel institutions appears to be a political ploy to bypass or short-circuit the democratic institutions, which are no longer under the control of the socio-economic elite, due to the reservation policies.

Notes

1. The proposed watershed guidelines recommend a raise in the per hectare expenditure from the existing Rs. 6,000 (US$ 150) to Rs. 12,000 (US$ 300).
2. Most of the earlier works concentrate on the livelihood strategies at the household level (for a review see, Ahmed and Lipton (nd), rather than linking SRL issues with policy making. As a result, there is wide gap between bottom-up and top-down livelihood analysis (Shankland, 2000).
3. This section draws mainly from Soussan et al. (2000).
4. Participation may not be total in all situations due to divergent livelihood activities, such as migration, trans-humans, etc.

2

Watershed Management: The Context

Watershed development is almost as old as agriculture itself. There are ancient and noble traditions of collective, village-level water harvesting and distribution, soil conservation, and grazing and forestland management in every part of India. Some are still visible today, but generally these traditions have been eroded. The earliest example of soil conservation measures is the Bombay Plan. Systematic adoption of dry farming techniques dates back to the early decades of the 20th century. These were known as soil conservation methods used for controlling soil erosion in drought-prone regions. These methods were adopted on a scattered basis, more as relief measures (Shah, 1998). This piecemeal approach has continued till 1980s when the integrated National Watershed Development Programme for Rainfall Agriculture (NWDPRA) was adopted and launched. Successive Indian governments have recognised the value for watershed development, and have often sought to promote this where it is lacking.

The concept of watershed management involves planning the development of a resource region. It is essential to emphasise here the 'resource region' concept in the process. Resource region incorporates the private property as well as common property regimes and therefore the conflicts in resource sharing and use are quite natural without a proper property rights framework. The focus of planning is the optimal and sustainable use of the resources and here the focus is water, land and people. The approach of watershed treatment therefore is holistic and involves quite a few hydrological, economic and bio-social systems. Broadly, one can identify seven sub-systems interacting with the stakeholders, namely, silvi-horticultural, pastoral, livestock, agricultural, hydro-geological, administrative and social. These all have a dynamic setting and they interface at two levels. First, there are interactions within the bio-systems, as functions of the geographical and climatic conditions. In these interactions, the prevailing technology plays an important role. Usually, the results of the technological component are demonstrated under the laboratory conditions, but when it comes to testing or implementation of these on ground level, the institutional, operational, organisational and other social parameters assume greater importance. Being the components of behavioural sub-systems, a direct quantification of such parameters is not possible and therefore one has to resort to proxies represented by responses and opinions.

At the second level, the biological sub-system comes into the interface with the stakeholders, administrative and social systems. Therefore, the processes of implementation of the programme and people's participation in the programme become crucial determinants of the success. The World Development Report (1992) stressed the importance of a participatory approach in creating viable resource management institutions. Watershed development programme, being an area-based programme, can only be successful if there is an active support from the communities involved in the region. People's participation in the implementation of the programme becomes crucial, and a pure technocratic solution does not help in any resource-centred programme.

The NWDPRA was later modified in the light of the suggestions made by the committee of secretaries constituted to review the programme. Thus, in the year 1991, revised guidelines were issued under the name, WARASA, which included several important aspects. It is for the first time the programme gave importance to planning for the watershed and under primary activities preparation of a complete plan for the watershed was included. Secondly, the programme was made more people-oriented and participation of beneficiaries was encouraged through the programmes *Mitra Kisan* and *Gopal*. Thirdly, the technical bias of the programme was reduced and the programme was directed more towards providing economic benefits. Lastly, the programme was scaled up in its coverage and with a built-in monitoring and evaluation component.

In the Indian context, we have three types of models of implementation of watershed development programmes. The first type of model includes the state funded and implemented programmes having little to do with other non-governmental bodies. The second type is characterised by the programme taken up by groups of people or NGOs with/without outside funding. The third typology refers to the programmes undertaken by NGOs or groups of stakeholders with the state partnership.

Given the magnitude and spread of the watershed development programmes, several research studies were undertaken to examine the ecological and economic impact of these programmes across the country. An overwhelming majority of the studies have endorsed these programmes in terms of costs and benefits (Table 2.1). Some of them also highlight the less quantifiable ecological benefits (Singh, 1994; Deshpande and Ratna Reddy, 1991; Chopra, Kadeikodi and Murthy, 1989; Deshpande and Rajasekhar, 1995). These studies not only vindicated the economic viability of the

Table 2.1 *Economic Impact of Watershed Technology: Review of Studies*

Study/Year	*Region*	*Activity*	*Crops*	*Impact on*		
				Yield	*Net Income*	*B–C R*
1. Ram Mohan Rao et al. (1967)	Maharastra	Contour Bunding	Jowar (R)	+25%	—	—
			Bajra	+25%	—	—
	Tamil Nadu		Jowar (R)	+36%	—	—
			Bajra	+25%	—	—
2. Lal Gupta et al. (1970)	Varanasi (UP)	Soil Conservation	All crops	+112%	215%	4.6
3. Joshi and Seckler (1981)	Chandigarh	Rainwater Harvesting	All crops	—	Rs.1812/ha	—
4. Sarin and Ryan (1983)	Andhra Pradesh	Integrated Watershed	All crops	—	+4 –300%	—
	Solapur (Maharashtra)	-do-	Sorghum	—	+517%	—
			Castor	—	+600%	—
			Sorghum	+300%	—	—
5. Walker et al. (1981)	Mahaboob Nagar (AP)	-do-	All crops	+203%	—	1.37
	Medak (AP)	-do-	All crops	+130%	—	3.81
	Medak (AP)	-do-	All crops	+52%	—	3.02
	Akola (Maharashtra)	-do-	All crops	+28%	—	1.08
	Gulbarga (Karnataka)	-do-	All crops	+52%	—	1.03

6.	Ghodke (1981)	Tadapally (Andhra Pradesh)	-do-	All crops	—	+71%	—
				Sorghum	—	–45%	—
				Pulses	—	+1000%	—
				Pigeon Pea	—	+960%	—
				Fodder	—	+230%	—
7.	Gupta and Mohan (1982)	Rajasthan	Tree Plantation	Trees	—	Rs.1640/ha	—
8.	Tejwani and Babu (1982)	Farm Pond	Farm Pond	Jowar			
9.	Reddy and Kanwar (1985)	Andhra Pradesh	Agro-forestry	Agro-forestry	—	—	1.45
			Silvi-agriculture	Try Silvi-agriculture	—	—	1.30
			Silvi-pastoral	Silvi-pastoral	—	—	2.25
10.	Agnihotri (1985)	Shivalik Hills	Vegetative Cover	All crops	64 q/ha	— to 85q/ha	—
11.	Govt. of Punjab (1986)	Punjab	Soil Conservation	All crops	—	+84%#	—
				Maize	–13%	—	—
				Paddy	–30%	—	—
				Wheat	+16	—	—
				Potato	+4	—	—
12.	Itnal and Narayan (1987)	Bijapur (Karnataka)	Farm Pond	Jowar	—	+Rs.1300/ha	0.95
				Sunflower		+Rs.1800/ha	1.11
13.	Pant (1989)	Madhya Pradesh	Integrated Watershed	Sorghum	+127%	—	—
				Wheat	+111%	—	—

Table 2.1 (*contd.*)

Table 2.1 (*contd.*)

Study/Year	*Region*	*Activity*	*Crops*	*Impact on*		
				Yield	*Net Income*	*B–C R*
14 Deshpande and Reddy (1990)	Maharashtra	Integrated Watershed	Paddy	+18%	—	—
			Ragi	+34%	—	—
			Pulses	+7 %	—	—
			Bajra	+46%	—	—
			Wheat	+11%	—	—
			Jowar	–2%	—	—
			Sunflower	+64%	—	—
15. Rao (1990)	Andhra Pradesh	-do-	Paddy (K)	+54%	+13%#	—
			Paddy (R)	+135%	—	—
			Sorghum	+17%	—	—
			Pigeon Pea	+7%	—	—
			Castor	+61%	—	—
16. Singh (1991)	Karnataka	-do-	All crops	—	Rs. 1970/ha	—
17. Singh, et al. (1991)	Punjab	-do-	Forestry	—	— 2.74	
			Ani. Husbandry	—	— 1.14	
			Soil Conservation	—	Gross Margin	0.90
	Integrated		Horticulture	—	Rs. 825–2780	7.05
	Watershed		All crops	—	— 0.95	
18. Mahnot et al. (1992)	Rajasthan		Maize	+21%	—	1.03
			Wheat	+20%	—	to
			Oilseeds	+52%	—	8.37

19. Singh et al. (1993)	Kandi (Punjab)	Integrated Watershed	Maize	+5-14 q/ha	—	1.72 (avg.)
			Paddy	+5-13 q/ha	—	
			Blackgram	+4-6 q/ha	—	
			Wheat	+8-22 q/ha	—	
			Gram	+4-9 q/ha	—	
			Mustard	0-8 q/ha	—	
20. Singh et al. (1995)	Udaipur (Rajasthan)	-do-	Maize	+2 q/ha	+Rs.1100 per year	1.76 (avg.)
			Paddy	+2 q/ha		
			Jowar	+2 q/ha		
			Blackgram	+4 q/ha		
			Wheat	+2 q/ha		
21. Nalatawadmath et al. (1997)	Bellary (Karnataka)	-do-	Bajra	+16 q/ha	+50%	1.75 (avg.)
			Jowar	+13 q/ha		
				+22 q/ha		
22. Joshi and Bantilan (1997)	ICRISAT Asia Centre	-do-	Sunflower Chickpea	—	+40%	—
23. Kerr (2002)	Maharashtra	-do-	All plots	—	+13%	—
	AP		All plots	—	+12%	—

Note: Till the year 1991 studies are taken from Deshpande and Reddy (1991a).
Gross income.

programme but also underlined watersheds as the only alternative to the development of rainfed agriculture in India. In fact, some of the studies even proved that watershed development programmes scored over the traditional intervention programmes like IRDP/JRY/NREP in terms of employment generation and natural capital regeneration in moderately degraded regions (Chopra and Kadekodi, 1993). In fact, it was suggested that JRY should adopt the watershed development programmes instead of taking up purely employment generating programmes (Bhatnagar, 1996). Besides, watershed development programmes are more appropriate in providing ecological sustainability in the long run.

Although the economics of watershed technology is unambiguously in its favour, the magnitude of its impact differs across regions and locations. The impact of watershed technology is observed to be more effective in scarcity regions when compared to assured rainfall regions (Deshpande and Ratna Reddy, 1991). On the other hand, adoption of the technology itself might be a difficult proposition in extreme scarcity conditions, as poor households living on the margin can hardly afford to follow conservation practices, such as halting grazing their animals (Singh, 1991). This is mainly due to a long gestation for rearing benefits from the technology. Further, the favourable picture depicted by most of the studies is deceptive, caused by bias in selection, i.e., purposively taking a successful watershed programme for evaluation. On the contrary, the overall picture is hardly rosy, the success rate in some of the states being as low as 15–20 percent. Deeper probe into these differences brings out interesting insights that watershed management ought to be differentiated from watershed development.[1]

While watershed development is associated more with technology, watershed management is more of a philosophy. While the success of watershed development as a technology is well established, the philosophy of watershed management is proving to be the main bottleneck for the wider success of the programme. Watersheds have been studied from various perspectives, such as economic efficiency of water use and investments, flood run-off, soil erosion, sedimentation, ground water recharge, socio-political dimensions etc. (Dixon, 1992). Understanding the interplay between land, water and people is equally important in studying watersheds. Therefore, watershed management is more than just the cost-benefit analysis of investments. The main distinction between watershed development and other traditional developmental programmes is that the former is essentially a community-based one. Watershed development technology requires large areas often cutting across households and even villages for its adoption. Hence, its adoption and success critically hinges upon inter-village as well as intra-village cooperation. In other words, collective participation and action is a critical ingredient for successful watershed management. This throws up a wide range of issues, such as social organisation and property rights, which require careful scrutiny. The problem of property rights arises in dealing with the treatment of common lands. Another distinctive feature of watershed technology is its relatively long gestation period. That is, farmers have to wait for 5–7 years to get benefits. This aspect further makes watershed management difficult.

Social organisation and its sustainability are linked to the allocation of property rights and the distribution of benefits across different sections of the community. In other words, whether property rights are defined clearly and equitably rather than who has the rights—individuals or groups. Unless property rights are defined clearly and equitably, it is difficult to ensure sustainable resource management even under community management. Allocation of rights and distribution of costs and benefits are the most important among the rules and regulations in managing the commons. These distributional aspects are important and affect the monitoring costs to a large extent. If solved to the satisfaction of all socio-economic communities in the group, they would reduce the costs of monitoring. For, free rider attitudes are more prevalent under institutional arrangements where costs and benefits are distributed unequally across households. Those who are on the other extreme (deriving least benefits) tend to assert their use rights inappropriately, verging on encroachment. That is, when people view an established system as inequitable according to established social standards, they have incentives to undermine it (Hanna, 1996). Similarly, grazing restrictions go against the interests of herders while they benefit the landholders (Reddy, 2000; Turton, 2000). On the contrary, small and marginal farmers tend to benefit from restrictions on groundwater exploitation while large farmers stand to loose (Reddy, 2000). Such contradictions need to be addressed in order to sustain collective action. Therefore, it is necessary not only to involve in the process but also show benefits (tangible economic) to all sections of the community. This aspect does not find articulation in the context of watershed development.

Impact of Watershed Development: A Review

As mentioned earlier, numerous studies have highlighted the positive impact of watershed development programmes on crop yields, cropping intensity and cropping pattern changes. Review of existing studies in this regard indicates variations in the magnitude of impact across regions and crops (Table 2.1). The magnitude of impact is also dependent on the nature of the components adopted.[2] All the studies, however, have shown that net incomes have gone up substantially and have favourable benefit-cost ratios. Recent years have revealed stabilisation of B–C ratios at around 1.75.

Impact assessment of watershed technology can best be accomplished by incorporating all the components. The study of Sukhmajiri watershed (Joshi and Seckler, 1981; Chopra et al., 1989) showed exemplary results of the integrated programme. The incremental benefits ranged from Rs. 1,800 to Rs. 2,000 per hectare. In a similar experiment, watershed projects in

Hyderabad, Solapur and Akola districts (Sarin and Rayan, 1983) recorded stabilisation of cash flow and substantial increase in productivity, incremental income and employment. Walker et al. (1990) also reviewed the overall impact of the application of watershed-based technologies at different locations in Maharashtra, Madhya Pradesh and Karnataka. Their results indicated incremental net income ranging between 49 and 203 percent of the base level. The B–C ratio worked out in the range of 1.08 to 3.81 across the locations.

Significant changes in the household economy were noted in an analysis of the state level programme of Comprehensive Watershed Development Programme (COWDEP) in Maharashtra (Deshpande and Ratna Reddy, 1991). The study analysed data covering 30 blocks in the state and pointed out concentration of only a few components but overall good results of the watershed technology. It was noted that employment generated in each of the watersheds ranged between two and thirty thousand man days depending on the agro-climatic conditions and that the crop pattern, crop intensity, proportion of wasteland and yield per hectare changed substantially. Increased moisture availability has been reported in the watershed regions. The study also made a comparative analysis of the cases of active beneficiary participation as against the passive participations. It was noted that participatory process acts as a powerful catalyst for the programme a result supported by Singh (1991) and Chopra et al. (1989).

In another detailed study of Maharastra (Deshpande and Ratna Reddy, 1991) covering three agro climatic zones (scarcity, moderate rainfall and assured rainfall), revealed differential impact of watershed technology. In the *scarcity zone* watershed technology has led to intensification of agriculture, higher diversification, risk spreading and increased stability in yield levels. Small and marginal farmers of the project area gained on income front compared to their peers from the non-project areas. *Moderate rainfall zone* also showed similar results. Except in the case of jowar and paddy the watershed region had a distinct edge over the control region although the latter had a slightly higher area under irrigation. Beneficiary group also showed higher net incomes. However, the level of income inequality was higher in the programme area while the reverse was true in the case of scarcity zone. *Assured rainfall zone* within the watershed region also showed lower inequalities. This zone is characterised by high intensive agricultural practices and high remunerative crops. Farmers response in this zone indicated increased yield rates with greater stabilisation, increased income, higher wages and employment. A recent study of Maharashtra and Andhra Pradesh (Kerr, 2002) brought out the impact differentials across different types of watershed projects. It was observed that NGO and NGO–GO watersheds had done exceedingly well in terms of net farm returns compared to government watersheds or even World Bank/ICAR watersheds. NGO watersheds are conceived and implemented with the support of external funding, while NGO–GO watersheds are implemented by NGOs with government funding. Government watersheds are funded by the State Government and implemented by the line departments as per the existing guidelines. An exhaustive review of 311 case studies (Joshi et al., 2005) revealed that cost-benefit ratios are found to be largely positive in medium rainfall (701–900 mm) and low income regions. In the drier areas, while water scarcity encourages collective harvesting, the extreme shortage of water and low rainfall patterns seem to diminish the returns from watershed interventions. In areas with high rainfall, the marginal net benefits from improved water and soil management seem to be quite modest. However, all the watersheds covered in these studies were implemented prior to the new watershed guidelines came into effect in 1994–95. The participatory aspect was not emphasised in the earlier guidelines.

Thus, the existing literature on watershed programmes is overloaded with evaluation of economic and ecological benefits. Though every study suggested that collective action and people's participation were necessary for sustainable watershed management, it remained as a more cursory note at the end of each study. Despite this, collective action and people's participation had never been central to the implementation of watershed development programmes till the mid-1990s. Further, for a long time, the theoretical frame for collective action was stuck at the famous 'group size syndrome' (Olson, Jr., 1965). Olsan's seminal work employs too narrow a framework to explain the present-day collective action situations. Nevertheless, group size is among the most important factors explaining collective action. A few studies based on Olson's framework also tried to explain people's participation in watershed management in India (Singh, 1991; Deshpande and Ratna Reddy, 1991).

Watershed Development in Andhra Pradesh

Andhra Pradesh (AP) is the fifth largest state in India, both in area and population. Bounded by Madhya Pradesh, Chattisgarh, and Orissa in the north, the Bay of Bengal in the east, Tamil Nadu and Karnataka in the south and Maharashtra in the west, AP forms the major link between the north and the south of India. The northern area of AP is mountainous. The highest peak Mahendragiri rises 1,500 m above the sea level. The climate is generally hot and humid. Average rainfall in the state is 925 mm. The Krishna and the Godavari are the major rivers in the state. With a 970-km coastline, AP is the largest maritime state in India. It consists of three distinct regions: (a) Coastal region, made up of nine districts, (b) Rayalaseema region, consisting of four districts, and (c) Telangana region, consisting of the capital Hyderabad and nine adjoining districts. In AP there are extensive areas of rainfed agriculture, which could potentially benefit from the sort of approaches seen elsewhere. Watershed development programmes in AP have been implemented for many years. In order to combat the frequent recurrence of drought in the state, Drought-Prone Area Programme (DPAP) was introduced in the year 1976, as a centrally sponsored scheme with matching state share of 50:50. Integrated Wasteland Development Programme (IWDP) was introduced in 1991 with 100 percent central assistance. The wasteland development programmes taken up before April 1995 have not performed well, mainly because they had been planned and implemented on departmental basis by government officials and in isolated patches, without any regard for the complete micro-watershed principle or for people's participation (GoAP, 2001).

The renewed watershed programme envisages a great opportunity for improving the productivity, profitability and sustainability of dry farming areas through social mobilisation. Rainfed agriculture should be based on watershed as the unit of development to become productive. Watershed is not a technology but a concept, which integrates conservation, management and budgeting of rainwater through simple but discrete hydrological units. Simultaneously, watershed supports a holistic framework, which means the combined application of technologies on soil and water conservation with improved crop varieties, farming systems and agronomic management, taking into account both arable and non-arable land. Water resource development, management, harvesting and equity in sharing form the nucleus of watershed development (GoAP, 2001).

With assured availability of water, farmers get motivated to accept more profitable, sustainable and innovative farming systems. Water availability has also catalysed the adoption and spread of value-added activities in the entire area of the watershed, such as horticulture. Cropping systems need to be tailored to suit different rainfall-cum-soil zones. Watershed development is the only solution to ensure drought-proofing and to mitigate the distress caused by frequent droughts. In view of these benefits, a 'massive' programme for development of all the degraded lands in Andhra Pradesh in 10 years was launched during 1997(GoAP, 2001). The action plan for development includes wetlands, degraded lands (i.e., dry lands which are being cultivated under rainfed conditions) and degraded reserve forests. It is envisaged to develop 10 million hectares of degraded and wastelands, with an outlay of about Rs. 4,000 crore (US$ 888.89 million) from 1997 to 2007 at the rate of 1 million hectares every year. However, only a little over 50 percent of the target has been achieved till March 2007 (Table 2.2) at a cost of about Rs. 2,000 crore.

Table 2.2 *Watersheds under Implementation since 1995–96*

Year	*Total watersheds*	*Area (in M ha)*
1995–96	1248	0.600
1996–97	436	0.209
1997–98	767	0.369
1998–99	1669	0.803
1999–00	782	0.376
2000–01	1825	0.878
2001–02	552	0.265
2002–03	1007	0.484
2003–04	775	0.373
2004–05	517	0.248
2005–06	755	0.363
2006–07	750	0.361
Total	11083	5.329

Source: Status Reports, Commissioner of Rural Development, Government of Andhra Pradesh, Hyderabad.

Prior to the implementation of new watershed guidelines, an area of 4.19 lakh hectares. was treated under DPAP in the state. However, after the new watershed guidelines have come into force from 1995–96 onwards, a total of 2,090 watersheds involving an area of 10.45 lakh hectares have been introduced. After the launch of the 10-year perspective plan, another 5,887 watersheds in wastelands and forestlands covering an area of 18.22 lakh hectares have been added. As a result, as on 1st April 2005, an area of 4.2 million hectares with an expenditure of Rs. 1692 million, have been brought under the programme (Table 2.3). It is also proposed to take up the development of forestlands in fringing villages falling within the boundary of watersheds. The Watershed Development Committees (*Vana Samrakshana Samithis*) have taken up the works as per the revised guidelines. The programmes under DPAP/DDP/EAS/IWDP/AP Hazard Mitigation/VSS are integrated with watershed programmes.

In the last decade, AP has remained in the forefront with regard to implementation of watershed development programmes. The programmes of dry land development in the state have undergone a major change since 1995–96 with the introduction of new watershed guidelines, based on the recommendations of Hanumantha Rao Committee Report. The main principle adopted in the guidelines lays special emphasis on the active mobilisation and participation of the stakeholders in the programme, including planning, implementation and subsequent management. The guidelines specify how watersheds are to be developed, using the micro-watershed (500 ha) as the basic unit for treatment. Of the 23 districts in AP the DPAP is under implementation in 17 districts. Over the late 1990s the approach has been continuously modified in the light of experience. The districtwise break-up of watersheds is presented in Table 2.3.

Andhra Pradesh has taken up the watershed development programmes by strictly adhering to the new watershed guidelines since 1995–96.[3] As per the guidelines implementation of the watershed has to be completed in four years covering 500 hectares of area with an outlay of Rs. 20 lakh per watershed (Rs. 4,000 per ha).[4] Desert-prone districts like Anantapur receive Rs. 22.5 lakh per watershed (Rs. 4,500 per hectare) due to their unfavourable agro-climatic conditions. The average area under watershed is limited to about 500 hectares in line with the guidelines. Twenty-two districts have been covered under this programme till 2001–02. In terms of distribution across districts,

Table 2.3 *Watershed Development Programmes in Andhra Pradesh across Districts (1995–96 to February 2005)*

District	*No. of watersheds*	*Area (in lakh ha)**	*Area per watershed (in ha)**	*Amount allocated (Rs. in lakh)*	*Amount spent (Rs. in lakh)*	*Percent of utilisation*
Srikakulam	360	1.5	457	567.56	295.34	52.0
Vizianagaram	166	0.7	426	187.89	177.72	94.6
Visakhapatnam	111	0.6	557	152.62	111.47	73.0
East Godavari	137	0.6	441	187.08	176.99	94.6
West Godavari	28	0.1	462	50.00	38.26	76.5
Krishna	262	1.1	441	0.00	0.00	0.0
Guntur	52	0.2	441	142.64	100.70	70.6
Prakasam	820	3.8	465	2616.99	2128.05	81.3
Nellore	313	1.3	441	387.29	159.12	41.1
Chittoor	688	3.3	491	1575.55	791.27	50.2
Kadapa	474	2.0	431	1225.99	807.42	65.9
Anantapur	1204	5.0	423	4352.12	3488.50	80.2
Kurnool	981	4.3	442	2050.02	1412.95	68.9
Mahabubnagar	1077	4.4	410	2437.02	1868.16	76.7
Ranga Reddy	497	2.2	454	1576.69	1191.11	75.5

Table 2.3 *(contd.)*

Table 2.3 *(contd.)*

District	*No. of watersheds*	*Area (in lakh ha)**	*Area per watershed (in ha)**	*Amount allocated (Rs. in lakh)*	*Amount spent (Rs. in lakh)*	*Percent of utilisation*
Medak	441	2.0	458	1011.44	414.06	40.9
Nizamabad	81	0.3	449	439.70	246.58	56.1
Adilabad	593	3.0	506	746.81	785.06	105.1
Karimnagar	122	0.6	470	242.74	99.29	40.9
Warangal	144	0.6	441	226.68	167.59	73.9
Khammam	255	0.7	273	429.87	301.44	70.1
Nalgonda	831	3.7	449	2964.06	2158.95	72.8
Andhra Pradesh	9637	42.0	446	23570.76	16920.03	71.8

* These are rough estimates and not exact figures.

Source: Status Report on Watersheds, Commissioner of Rural Development, Government of AP, October 2005.

coverage is higher in dry districts. Though there are variations across districts, the utilisation ratio is about 72 percent, which varies from 41 percent in Karimnagar and Medak districts to 105 percent in Adilabad district (Table 2.3). Till 2006–07 the number of watersheds initiated in the state stood at 11,083 and covered about 75 percent of the unirrigated area (Table 2.4). Though the coverage is impressive, it would have been better if some of the low irrigated districts like Anantapur and Kurnool, where the coverage is less than state average, were given greater priority.

Though we do not have accurate data on the coverage of watershed programme by socio-economic groups of population, the role of these groups in the management of the programme at the village level is indicative of the dominance of rich and elite classes (Tables 2.5 and 2.6). Non-poor people occupy the coveted positions of president and chairman in number disproportionate to their numerical strength. Some one among the poor generally occupies the paid job of secretary. Upper class dominance is conspicuous in every sphere. Forward communities occupy all the three positions (chairman, president and secretary) disproportionately while backward, scheduled castes and tribes get much less than their due share in these positions. The dominance of the rich and the elite on the watershed committees is often seem as motivated schemes to bypass the reservation policy in the PRIs (Reddy and Jenkins, 2003). For, the advent of reservation policy has resulted in weakening the elite politically, as they are not allowed to contest in the reserved category.

The current approach enables identification of the wastelands superimposed as it is by the village boundaries. Simultaneously, mobilisation of the community into Self-Help Groups (SHGs) has been taken up all over the state. Of the total 330 blocks having allocation of EAS funds, 94 are DPAP blocks and 16 (whole of Anantapur district) are DDP blocks. The 330 blocks have been grouped into 1,104 mandals for administrative convenience. Watershed and related activities in all these

Table 2.4 *Rainfed Area under Watershed Programmes*

(in 000 ha)

District	*Gross cropped area*	*Gross irrigated area*	*% of irrigated area*	*Unirrigated area*	*% of unirrigated area covered by WSP*
Srikakulam	1390	180	46.2	210	100.7
Vizayanagaram	383	141	36.8	242	41.7
Visakhapatnam	361	125	34.6	236	23.0
East Godavari	747	475	63.6	272	27.2
West Godavari	709	622	87.7	87	29.9
Krishna	715	443	62	272	52.6
Guntur	813	408	50.2	405	8.5
Prakasam	650	215	33	435	104.3
Nellore	360	274	76.1	86	193.6
Chittoor	457	198	43.3	259	144.2
Cuddapah	498	179	35.9	319	94.3
Anantapur	1169	154	13.2	1015	73.2
Kurnool	991	231	23.3	760	70.19
Mahaboobnagar	833	211	25.3	622	85.8
Ranga Reddy	278	83	29.9	195	143.6

Table 2.4 *(contd.)*

Medak	525	177	33.71	348	85.0
Nizamabad	402	280	69.7	122	48.8
Adilabad	565	110	19.5	455	71.8
Karimnagar	694	484	69.7	210	37.1
Warangal	613	391	63.8	222	40.8
Khammam	523	241	46	282	55.1
Nalgonda	686	374	54.5	312	144.3
Andhra Pradesh	13362	5996	44.9	7366	75.2

Sources: 1. Directorate of Economics and Statistics, Hyderabad., 2005–06.
2. Status Reports, Commissioner of Rural Development, Government of Andhra Pradesh, Hyderabad.

Table 2.5 *Families involved in the Watershed Programmes by Economic Classes*

Category	*Total*	*Chairman*	*President*	*Secretary*
Non-poor	141249	474	420	236
	(12.4)	(25.1)	(21.5)	(10.4)
Poor	997921	1414	1534	2027
	(87.6)	(74.9)	(78.5)	(89.6)
Total	1139170	1888	1954	2263
	(100)	(100)	(100)	(100)

Note: Figures in parentheses are percentages.
Source: Status Report, 1998, Department of Rural Development, Government of Andhra Pradesh, Hyderabad.

Table 2.6 *Families Involved in the Watershed Programmes Social Status.*

Category	*Total*	*Chairman*	*President*	*Secretary*
Scheduled Castes	217290	128	123	244
	(19.1)	(6.8)	(6.3)	(10.8)
Scheduled Tribes	126652	160	209	191
	(11.1)	(8.5)	(10.7)	(8.4)
Backward Castes	454817	608	626	693
	(39.9)	(32.2)	(32.0)	(30.6)
Other Castes	340411	992	996	1135
	(29.9)	(52.5)	(51.0)	(50.2)
Total	1139170	1888	1954	2263
	(100)	(100)	(100)	(100)

Note: Figures in parentheses are percentages.
Source: Status Report, 1998, Department of Rural Development, Government of Andhra Pradesh, Hyderabad.

mandals have to be carried out with the resources available under NWDPRA, DPAP, IWDP, JFM, EAS, etc. (for details on implementation and organisational structure, see Chapter 4). Prior to the advent of the new watershed guidelines, an area of 14.93 lakh hectares (a total of Rs. 406.05 crore allocated) land was treated (2,966 watersheds) under DPAP programme in the state. Similarly, under the EAS scheme an area of 9.06 lakh hectares coming under 1,884 watersheds was treated at an outlay of Rs. 409.81 crore (Table 2.7).

Past Experience

There are, hitherto, a few studies that recorded the initial experience of watershed development programme under the DPAP, which have put into doubt whether macro-objectives have been achieved to a satisfactory level (WASSAN 2001, MANAGE 2000, ORG-MARG 2001). These studies have identified 'technical' problems as the main lacuna in the programme. Some of the important issues included are discussed as under:

(a) *Size of watershed area:* As per the guidelines, the size of the any watershed should be approximately 500 hectares, but since the watershed is a geographical boundary, depending on the intensity of degradation, there should be flexibility in deciding the size of the watershed either more or less. Treatment of the micro-watersheds should be in line with the macro-watersheds. In other words, the process of treating micro-watershed should be co-terminus with the treatment of macro-watershed. In the absence of such planning, i.e., treating patches of micro-watersheds of a macro-watershed, micro-watersheds will not sustain.

(b) *Duration of the programme:* The duration of the project is four (now 5) years, although it requires at least seven years. This would include pre-preparatory and preparatory phases, each for one-year duration, an execution phase of four years followed by a withdrawal phase of one year. During the preparatory phase,

Table 2.7 *Status of Watersheds under Different Schemes in Andhra Pradesh (1995–96 to March 2007)*

Scheme	*Funding Agency*	*No. Projects/WS*		*Area Covered/ (in lakh ha)*	*Amount Spent (Rs. crore)*	
DPAP	Department of Land Resources, GoI	4242	(38.3)	20.41	707.32	(35.4)
DDP	Department of Land Resources, GoI	1054	(9.5)	5.07	176.93	(8.9)
IWDP	Department of Waste Land Development, GoI	1449	(13.5)	7.21	242.17	(12.1)
EAS	Department of Land Resources, GoI	1884	(17.0)	9.06	409.81	(20.5)
APHM	World Bank	100	(0.9)	0.48	22.15	(1.1)
RIDF VI	NABARD	1214	(11.0)	5.84	107.80	(5.4)
RIDF VIII-I	NABARD	277	(2.5)	1.33	34.64	(1.8)
RIDF VIII-II	NABARD	258	(2.3)	1.24	41.94	(2.1)
WDF	Government of India and NABARD	55	(0.5)	0.26	4.22	(0.2)
APRLP	DFID, UK	500	(4.5)	2.40	250.27	(12.5)
All		11083	(100)	53.3	1997.25	(100)

Note: Figures in parentheses are percentages.
Source: Status Report, Commissioner of Rural Development, Government of Andhra Pradesh, Hyderabad.

the community could be mobilised through awareness camps, exposure visits, identifying their needs and priorities with participatory approaches and introduction of small entry point activities. During the preparatory phase, the action plan with necessary socio-technical surveys could be carried out with some immediate entry point activity. Prior to the execution phase, the necessary monitoring and evaluation of the previous phases should be undertaken. Based on the impact (if positive), then, the project implementing agency (PIA) can be directed to implement the programme in four years. After a critical evaluation of the activities carried out during the execution phase and the level of community participation, the PIA may withdraw from the project by handing over the assets to the existing watershed committees and user groups.

(c) *PIA operational constraints*: Each PIA is being given 10 to 12 micro-watersheds to implement the programme. Since most of the PIAs do not have that much infrastructure to implement the programme successfully, the number of watersheds provided to an individual PIA should be optimised on the basis of the potential of PIA.

(d) *Rate per unit*: Initially (1991–95), the rate for developing a watershed per hectare used to be Rs. 4,000, which has revised to Rs. 6,000 from the year 2001–02. These rates are adjusted as per the long-standing demand from the implementing agencies. This was necessary given the inflation rate and the increased demand for labour after the advent of watershed, at least temporarily, in the villages.

(e) *Administrative and financial arrangements:* Watershed programme requires continuous flow of funds in the implementation phase while DRDA releases the funds in seven instalments, which has an adverse effect on the smooth functioning of the programme due to scarcity of money. Thus, the release of the instalments should be based on actual cost to be incurred of a specific physical activity in the programme. In addition to this, the funds for administrative activities should be more than 15 percent of the programme budget.

(f) *Landless households:* There is no provision for empowering the landless communities in the watershed area. The direct benefits go to the landowner beneficiaries, whereas landless people get indirect benefits from the wage employment. Many watersheds comprise common/community lands and the benefits out of them should go to the landless people. Moreover, there should be a provision to help them financially through revolving fund to enhance their entrepreneurship.

The importance and the scale at which watershed development programme was initiated in Andhra Pradesh are unprecedented and laudable. At one stage the state was drawing about 50 percent of the central funds allocated to watershed development for the country as a whole. This, in turn, has helped in scaling up of the programme at the state level. In the process it has gained the advantage of an early starter. Given the extent of coverage, this programme could place the state firmly on a higher agricultural growth trajectory, provided the programme is implemented effectively and could achieved the desirable results. For this to happen, the progamme ought to be supported through appropriate policies, institutions and implementation procedures. The following chapters address these issues in detail prior to taking up the impact assessment.

Empirical Setting

The empirical base for this research comes from our extensive research in various parts of Andhra Pradesh for the past seven years. The analyses presented here were drawn from mainly three studies supported by Department for International Development (DFID), UK, Ministry of Rural Development, Government of India and Overseas Development Institute (ODI), London, UK. Extensive and intensive fieldwork was carried in fifteen villages spread over five districts located in coastal, Rayalaseema and Telangana regions of Andhra Pradesh (Table 2.8). Besides, a number of watershed villages in various mandals across the sample districts were visited for the purpose of validation and cross-checking our findings in the sample villages where we have conducted the intensive study (see Figure 2.1).

Both qualitative and quantitative information was elicited. Participatory Rural Appraisal (PRA) exercises, such as group discussions, social mapping, resource mapping, wealth ranking, transect walks, discussions with Watershed Associations/ Committees, were carried out. Besides, discussions with MDT members, PIAs, project directors at the district level were helpful to get an overview of the situation. This process also helped us

Figure 2.1 *Location of Study Watershed Mandals (Villages)*

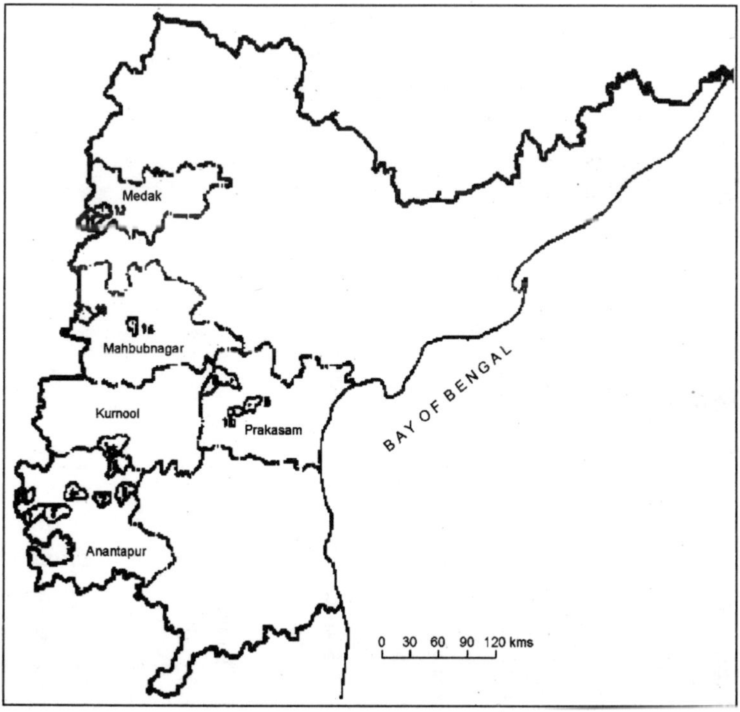

Table 2.8 *Location of the Sample Watersheds*

District/Name of the Watershed Village	*Mandal*	*Implementing Agency (PIA)*	*Year of Starting*	*Year of Completion*
PRAKASAM				
(a) Tadivaripalli	Tarlupadu	DPAP-GO-Markapur	1994	2000
(b) P. Bommalapuram	Dornala	SNIRD- NGO-Ongole	1995–96	2000
(c) Lingapuram	Cumbhum	PRRD-GO-Cumbum	1996	2000
ANANTAPUR				
(a) Mallapuram	Kalyandurgam	Rural Development Trust (RDT)	1995–96	2000
(b) Kannepalli(A)	Brahma Samudram	MDT-GO-Kalyandurg	1998	2001
(c) Mamdoor	Brahma Samudram	RDT-NGO-Kalyandurg	1995	2000
(d) Seeboi	Kalyanadurg	RDT-NGO-Kalyandurg	1996	2000
KURNOOL				
(a) S. Rangapuram	Peapully	Weaker Community Upliftment Service Society (WCUSS)	1995–96	2000
MAHABUBNAGAR				
(a) Tipaspalle	Utkoor	Mahila Samata Society (APMSS)	1995–96	1999

(b) Mamidimada	Khilla Ghanapur	Villages in Partnership (VIP)	1995–96	1999
MEDAK				
(a) Sekhapur	Zaheerabad	KVK-NGO-Zaheerabad*	1996	2000
(b) Vanampalli	Jharasangam	KVK-NGO-Zaheerabad	1997	2000

* This is NGO-run Krishi Vigyana Kendra and hence falls under the NGO category.

in selecting the sample watersheds and finalising the structured questionnaire. Before and after as well as with and without approaches were used to evaluate the impact of the watershed development programme. Both these methods were used as complementary, as either of them is fraught with problems such as memory lapse in the case of before and after and estimation problems in the case of with and without approach (for an interesting analysis in this regard, see Ravallion, 2001).

Structured schedule was prepared in order to elicit information at the household level. About 1,000 sample households representing various socio-economic categories were interviewed. These sample farmers were selected using the probability proportionate sample (PPS) to wealth ranking or farm size depending on the situation. Sample households consist of beneficiary and non-beneficiary households for the purpose of with and without scenario analysis. At the same time, schedules were designed to capture before and after information from the same households. Various agencies, governmental as well as non-governmental, were involved in implementing the sample watersheds. This was used to compare and contrast the performance of government-implemented and NGO-implemented watersheds. The sample watersheds were selected after visiting a number of watersheds in the respective districts and consultations with the Project Directors, DRDA/DRD. Different criteria were used for selecting the sample watersheds depending on the purpose. For example, for the purpose of livelihood impact assessment the criteria include: (a) watershed should be completed, i.e., first batch watershed, and (b) watershed should be a successful or model watershed in terms of implementation and impact. The purpose here is that total impact can be assessed only in the technically completed watersheds. And, the selection of model or successful watersheds is not to herald the success stories but to assess the potential of watershed development in enhancing rural livelihoods when implemented under best conditions. For, these watersheds are implemented in manner that balances the technology and philosophy of watershed development. In other words, the PIAs are well aware of the importance of the participatory development philosophy. Some ongoing watersheds were also selected to assess the political economy aspects during the process of implementation.

Notes

1. It is necessary to define and distinguish some of the watershed-related terms such as watershed, river basin, integrated watershed management, watershed management practices and watershed approach:

   A *watershed* is a topographically delineated area that is drained by a stream system. It is a hydrologic unit that has been described and used both as a physical-biological unit and a socio-economic and socio-political unit for planning and implementing resource management activities.

   A *river basin* is similar to a watershed but larger in scale.

   Integrated watershed management is the process of formulating and implementing a course of action involving natural and human resources in a watershed, taking into account the social, political, economic and institutional factors operating within the watershed and its surroundings to achieve certain socio-economic and ecological objectives. The process would include: (a) establishing watershed management objectives, (b) formulating and evaluating alternative resource management actions involving various tools and institutional arrangements, (c) choosing and implementing a preferred course of action, and (d) through monitoring of activities and outcomes, evaluating performance in terms of degrees of achievement of the specific objectives.

   Watershed development deals with the changes in structural and non-structural activities taken up in a watershed and the resultant changes in ecological variables (such as land use, vegetative cover, *in situ* soil moisture, ground water level, etc.) and their economic impact. Usually, watershed development has nine land-based structural components:

   Watershed management deals with the changes in the institutional arrangements required for collective action situations (adopted with modification from Dixon, 1992).

2. Firstly, watershed apart from covering private areas also covers common areas because it is an area-based technology. Secondly, collective adoption of the technology is a necessary condition for complete implementation of the technology. Thirdly, given the nature of the technology, its management is a collective effort and hence a public good, i.e., once the technology, transcending the individual boundaries, is adopted, it acquires the characteristics of a public good. In other words, no participant can be excluded from deriving the benefits even if he does not participate or contribute towards maintenance (non-exclusion). Similarly, the benefits derived by one individual from the technology will not preclude others from deriving the benefits as they operate on individual properties. However, this may not apply in the case of resource created or developed due to the technology such as groundwater. Basically, the technology becomes a common good.
3. Prior to this, the National Watershed Development Project for Rainfed Areas (NWDPRA) has been introduced in 1990–91. Till 1996–97, under this programme, 94 watersheds covering 1.76 lakh hectares were treated with an expenditure of Rs. 5,116 lakhs.
4. These rates are now revised to Rs. 30 lakh per watershed (Rs. 6,000 per hectare).

APPENDIX

Table A2.1 *Categorywise Wasteland Area in Andhra Pradesh*

Category	*Total area (hectares)*	*% of total geographical area*	*% of total wasteland*
Gullied and or ravinous land	68529	0.278	1.40
Upland with or without scrub	1931075	7.825	39.56
Waterlogged and marshy land	67906	0.275	1.39
Land effected by salinity/alkalinity coastal/inland	56076	0.227	1.15
Shifting cultivation Area	1363	0.005	0.03
Under utilised/degraded notified forest land	2086912	8.457	42.75
Degraded pastures/grazing land	70929	0.287	1.46
Degraded land under plantation crop	5060	0.021	0.10
Sand-desertic/coastal	41542	0.168	0.85
Mining/industrial wastelands	7346	0.030	0.15
Barren rockey/ stony waste/ sheet rockey area	506349	2.052	10.38
Steep sloping area	38237	0.155	0.78
Total	4881324	19.78	100

Source: Status Report, 1998–99, Department of Rural Development, Government of Andhra Pradesh, Hyderabad.

3

Watershed Management: Policy Context

Policy Process

The policy environment and process paves the way for strengthening the existing policies or bringing in new policies for effective and speedy achievement of development goals. A wide debate on the need to respond to water problems, and recent droughts in particular, reflects serious problems in both rural and urban areas during times of variable rainfall. This reinforces the determination at the highest political level to be seen to be ensuring change in drought-hit areas. The effects of these problems are widely publicised and lead to an imperative to do something in this regard. This is reflected in the Prime Minister's statement of "ushering new green revolution in rainfed regions".

Dry land agriculture and watershed development have received policy attention during 1980s in post-independence era. The main point of departure for the policy analysis presented here is the 1994 National Watersheds Guidelines,[1] Haryali Guidelines of 2003, which are still the existing macro-policy reference point and the proposed Neeranchal Guidelines.[2] In fact, there are nine guidelines[3] over a span of 30 years reflecting the importance accorded to watershed development at the policy level. At the same time, it creates an impression that guidelines are treated as a panacea for all ills of watershed development, including implementation. One positive feature of these changing guidelines is the flexibility at which policies are adopted and corrected in a dynamic and evolutionary process where the basic approach set out in the guidelines has been adopted and extended in response to gained experience and emerging needs. Unfortunately, the pace at which the changes took place does not allow any time or space for stabilising the implementation process. In this chapter, we critically review the policy context at the national level and in Andhra Pradesh.

In Figure 3.1 we summarise the watershed policy process in India. It reflects a mix of field findings, stakeholder consultations and documentary reviews and is based on the analytical model of the policy process. The point of departure for the policy analysis presented here is the 1994 National Watersheds Guidelines, which are still the existing macro-policy reference point.[4] One feature of these guidelines is the flexibility given at both state and district levels to interpret them in terms of the specific form of watersheds development. In states like Andhra Pradesh, these guidelines are very much a point of departure, as there has been and still is a dynamic and evolutionary process where the basic approach set out in the guidelines has been adapted and extended in response to gained experience and emerging needs. The result is a drive to new approaches that represent major changes to the fundamental paradigm of watershed development. The Government of India modified these guidelines in 2003 and the new version is called 'Haryali Guidelines'. The new guidelines focus on the decentralisation of the implementation of the programme through Panchayati Raj Institutions (PRIs) as mandated by the 73rd and 74th constitutional amendments.

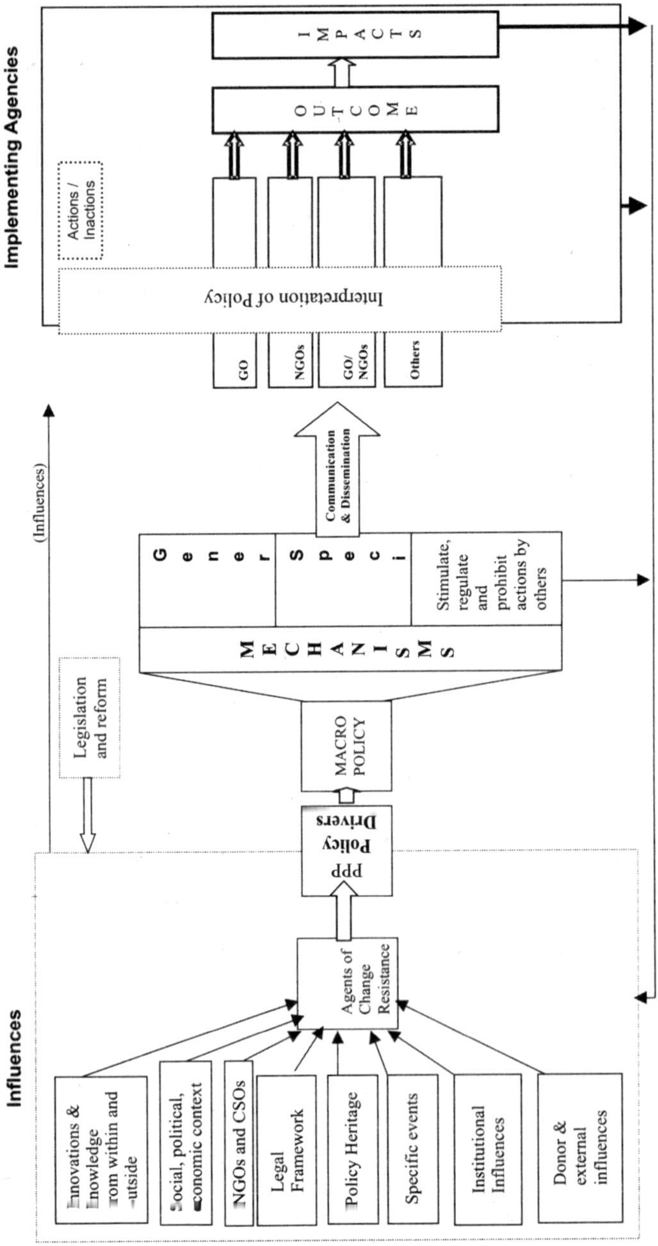

Figure 3.1 Policy Process and Implementation Framework

From 2003 onwards these guidelines are being followed in the state. For the purpose of analyses we have assessed the watersheds that were implemented under the 1994 guidelines.[5]

The flexibility and dynamism in adopting the watershed guidelines at the district level largely depends on the vision of the district administration (mainly the Collector and the Project Director—agents of change). Though dynamic officials are very few, the experience of such officials and districts reflects the flexibility embedded in guidelines and the state's readiness to experiment at the local level and learn from the experience. What lies behind this drive for innovation? Why has dynamic change become to characterise a system not noted for its flexibility or creativity? And, why does it take the specific form that it does, with watershed development seen as the leading programme along with programmes such as self-help groups (SHGs) and joint forest management (JFM), a key in approaches to the reduction of poverty in the semi-arid rural areas of the state? Several factors seem to be driving this process (policy drivers).

First of all, there is a state-level political process that creates openness to innovation and climate of reform. That there is a strong policy debate on water management and watershed development is reflected in the priority given to this issue by the state that identifies watershed development as a key to the promotion of sustainable livelihoods for the poor. A second policy driver is the existence of generally good governance and efficient administration that means that policy intentions can be translated into actions. This is far from true in a number of Indian states. The absence of decentralisation in terms of devolution of powers to PRIs is seen by some as a hindrance to the process of development and sustainability of good governance, in particular at the local level (Manor, 2001). The central government could well take issue with this point and good governance might also be questioned. However, the underlying causes are less widely discussed and some issues (especially the effects of unsustainable groundwater use for irrigation) seem to be consciously avoided even at the central level. In fact, sustainability and equity in water resource management continue to be the daunting problems in the absence of policy initiatives in this direction.

Thirdly, the active support of donors, which responds to the combination of the existence of clear need in parts of the country and the capability to implement donor programmes. In particular, the openness to new approaches in both the content and the implementation modalities of donor support is appealing to many donors. This combines with the high level of government expenditure in programmes that means donor support can be complementary to, rather than a substitute for, state development initiatives. Fourthly, the existence of several models of watershed development in India that are widely publicised (including in the mass media) and strongly advocated by leading figures in academia, policy-oriented NGOs and government. That this is seen as an indigenous 'Indian' solution that builds on long tradition in many areas is critical in the attention these models receive. But, the approach is to learn from these models rather than trying to emulate them. This approach of lesson learning from the best practices within a state, country and outside injects dynamism into the process of implementation. These learnings mainly come from the innovations of NGOs, who innovate using the local knowledge. The involvement of dry land farmers as policy drivers is rather missing in the Indian context. The innovations and adaptations of these farmers are reflected in the knowledge and innovations of the NGO sector.

Furthermore, the existence of effective NGOs and civil society organisations (CSOs) in many areas and the willingness of these groups to enter into partnership with the state governments to implement watershed development programmes. Indeed, some of the leading NGOs have their own watershed programmes independent of the state government again reflecting the widespread attention that watershed development has received. Some of the NGOs have their own models of watershed development and implementation, which are incorporated into watershed guidelines.

Recent Watershed Policies: A Critique

The 1994 guidelines are viewed as landmark in watershed development in India in many respects. These guidelines formalised participation from being a mere catch phrase through making the involvement of all sections of the community as a prerequisite. Almost all the available studies have identified the process of implementation, low levels of participation and sustaining the tempo, as critical inputs for achieving the objectives. As far as implementation is concerned, despite the emphasis on participatory approaches in the 1994 guidelines, only the NGO-implemented watersheds have done better, as they follow intensive approach when compared to the government (line departments) implemented ones. Of course, among the NGOs, there are variations, due to proliferation of NGOs in the post-1994 scenario due to the scaling up of the programme, especially in states like Andhra Pradesh. At the same time, one can find some better implementation in the government implemented watersheds. Effectively, the performance of the watershed development programme is satisfactory only in 15–20 percent of the watersheds. This scenario is no different from that of the pre-1994 guidelines.

A comparative assessment of the three recent watershed guidelines, including the proposed guidelines, is attempted to assess the merits of the proposed Neeranchal Guidelines. Our objective here is to examine the likely contribution of the proposed guidelines towards improving the implementation of the programme in the light of the past experience and highlight the missing aspects in the proposed NASDORA. A closer look at the three guidelines does not really indicate any major deviations in content and spirit of the programme (Table 3.1). There are six major changes in the proposed guidelines, viz., (i) creation of NASDORA; (ii) enlarging the size of watershed and making

Table 3.1 *Summary of MRD Watershed Development Guidelines*

Item	*MoRD Guidelines (1994)*	*Haryali Guidelines (2004)*	*Proposed Neeranchal Guidelines (2006)*
Objectives	Economic development through regeneration of natural resources in drought-prone areas. Integrated treatment of both –non-arable and arable lands on watershed basis.	Stressing the physical nature of the watershed development and the central role of the Gram Panchayats in overall economic development.	Providing sustainable rural livelihoods through overall development centred around watershed development (harnessing, conserving and developing natural resources, i.e., land, water and biomass.
Selection of watersheds	Places where people's participation and voluntary contributions are forthcoming. The area should have acute shortage of drinking water, preponderance of SC/ST population and wastelands. Only micro-watersheds of 500 ha each are selected. In case of more than one micro-watershed in a block, these need not be contiguous.	Same as 1994 guidelines. Contiguity with existing watersheds is favoured (and is one of the criteria used for watershed selection).	Same. Plus: Positive history of women's agency and community action. Micro-watershed will be a part of the mili-watershed (4–10 thousand ha) identified by the district watershed management team.

Institutional arrangement			
(a) National	MoRD	Same	NSDOR (supported by apex stakeholders council/ governing board)
(b) State	Review Committee under the chairmanship of the Chief Secretary.	Same	State Level Governing Board
(c) District	DRDA/DPAP. A District Watershed Advisory Committee which offers guidance on issues of implementation, including PIA selection.	ZP or DRDA/DPAP	District Watershed Development Agency, supported by Zila Panchayat (ZP).
(d) Watershed	GO or NGO can be selected as the PIA at the watershed level. A multidisciplinary watershed development team to assist the PIA. Watershed association, which shall be a registered body. This will be supported by a	Grama Panchayat and NGO in the case of requirement. Grama Sabha will act as watershed association. Watershed committee is discontinued. A multi-disciplinary watershed development team to assist the PIA directly.	Village watershed committee (elected body) will implement the watershed, supported by mili-watershed council, watershed development team, Gram Sabha and women's watershed councils.

Table 3.1 (contd.)

Table 3.1 (*contd.*)

Item	*MoRD Guidelines (1994)*	*Haryali Guidelines (2004)*	*Proposed Neeranchal Guidelines (2006)*
	watershed committee (elected body) with representatives from self- help groups (SHG), user groups(UG), women, GP and WDT, etc.		VWC would have maximum 20 members- 50% women and 33% SC/ST; and representation from SHGs, and UGs, GP and WDT. VWC would function as a subcommittee of the Gram Panchayat.
Funding Pattern	Rs. 4,000–4,500 per hectare at DRDA level Watershed Works: 80% Social & Human Development: 10 % Administrative overheads: 10%	Rs. 6,000 per hectare (from 2001 onwards) at DRDA/ ZP level Watershed works: 85% Social & Human Development: 5% Administrative overheads: 10%	Rs. 12000 per hectare at DRDA/ZP level Watershed works: 80% Social & Human Development: 8% Impact assessment: 2% Administrative overheads: 10%
Flow of funds	GoI, MRD to DRDA-PIA	Same	NSDOR - State Boards - DWDA- VWC

Cost Sharing	Compulsory, 5% in respect of CPR and 10% in respect of private lands of general category and 5% for the SC/ST.	Same	Same
Time period	4 years	5 years (increased in 2001)	8 years (2+4+2)
Role of NGOs	Can be one of the implementing agencies for a group of 10 or 12 MWS	Limited to group formation and social mobilisation. PIA where GP and / or ZP capacity is not adequate	Importance of NGOs is recognised and restored to pre-Haryali level.
Watershed Development Fund	Concerned WDT to take care with the help of the watershed committee. To support this activity, watershed development fund is to be created and cost contributions will go to this fund. No operational rules were prepared.	Same	Operation rules of the fund should be prepared by VWC and ratified by the Gram Sabha. 50% of the fund should go to towards maintenance of common assets. Remaining should be used as revolving fund for giving loans to the villages, who have contributed
Gender	This question is addressed in the guidelines but strategy has not been spelt out clearly	Same	gender quota of 50% in VWC is introduced. Separate women WC is introduced to support VWC.

Table 3.1 (contd.)

Table 3.1 (*contd.*)

Item	*MoRD Guidelines (1994)*	*Haryali Guidelines (2004)*	*Proposed Neeranchal Guidelines (2006)*
Equity	This question has been addressed by giving use rights for poor and SC/ST in the CPRs. But no strategy is defined or suggested.	Same	Livelihoods component is added for the benefit of poor. But no specific strategies for sharing the common resources like water.

Source: GoI, 1994, 2003, 2006.

the micro-watersheds part of a milli-watershed (4–10 thousand ha); (iii) adding a livelihood component with financial allocations and making it a comprehensive rural development programme; (iv) increasing the duration of the programme from 5 to 8 years; (v) special provision for women and weaker sections by providing 50 percent and 33 percent quota respectively in VWC and also the creation of women watershed councils; and (vi) doubling the financial allocation, i.e., from Rs. 6,000 to Rs. 12,000 per hectare.

The creation of an apex body – NASDORA – is a step in the direction of consolidating and re-emphasising the importance of rainfed areas. However, it has a narrow mandate of managing primarily central government funded watershed programmes with overarching goals of ensuring access to drinking water and sustainable livelihoods to the local population (GoI, 2006: 113). Certainly watershed development is not a panacea for the problems of rainfed farming. It is a necessary but not a sufficient condition to address the problems of these areas (Reddy et al., 2004). Therefore, one expects a much broader mandate for the NASDORA and watershed could have been made sub-component under its purview.

Even for addressing the livelihood issues, the need for departmental integration, which is being talked about for more than a decade, is a precondition for making watershed development central in the context of overall rural development. This integration should take place from top to bottom. Sustainable resource management or ecological balance can be attempted only if there is coordination between land, water, forests and people. Presently, each one is dealt under a separate ministry with numerous departments dealing with sub-sectors, while ideally all should be under one administrative unit. Moreover, sustainable resource management would be meaningful at the river basin level with an integrated river basin approach. Integration of water bodies like tanks with watershed development is vital for integrated resource management in the rainfed areas. Presently, tank rehabilitation and watershed programme are carried out separately and simultaneously. Watershed development could obstruct water flows into the downstream tanks, at least in the short run, making the tank renovation redundant. Similarly, tank renovation in the absence of watershed treatment in the catchment areas may be ineffective due to high rates of silting.

The report also talks about making these bodies professional. But most of the managers are expected to come from the line departments on deputation. The evidence of the performance of these professionals from line departments as PIAs in the ongoing watersheds questions the kind of professionalism they can bring in. This is not a new approach. The Karnataka Dry Land Development Board had done this experiment with mixed results. The possibility of attracting professionals from NGOs is constrained by the availability of good NGOs. And attracting from market is more complex given the salary structures in the corporate sector. The experience of the DPIP in Andhra Pradesh, where such approach is followed, is not very encouraging even in the absence of any subsidy involved.[6] In the end, implementation of the programme depends critically on the government bureaucrats and the NGOs. The 80:20 syndrome perpetuates.

While the creation of milli-watersheds makes ecological sense, it not only complicates the administrative process but also militates against participatory philosophy. One of the main reasons for adopting micro-watersheds of 500 hectares is for facilitating participation, which is a prerequisite for watershed development. Lack of participation was one of the bottlenecks in the case of earlier watershed programmes, which were bigger in size cutting across number of village boundaries. Even in small watersheds number of conflicts arise in the process of prioritising the works, nature of works, etc. These conflicts often result in the dilution of technical guidelines of works. In the case of milli-watersheds coordination of about 20 VWCs is required in dealing with upstream-downstream externalities and ridge to valley treatment. Inter-village coordination problems are observed in the case of water user associations in Andhra

Pradesh for similar reasons (Reddy and Reddy, 2005). The absence of property rights in common resources like water and grazing lands may aggravate the inter-village conflicts. There is a need for clarity on how micro-watersheds would be integrated administratively into the mili-watersheds.

The proposed guidelines institutionalised the livelihoods dimension by allowing 20 percent financial allocations for the livelihood component. Livelihoods are already a part of watershed development in watershed-plus or livelihood approaches that are being adopted in many states like Andhra Pradesh and Orissa where the DFID-funded livelihood programmes are linked to watershed development. Our discussions with the district level officials revealed that this would dilute the main purpose of the watershed development, i.e., soil and water conservation. They argue that while there are numerous programmes addressing poverty and livelihoods, why to add this to watershed also. While the rationale for adding livelihood approach to watershed development programme is to enhance the benefit flows and to spread the benefits, there could be a danger of overshadowing the basic programme and thus increasing the expectations from the programme. This, in turn, may pull down the ultimate monitoring and evaluation ratings of the programme.

But, the larger question is whether adding the livelihood component, in the absence of clearly defined property rights in resources (especially water), could ensure sustainable livelihoods? Watershed development per se can result in substantial gains in widespread livelihood improvements only in the regions where there would be significant improvement in water availability and irrigated agriculture. This is possible in the regions where average annual rainfall is above 700 mm (Deshpande and Reddy, 1991; Joshi et al., 2005). Even in these regions, the spread of benefits would be limited unless resource management strategies are followed. Managing water resources is crucial for improving land and water productivities. Most of the proposed livelihood components, such as lift irrigation, livestock, agro-processing, etc., in the third phase are linked to water. Unless water resources are managed judiciously and equitably, the spread of livelihood benefits will be limited, as most of these regions are dependent on groundwater, irrigation. On the contrary, the improved economic returns to water may further aggravate the inequities in access to water. Though the report reviews the equity issues associated with groundwater, it is silent on the strategies to bring in the equity. The equity safeguards provided in the guidelines are neither new nor effective in practice (Vaidyanathan, 2006). The continued supply side focus of the policies in the absence of demand management and clearly defined property rights in common resources would perpetuate the inequities.

One issue raised at a policy level is the need to ensure better access to the benefits of watershed development for landless and land-poor people by 'de-linking' access to water from landownership; in other words, to treat water as a public good to which all sections of the community have equal rights and entitlements. This calls for a change in the existing structure of property rights and bringing groundwater under the common property management regime. The formal water user associations that are in place in a number of states would come in hand in addressing this issue. That is, groundwater should be brought under the purview of water user associations. To achieve this may require primary legislation. It certainly requires a clear property rights fostered on institutional basis at the community level through which these rights could be translated into access to water resources.

Duration of the programme is increased to eight years, which is a necessity in the case of watershed development due to its long gestation period. Importantly, initial community mobilisation phase is increased to two years from the existing one year. Though this gives more time for establishing the most needed participatory process, there is no provision in the guidelines to how this is strictly adhered to, except for monitoring and evaluation. Experience shows that in majority of the cases the preparatory phase was limited to three months instead of 12 months. Most of the PIAs blame administrative process, which takes more time for releasing the funds. On the other hand, established NGOs are comfortable, as they have been working with the communities prior to the advent of the programme and hence they do not require more time to catch roots (Reddy et al., 2005). In the case of GO-PIAs there is a need for strict monitoring during this phase in order to make sure that social development gets priority in the process of implementation.

One of the most serious concerns, in our view, is the enhancement of allocation from Rs. 6,000 to Rs. 12,000 per hectare. Rent seeking has become a common phenomenon in the watershed programmes. Mushrooming of NGOs in states like Andhra Pradesh, Karnataka and Madhya Pradesh was attributed to the significant cash flows in watershed programme. In a detailed study on pro-poor policies and watershed development, the nexus between politicians, PIAs and contractors was brought out clearly (see Chapter 9). There is blurring of the lines between inter-group conflicts based on economic divisions and those based on political differences. In effect, the means by which watershed programmes have been permitted to operate has assisted this percolation of money politics down to the base of political pyramid. This was the situation when funding was Rs. 30 lakh per watershed.[7] One can imagine the plight with Rs. 60 lakh per watershed.

However, this is not to argue that the financial requirements are any less in the rainfed regions. In fact, we argue against the planned increase in user contribution in the watershed programmes as proposed in the plan documents.[8] User contribution is expected to go up to 25 percent during the 11th Plan period, to 50 percent during the 12th Plan period and to 75 percent during the 13th Plan period. While this approach is embedded in the economic rationale of cost sharing, it faults on plan objective of social justice and equity. For, (a) the magnitude of investments in watershed development programmes (WDP) is much less (Rs. 12,000 per hectare), when compared to providing canal irrigation (Rs.1–2 lakh per hectare); and (b) the benefits from WDP are visualised only in the long run and uncertain in nature while the benefits from canal irrigation are immediate and dramatic.[9] Despite substantial benefits the pricing of canal water is ridiculously low covering not even a third of the operation and maintenance costs let alone capital costs. It is unfair to apply economic/market principles of higher contribution in the backward and poverty-stricken regions while leaving developed and rich regions as spoiled kids of the benevolent state. While arguing against enhanced cost recovery from WDP beneficiaries, it is necessary to ensure proper implementation of the programme and its sustainability. The guidelines should have introduced stringent procedures/checks ensuring accountability and transparency. Social accounting and transparency should have been made mandatory using the recent Right to Information Bill.[10]

Another significant policy issue is that a range of other policies, like power, agriculture, water, etc., also influence watershed development. In some states, power pricing (which greatly influences irrigation levels), the guaranteed purchase of rice and changes in agricultural subsidies and other protection measures greatly influence the ways in which the benefits (and especially the extra water available) from watershed development are used. While some policies (like water pricing) strive to improve the economic efficiency of water, agricultural price policies indirectly promote inefficient water use practices. The case in point is the support price mechanism, especially for paddy, which encourages farmers to grow more of paddy crop, which is highly water intensive, through keeping paddy prices artificially high. This results in excessive and inefficient use of water resources. More value addition could be achieved through the reallocation of water to other crops. This would also facilitate more equitable distribution of the resources. Similarly, in the case of groundwater, the policy of subsidised power tariff structure for agriculture is resulting in the widespread degradation of the resources. These policies are set and administered by different branches of government than those responsible for watershed development, reflecting the problems that come from institutional fragmentation.

Therefore, pro-poor policies need to be more comprehensive in terms of resource or policy integration. Coordination, if not integration, between various departments that deal with natural resources is a pre-condition for drawing up appropriate policies. Unless the bottlenecks in effective implementation are identified and corrected, there is no rationale for adding more guidelines. One fails to understand how the proposed guidelines can ensure better implementation when earlier two failed to do so. Instead of correcting the problems at the implementation level, new implementation structures are invented. As long as these structures have to operate in the same environment (socio-economic, political and policy), the expected outcomes will not be very different. Therefore, attempts should be made in the direction of changing the implementation environment. On the whole, the proposed guidelines are neither comprehensive enough to tackle the complexities of rainfed agriculture nor deep enough to improve the implementation of the programme. Instead of adding to the list of guidelines, the focus should be shifted to implementation and governance issues.

Policy Process: Andhra Pradesh Experience

In this section we attempt to summarise the findings of the analysis of the watershed policy process in Andhra Pradesh. It reflects a mix of field findings, stakeholder consultations and documentary reviews. The analysis of the policy process concludes with a number of policy recommendations that are intended to contribute to the existing dynamic debate on the future of this and related policies in AP and elsewhere.

The importance of water and watershed management in AP is reflected in the priority given to this issue by the earlier political regimes that identified watershed development as a key to the promotion of sustainable livelihoods for the poor in the

'Neeru-Meeru' (Water and People) poverty eradication campaign. It is also reflected in the formation and composition of the state-level Water Conservation Mission, which was constituted in 2001 to provide innovative thinking on how to counter the widespread water problems in AP. These programmes are supported by legislative support such as the formation of water user associations for managing surface irrigation and the recent legislation on 'land, water and trees', which is more comprehensive in nature. This new legislation is focused on groundwater resources. It requires the registration of all new wells. Though the legislation strengthens the regulation of groundwater, it does not provide the basis for improving the situation where wells already exist and nor does it really address land, water and trees in an integrated manner.

The Water Conservation Mission has initiated a series of consultations to prepare the Andhra Pradesh Water Vision. The June 2002 update of progress in developing this issue identified questions of the quantity, sustainability and security of water supplies now and in the future. The consultation process led to the preparation of the final vision in 2003. This process provides a context within which the analysis of policy trajectories in the state should be considered. The new government that had come to power in 2004 has not only continued the earlier emphasis on watershed development but also strengthened it further through new initiatives, such as irrigation development, extension services, improved credit in rural areas, seed distribution, etc.

Andhra Pradesh has prepared a vision 2020 document in 1999, which sets goals to be achieved by the year 2020 in various fields. Some of these goals are more ambitious than that of Millinium Development Goals. Besides, the state has the process guidelines for watershed development setting the objectives for watershed development in the state. Though AP follows the national guidelines in spirit, it has developed its own process guidelines in 2004 to operationalise the central Haryali Guidelines and also to link the watershed development programme

WDP with its own vision. The Andhra Pradesh Rural Livelihoods Programme (APRLP), supported by the DFID, UK, mainly influenced the process guidelines. The APRLP or the process guidelines are a head of the national guidelines in terms of integrating rural livelihoods into watershed development. These objectives and goals at the state level can be compared with the expected contribution, direct as well as indirect, of the WDP. The juxtaposition of the contributions of WDP with the development goals set by the "Process Guidelines for WDP" (GoAP, 2002), the goals for 2020 as set by the state government in "Vision 2020" (GoAP, 1999) and the "Millennium Development Goals" (MDGs) would help in establishing the linkages between the MDGs and the state's leading sectoral programme, i.e., WDP (Table 3.1). While the goals set out in various documents do not completely match, there is considerable similarity. The direct and indirect contributions of watershed development indicate the potential range. WDP contributes directly and prominently towards achieving the goals of rural poverty, hunger and environmental sustainability, whereas it contributes indirectly towards achieving the goals of gender equity, literacy and health, though the process guidelines of WDP are silent on these aspects. However, the spill over effects or externalities of WDP are strong enough to have an impact on the other goals as well.

Key Policy Challenges: Learning from Experience

The management of small-scale watersheds in India has a long history, with many traditional village-based systems that were integral to the livelihoods of rural communities. These traditional systems have often broken down and tended not to be recognised until recently, with the 'modern' era of watersheds development emerging in the last 40 years to be the main approach to improving land and water management, particularly in many of the semi-arid parts of the country. This approach has had many successes, particularly the severe degradation of land and water resources

Table 3.1 *Linkages between MDGs, Vision 2020 and Watershed Development in Andhra Pradesh.*

Millennium Development Goals	*Andhra Pradesh's Vision 2020*	*Andhra Pradesh's Process Guidelines for WDP*	*Watershed Development's Contribution*	
			Direct	*Indirect*
Poverty: to halve by 2015 the proportion of the world's people whose income is less than $1 per day	• Eradicate poverty and take care of its old, vulnerable and generally needy. • Create the resources people need, such as capital and infrastructure, to transform their own futures. • Embrace innovation and the latest know-how to grow crops, produce goods and provide high quality services	• Promoting the overall economic development and improving the socio-economic conditions of the resource poor and disadvantaged sections inhabiting the programme areas. • Employment generation, poverty alleviation, community empowerment and development of human and other	• Water as a factor of production in homestead gardening, agriculture, dairy, horticulture, floriculture, aquaculture, industry and in many other types of economic activity. • Investments in water infrastructure and services as a catalyst for local	• Reduced vulnerability to water-related hazards boasts investments, production and development. • Reduced ecosystem degradation boosts local-level sustainable development. • Improved health from better quality water increases productive

		economic resources of the village.	and regional development.	capacities.
Hunger: to halve by 2015 the proportion of the world's people who suffer from hunger.	• Enable its farmers, entrepreneurs and professionals to make agriculture flourish and build thriving industries and service businesses.	• Developing wastelands/ degraded lands, drought prone and desert areas on watershed basis keeping in view the capability of land, site conditions and local needs.	• Water as a direct input for expanded staple food production. • Sustainable production of fish, tree crops and other foods gathered in CPRs. • Reliable water for agricultural cash crops, horticulture, livestock, fisheries, etc. • Employment creation allowing landless to buy food	• Ensure ecosystems integrity to maintain water flows to food production. • Reduced urban hunger by cheaper staple food from more reliable water supplies.
Universal Primary Education: to ensure that, by	• Enable its people to learn, earn, and lead healthy and productive lives.	• Simple, easy and affordable technological solutions and		• Improved school attendance from improved health

(contd.)

Table 3.1 (*contd.*)

Millennium Development Goals	*Andhra Pradesh's Vision 2020*	*Andhra Pradesh's Process Guidelines for WDP*	*Watershed Development's Contribution*	
			Direct	*Indirect*
2015, children everywhere will be able to complete a full course of primary schooling.		institutional arrangements that make use of, and build upon, local technical knowledge and available materials.		and reduced water carrying burdens, especially for coupled with income effects.
Child Mortality: to reduce by two-thirds, between 1990 and 2015, the death rate for children under the age of five years.	• Give its children a happy childhood and every opportunity to achieve their full potential.		• Improved quantities and quality of drinking and domestic water and sanitation reduce main morbidity and mortality factor for young children.	• Improved nutrition and food security reduces susceptibility to diseases.
Maternal Mortality: to	• Promote small families for a		• Improved cleanliness, health	• Improved health and nutrition

reduce by three-fourths, between 1990 and 2015, the rate of maternal mortality.	healthy and wealthy society.		and reduced labour burdens from improved access to water reduce mortality risks.	reduce susceptibility to anaemia and other conditions that affect maternal mortality.
Major Diseases: to halve, by 2015, halted and begun to reverse: • The spread of HIV/AIDS • The scourge of malaria • The scourge of other major diseases that affect humanity			• Better water management reduces mosquito habitats and malaria incidence. • Reduced incidence of range of diseases where poor water management is a vector.	• Improved awareness, especially among women, reduces susceptibility to HIV/AIDS and other major diseases.
Environmental Sustainability:to stop the unsustainable	• Safeguard its environment and make its villages and cities clean,	• Mitigating the adverse effects of extreme climatic conditions of the	• Improved water management, including pollution control	• Development of integrated management within river

(contd.)

Table 3.1 (*contd.*)

Millennium Development Goals	*Andhra Pradesh's Vision 2020*	*Andhra Pradesh's Process Guidelines for WDP*	*Watershed Development's Contribution*	
			Direct	*Indirect*
exploitation of natural resources and to halve, by 2015, the proportion of people who are unable to reach or to afford safe drinking water.	green and safe to live in.	resource poor and disadvantaged sections inhabiting the programme areas. • Restoring ecological balance by harnessing conserving and developing natural resources, i.e., land, water and vegetative cover.	and sustainable levels of abstraction, are key factors in maintaining ecosystems integrity • Actions to ensure access to adequate and safe water for poor and poorly-serviced communities	basins creates conditions where sustainable ecosystems management possible while upstream-downstream impact mitigation is taken care off.
Develop a Global Partnership for Development	• Make its government simple, transparent, accountable and responsive.	• Sustainable community action for the operation and maintenance of assets created and further	• Sustainable development, linking environmental protection to poverty	• Practice of global thinking and decentralised local action widely

	• Ensure that its people continue to have a strong voice and role in the governance of their state.	development of the potential of the natural resources in the watershed.	alleviation and good governance, widely supported. • Partnerships based on environmental programmes are a basis for wider agreements, nationally and internationally.	supported • Improved knowledge, understanding and confidence creates basis for partnerships.

halted and even reversed in many semi-arid areas and clear gains in terms of agricultural production, labour demand, migration and income in rural communities where watershed development has been implemented. Despite these successes, the accumulation of experience and analysis of the policy process and impacts in AP and elsewhere has identified limitations to the existing mainstream approach that need to be taken into account in the further evolution of watershed policies and approaches.

Watershed development has particularly taken off during the last decade or so, with the 1994 National Guidelines providing the framework within which this expansion has taken place. The recent Government of India Working Group on Rainfed Agriculture estimates that the total area covered by watershed programmes was about 45.58 million hectares by March 2005, about 40 percent of the total potential area, at an investment of Rs. 1,70,370 crore (GoI, 2008). Annual expenditure on watershed development during 10th Plan is about Rs. 2,300 crore (MoRD, 2006). Although this represents a substantial achievement, given that this progress has taken over 40 years, the speed of implementation of watershed programmes, the ability to scale up successful experiences is clearly a major policy issue.

In particular, the need for effective on-the-ground implementation capacity is recognised as an important constraint in many areas, both from government agencies and from NGOs, which are intended to be the main project implementation agencies (or PIAs). This is recognised in AP and is reflected in the focus within the APRLP on the development of capacities at district level and below. This constraint is also reflected in the quality of watershed implementation, which at its best can be a flexible and empowering process that can transform the livelihoods and resource base of poor communities. This is too often not the case, however, with many watersheds that are implemented following a rigid and prescriptive model. In particular, the guideline figures for both the size (500 ha) of a watershed and the amount spent (Rs. 20 lakh, now revised to Rs. 30 lakh) per watershed have been rigidly applied in many places regardless of local needs or conditions. In some cases, the actual implementation is far from satisfactory, with little effort to engage local communities or implement interventions to an adequate quality.

Although there are exceptions, much watershed development has concentrated on physical interventions such as contour-bunding and check-dams that are intended to improve groundwater recharging and reduce land and soil degradation. These physical interventions are often not balanced against non-structural measures or measures to improve the production process or open up new livelihood opportunities. These measures include policy changes that bring in cropping pattern shifts and changes in livelihood patterns. The need to widen the scope of activities in watershed programmes is reflected in the "watershed-plus" approach, developed under APRLP, in which a wider range of interventions is considered, but this is still recognised as limited and there are active strategies to develop the approach yet further. The development of a process to widen the scope of possible interventions and root the choices made more effective in local conditions is critical for the further evolution of watershed policy.

Equity is seen as a major policy issue, with past watershed programmes often failing to reach the poorest households and disproportionately benefiting the better off sections of the community. This is reflected in the pattern of expenditure on different activities in watershed programmes, with an estimated 70 percent of funds used for land and water management interventions that predominantly benefit larger farmers and only 7.5 percent being used to support the livelihoods of poor and landless families (GoI, 2001). There is thus need to more effectively target the requirements and potentials of landless and land-poor (especially those with rainfed lands on upper slopes) families and of women, if watershed development is truly to become the catalyst for a wider process of local-level development and poverty reduction.

Several approaches are considered for addressing the equity issues, though these are mainly technical in nature and hence their impact is limited to physical coverage rather than actual benefits. Moreover, the focus in these approaches continues to be on landed households. One such approach is 'ridge to valley' treatment of the watershed basin. This approach gives preference to small and marginal farmers, who are located on the degraded slopes of the higher reaches of the watershed. Another approach is to treat the entire land in the village rather than restricting to 500 hectares. This approach, adopted under the APRLP, facilitates the coverage of all the sections of the landed households and ensures better participation and cooperation. Besides, APRLP is also focusing on the landless households in the community through initiating specific programmes for them. These aspects are being incorporated at the national level in the proposed Neeranchal Guidelines.

One issue raised at a higher policy level in both the country and the state is the need to ensure better access to the benefits of watershed development for landless and land-poor people by 'de-linking' access to water from landownership; in other words, to treat water as a public good to which all sections of the community have equal rights and entitlements (Reddy, 2002). To achieve this may require not only primary legislation, but also a clear institutional basis at the community level through which these entitlements are translated into access to water resources.

There are also concerns over the sustainability of many interventions made and benefits gained, with the mid-term appraisal of the 9th Plan by the Planning Commission (GoI, 2000) stating that, for watersheds surveyed in Maharashtra and AP, "increase in agricultural production did not last for more than two years. Structures were abandoned because of lack of maintenance and there was no mechanism for looking after common lands". The situation has not changed much during the 10th Plan. This picture is corroborated by other studies, with the root cause of poor sustainability seen as the failure to effectively engage local people in the process. This issue of local-level 'ownership' of the process has major policy implications too.

A final major lesson from past experiences is that watershed development is not influenced by watershed policies alone. In particular, a range of other policies influence agriculture, water management and land management. In AP, power tariffs (which greatly influences irrigation levels), the guaranteed purchasing scheme for rice and changes to agricultural subsidies and protection measures greatly influence the ways in which the benefits (and especially the extra water available) from watershed development are used and the response of communities to watershed programmes is made. While the recent water policies in the state strive to improve the economic efficiency of water, agricultural price policies tend to promote inefficient water use practices. The case in point is the state intervention in paddy markets to hedge against the falling prices when there is glut in the market. The support price mechanism, especially for paddy, encourages the farmers to grow more paddy, which is highly water intensive, through keeping the paddy prices artificially high. This results in excessive and inefficient use of water resources. More value addition could be achieved through the re-allocation of water to other crops. This would also facilitate more equitable distribution of the resource. This raises the notion of the need to better understand the water intensity of different patterns of water use in production. This is a concept that has been widely used in relation to energy for many years. Adapting the idea to reflect the dynamics of an even scarcer resource, water, would provide a basis for more informed decision-making on production choices and water allocations.

Similarly, in the case of groundwater, the policy of subsidised or free power tariff structure for agriculture is resulting in the widespread degradation of the resources. There are no policies, except for some regulatory ones linked with institutional credit, dealing with groundwater despite the fact that groundwater is the single largest source of irrigation in the state. Groundwater is conspicuously missing in the recent water user association legislation. Even in the context of *Neeru-Meeru* programme the stress is more on supply side, i.e., recharging the aquifers rather than managing the resources in a more efficient and equitous manner. These different policies are set and administered by different branches of government than those responsible for watershed development, reflecting the problems that come from institutional fragmentation.

Challenges for Watershed Policy

The dynamic approach to watershed policy development in AP is one that needs to be renewed and further developed as an incremental process. How this takes place and the factors that drive this process will go far to determine whether the potential of watershed development to be a driving force for local-level development in semi-arid areas of the state will be realised. This conclusion elevates even at the policy, rather than the local, level as being determinant of success in watershed development. This is not to deny the importance of local developments. It rather reflects that what happens at the local level is greatly determined by the policy framework within which they take place.

The analysis presented above identifies a series of factors that inform and influence policy development. Not least of these is a genuine and concerted determination at the central political level to local-level development. What consequently becomes a core issue is the knowledge and understanding that drives this central level debate. In particular, the process through which feedback from implementation to policy development is a critical issue. This must be transparent and inclusive, with the needs and experiences of all stakeholders reflected in the feedback.

Policy development needs to be informed and guided by the effectiveness of on-the-ground experiences in the implementation of existing approaches. This is especially true where, as in the watershed programme in AP, innovations are often developed through pilot schemes. Those elements that do work need to be consolidated and scaled up to cover the whole programme, whilst actions to reconcile limitations need to be identified and incorporated into policy changes. But, the impact of many innovations is intermeshed with other aspects of rural development and takes time to manifest themselves.

The nature of links between the ground and the policy process will become even more critical where watershed development becomes more flexible and locally rooted. This is essential (and is recognised in the report of the 10th Plan Working Group, GoI, 2001) if the limitations that come from the normative approach and characterises existing guidelines are to be overcome. There are a number of dimensions to this that need to be worked through changes in watershed policy at all levels.

Andhra Pradesh's approach to watershed development is unique. It is a 'top-down model' with a 'bottom-up' approach. The success of this model would have important macro-policy implications. The main advantage of this is its scale and spread, which is a departure from the earlier success cases of small and experimental types. Success of this approach means bringing down the duration of the programme. However, as discussed above, there are lacunae in the programme implementation that need attention in order to make it a fairly successful and sustainable programme.

The importance and the scale at which watershed development programme was initiated in AP are unprecedented and laudable. At one stage the state was drawing about 50 percent of the central funds allocated to watershed development for the country as a whole. This, in turn, has helped in scaling up of the programme at the state level. In the process it has gained the advantage of an early starter. Given the extent of coverage, this programme could place the state firmly on a higher agricultural growth trajectory. More importantly, successful implementation of this programme would open a new chapter in development economics, i.e., 'top-down' participatory approach at the macro-level is possible as well as sustainable. This calls for a detailed assessment of the programme, which is the main objective of this study. As far as watershed development is concerned the main pillar is the institutional structure and its sustainability that forms the subject of the next chapter.

Notes

1. The 1994 guidelines were revised in August 2001. Changes such as increasing the time span from 4 to 5 years are made to the 1994 guidelines.
2. The Parthsarathy Committee submitted its report in January 2006, but it is yet to be approved and converted into guidelines.
3. These include the guidelines for (i) Operations Research Projects in mid-1980s; (ii) World Bank Aided Projects, 1985–86; iii) National Watershed Development Programme (NWDP), 1986–88; (iv) National Watershed Development Programme for Rainfed Agriculture (NWDPRA), 1989–90; (v) Ministry of Agriculture's WARASA guidelines in early 1990 after modification by the committee of secretaries; (vi) Ministry of Rural Development guidelines, 1994, revised in 2001; (vii) Haryali Guidelines, 2003; (viii) World Bank-DFID-GTZ guidelines; and (ix) the proposed Neeranchal Guidelines.
4. The revised guidelines are issued in August 2001. Changes such as increasing the time span from 4 to 5 years and per hectare allocations from Rs. 4 to 6 thousands are made to the 1994 guidelines.
5. All our references to guidelines in the paper are to 1994 guidelines, unless otherwise mentioned.
6. Field experience revealed that the community coordinators hired from the market for the purpose of organising the self-help groups have got in to the culture of commission agents, i.e., demanding a cut from the groups whenever a loan is sanctioned.
7. We aregue that there are other ways of increasing funding in rainfed regions rather than putting every thing in watershed development.
8. The guidelines do not take the cognisance of this while talking about user contribution.

9. Here we are talking about access to water viŝ-a-viŝ watershed treatment at the farm level. It naïve to think that getting canal water needs longer period due to time taken for constructing the dam. Farmer is concerned with the gestation of his investments, time or money.
10. Though the report narrates at length, like an academic exercise, how good governance can be attained, it fails to suggest any concreted steps to improve good governance. Policy guidelines should be more specific unlike an academic review of issues from literature. In fact, the lengthy report is rather vague in pinning the issues and addressing them up front. The report writers should have seen the clarity and breavity in the 1994 guidelines.

4

Watershed Management: Institutional Context

While the success of watershed development as a technology is well established, the process of watershed management is proving to be the main bottleneck for the widespread success of the programme. Watersheds have been studied from various perspectives, such as economic efficiency of water use and investments, flood run-off, soil erosion, sedimentation, groundwater recharge, socio-political dimensions, etc. (Dixon, 1992). Understanding the interactions between land, water and people is equally important in studying watersheds. Therefore, watershed management is more than just the cost-benefit analysis of investments. The main distinction between watershed development and other traditional developmental programmes is that the former is based essentially on community-natural resource interface. Given the nature of the technology, watershed development requires large areas cutting across households and even villages for its adoption. Hence, its adoption and success critically hinges upon inter-village as well as intra-village cooperation. In other words, collective participation and action is a critical ingredient for watershed management. This throws up a wide range of institutional issues, such as social organisation, property rights, etc., that need careful scrutiny in order to sustain the programme. Institutional aspects become important in the case of common resource interests transcending across households, communities and even villages. For instance, the problem of property rights arises when dealing with the treatment of common land and water resources.

The 1994 watershed guidelines have recognised that the involvement of all sections of the community (collective action) is a prerequisite for sustainable watershed management. Implementation is decentralised with a mix of 'bottom-up' and 'top-down' approaches. In the case of scaling up, the guidelines have also suggested that implementation should be handed over to PRIs when they are equipped with capacities. Almost all the available studies have identified the process of implementation and sustaining the tempo as critical inputs for achieving the objectives. In general, people's participation in the programme is observed to be very poor, which is reflected in the recommendations of the National Advisory Committee to the UPA government. As far as implementation is concerned, despite the emphasis on participatory approaches in the guidelines, only the NGO-implemented watersheds have done better, as they follow intensive approach when compared to the government (line departments)-implemented ones. On the whole, about 20 percent of the watersheds are implemented by NGOs, while the rest are implemented by the line departments. This ratio, however, would have further tilted in favour of the line departments after the advent of Haryali Guidelines. Of course, among the NGOs, there are variations, owing to the proliferation of NGOs in the post-1994 scenario and scaling up of the programme, especially in states like Andhra Pradesh. Here, we address the institutional issues that arise in the context of watershed management.

Property Rights and Collective Action

Often, poverty can be termed as resource or asset poverty, which is a situation where poor people, because of their limited access to resources/assets, face constraints in investment possibilities to improve the assets (make them more valuable) and accumulate resources/assets (Di Gregorio, 2004). Property rights over natural resources are fundamental in shaping the livelihoods of rural poor. Rural poor are often found to possess the weakest property rights, such as secure rights over land, water, trees, livestock, fish, genetic resources, etc. The proponents of property rights school argue that assignment of exclusive property rights gives necessary approval and control over the resources and, thus, will assure the right holder of the future benefits of investment and careful management and bear the losses incurred by misuse of the resources. As a result, secure property rights provide a strong incentive for sustainable resource management.

Although property rights are necessary and relevant in many circumstances, these alone may not result in poverty alleviation (Saliem, 2004; Mwangi, 2004). That is, property rights are necessary but not sufficient for poverty alleviation. Other resources (credit, human skills, infrastructure, markets, etc.) are needed to complement the rights in resources that one requires to make sound investment decisions for overcoming poverty. Most poor happen to be mal-resourced in terms of land, having some parcels that can barely favour any surplus production or even meet the basic subsistence needs. Improvements to such degraded lands depend on injections from off-farm income, at least in the early stages of farm development (Shiferaw et al., 2005). Again, the poor lack access to such income, which further limits their choices to move out of primitive agricultural production. Thus, property rights in themselves have not and do not always translate to increased productivity and incomes for alleviating poverty (Kariuki, 2004; Pasha, 2004).

Assigning property rights may result in a 'zero sum' game as they exclude groups of people. Or, any changes in the existing property regimes tend to produce gainers and losers. Change in property rights has redistribution effects, as assigning exclusive property (to individuals or groups) will automatically exclude others from sharing the benefits that are accustomed to use the resource before the assignment/change of rights. In many cases, it is the poor who get excluded, as is the case with the watershed development programmes in India (Meinzen-Dick, 2004; Reddy et al., 2004). However, who loses and who gains depends on the type of resource and the nature of changes in property rights, i.e., moving from individual to group or vice versa (Reddy, 2000). Besides, the zero sum characterisation of property assignment may be a possibility initially, as opportunities may widen for those excluded after sometime (Colfer, 2004; Di Gregorio, 2004; Mwangi, 2004). By re-contracting rights in different ways, disadvantaged actors may create opportunities to amend their initial disadvantages into a more beneficial arrangement for them. So, distribution of gains and losses may not be static (Mwangi, 2004; Meinzen-Dick, 2004). Bromley (2004), on the other hand, expresses doubts about the efficacy of better property rights arrangements that are assumed to induce enough new investment to bring forth gains that could be used to compensate those who have lost out. According to him, such situations are only Potential Pareto Improvements (PPI). If a section is powerful enough to execute exclusion, the probability is high that it will be able to exclude the marginal sections from the increased benefits (Husain, 2004). Tilting the scale in favour of poor (losers) even in the long run calls for collective action.

Most of the poor find themselves in poverty not due to the absence of property rights, but due to their inability to assert or change them through collective action. In most of the cases, the existing property rights that are embedded in political economy systems are biased against poor. Hence, collective action or social mobilisation is an important channel for asserting the rights of the poor. Collective action to solve poverty may be seen as a desperate effort by the extremely marginalised members of society to secure for themselves what the wider political-economic system has failed to provide for them (Bromley, 2004). Collective action could lead to poverty alleviation not only through asserting or changing rights over natural resources like land, water, etc., but also through asserting their right to information, share in the developmental programmes, etc. Often property rights framework considers the tangible assets or resources. In their present form property rights are self-limiting in alleviating poverty. Besides, collective action to assert or change the property rights in resources or assets is more complex and costly, as it threatens the existing socio-economic and political structures. Collective action and poverty are linked in two different ways. On the one hand, collective action can be the tool of the poor who are powerless and will provide a platform to express their voice. On the other hand, any kind of cooperation has costs and poverty reduces the ability of the poor to engage in collective action (Di Gregorio, 2004). The effectiveness of collective action in overcoming the socio-economic and political dynamics depends on the relative strength of the collective group in changing the political fortunes.

In the absence of such strengths, collective action may not necessarily guarantee success with respect to poverty alleviation. Communities are complex pluralistic entities, with members being part of different overlapping socio-economic and political groups. Such membership, especially in socio-economic groups, accords power that can be used for exclusion of weaker sections from collective action. This will certainly increase poverty and vulnerability. Political groupings tend to cut across income groups (poor/non-poor), especially in situations where poor are in substantial numbers. As long as socio-economic inequities and 'elite capture' are dominant phenomena in the system, institutional changes (including property rights) may not result in poverty alleviation, irrespective of the fact that these changes happen due to new ideas (Bromely, 2004) or due to social justice concerns (Birner, 2004). While donor communities and non-poor groups (Knox, 2004) can provide or raise pro-poor ideas and concerns, their implementation and effectiveness largely depend on the existing power structure. Experience in India[1] supports the fact that how pro-poor policies and donor conditionalities are diluted at the implementation level. Even the donors, to some extent, are responsible for this (Reddy, 2006).

Though, there is consensus regarding the role and importance of property rights and collective action in poverty alleviation, their importance, effectiveness and relative strengths in varying resource, socio-economic and political situations is less understood. Besides, there is no clarity regarding the linkages or synergy between property rights and collective action. These two are often treated as mutually exclusive rather than mutually inclusive or complementary. How necessary and sufficient the conditions of property rights and collective action in poverty alleviation? Can either or both of them ameliorate poverty? If so, under what socio-economic and political situations? Here, an attempt is made to understand the intricacies in the relations between property rights, collective action and poverty alleviation. Watershed development/management is the interplay between property rights, collective action and poverty alleviation.

Collective action is a prerequisite for watershed development, as it transcends across households and even villages. Hence, its implementation is critically linked with both inter-household and inter-village cooperation. Watershed encompasses private as well as common resources like land, water, forests, etc. The success of collective action, therefore, is linked to the allocation of property rights and the distribution of benefits from the common resources across different sections of the community. Watershed being a soil and water conservation technology, land and water resources are central to property rights and collective action. Moreover, being a land-based technology, watershed development has an inherent bias towards the landed or less poor communities. In this context, the role of property rights and collective action assumes greater importance.

Collective Action and Property Rights: Concepts and Linkages

Collective action is defined as "an action taken by a group of individuals to achieve common interests" (Marshall, 1998, as quoted in Di Gregorio, 2004). Often participation is used synonymously with collective action. There could be varying modes of participation, such as nominal, passive, consultative, activity specific, active, interactive and informed (Agarwal, 2001; GoI, 2006).[2] All these forms of participation do not result in collective action as defined above. Mere contribution by members does not merit collective action. Participation could be equated with collective action as long as long as "individual costs of participation are more than that of individual benefits". That is, there is an amount of "voluntary involvement and efforts for the sake of achieving a common good". What should be the size of the group that is involved in collective efforts? It varies depending on the nature of activity and resource itself. In the case of common resources like water, watersheds, etc., concerning the entire community, collective efforts of the entire community are necessary. Even majority involvement may not be effective in such cases. On the other hand, any number of individuals can be part of collective action when they are dealing with localised issues, like avenue plantations in the locality, managing a local pond, etc.

In the context of analysing the role of institutions involving collective action in the management of CPRs, institutions are understood as regularised patterns of behaviour between individuals and groups in society, or complexes of norms, rules and behaviours that serve a collective purpose (de Janvry, 1993). In the present context we use the term *institutions, formal and informal,* to identify local-level rules, regulations, norms and customs that emerged or evolved, either internally or with the help of external forces, in an historical process to solve the common problems in a village community. These may be in the form of watershed committees, user groups/associations or organisations to manage community grazing lands, water councils (*pani panchayats*) to manage irrigation and drinking water, forest councils (*vana panchayats*) to manage forest lands or resources and other grassroots organisations promoting such activities involving collective action for the common good.

The property rights school argues that private property is the most appropriate way to make individuals internalise the externalities and, therefore, a primary function of property rights is that of guiding incentives to achieve a greater internalisation of externalities (Demsetz, 1967 as quoted in Platteau, 1992). An efficient system of property rights should have three features: (i) universality, (ii) exclusivity, and (iii) transferability (Bromley, 1989a). It is argued that individuals with unique and absolute authority are assumed to act in a socially preferred manner in deriving the present stream of benefits. Therefore, individuals, rather than community, would be in a better position to allocate resources more efficiently and maximise societal returns. The property rights school also makes the contention that the institution of private property will spontaneously emerge in reality whenever a cost-benefit comparison makes it appear as more desirable than any other system (Baland and Platteau, 1996). In other words, property rights are developed to internalise externalities when the gains of internalisation becomes larger than the cost of internalisation (Demsetz, 1967, quoted in Baland and Platteau 1996).

Though it sounds logical that clearly specified property rights lead to better and efficient allocation of resources, individual property rights approach has some important drawbacks. Larson and Bromley (1990) show that the presumed optimality of individual property rights in natural resources is inconsistent with theoretical possibilities and empirical observations.

The argument is that resource degradation can be an optimal response to economic and environmental circumstances under a much wider range of property regimes than conventionally accepted. Further, the property rights approach underestimates the transaction costs involved in imposing and monitoring private property rights (Bromley, 1989a; Bates, 1989; Platteau, 1992). Establishing private property rights in common pool resources could have two important repercussions. First, it may not lead to an efficient allocation of resources due to the existing imperfections in capital and labour markets. Second, uneven distribution of rights would increase the ecological stress on the land if the majority of poor farmers were allotted rights in marginal and degraded lands (Gans, 1989). Besides, it would aggravate the existing inequalities due to the inequitable distribution of resources attached to land, such as groundwater. Further, distribution of such rights may be (dis)advantageous to certain communities/households due to their socio-cultural background.

Groundwater and grazing lands in watershed management epitomise such anomalies. Groundwater basin is a common pool resource in the sense that exclusion of multiple users (pumpers) is difficult and costly. Groundwater tables go down as water is extracted beyond optimum yield level (withdrawals exceed replenishing capacity of the aquifer) and may even lead to drying up of the aquifer in fragile environments. But, due to inequitable distribution of assets and inequitable access to man-made resources like capital across individuals, a few individuals in a community control groundwater. The capital intensity of groundwater extraction, makes it easier to exclude rival users. This feature is common in fragile resource regions where the high cost of groundwater extraction coupled with low and inequitable asset ownership, makes the resource privy to a few well-to-do households. This is similar to *technological externalities* (as termed by Ostrom, Gardner and Walker, 1994).

Heterogeneity in spatial distribution of groundwater creates the problem of assignment. But, it involves a further complication as land (under which groundwater lies) rights are privately owned. The intertwining of private and common resources results in further externalities, which can be termed as *legislative externalities*. Legislative externalities arise when there is no clear-cut legislation demarcating and protecting different property regimes. For instance, in India, property rights in land may be purely individual (highly concentrated), or purely collective (attenuated) though there exist many intermediate forms between these two extremes (Bell, 1990). On the other hand, while groundwater is a CPR in which rights are limited to use and income deriving, it is also sold and transferred along with land due to its link with land. But, legislation is not clear in specifying how groundwater should be managed judiciously and distributed equitably. As a result, farmers make private investment thinking that they have absolute rights to a groundwater basin beneath their land. Similarly, the spatial distribution of check-dams in a watershed may result in exclusion of downstream communities, at least in short run (assignment problems). On the other hand, common grazing lands are treated as common pool resources in most of the watersheds. But, the benefits from these lands are often going to the large farmers disproportionately due to the uneven distribution of livestock and consumption pattern (Reddy, 2001). As a result, poor have no incentive to join the collective efforts. These situations arise not only due to the nature of the resource but also due to the existing institutional arrangements. For, in other situations (California, USA), a groundwater basin is treated and used as a CPR in the pure sense of the term (Ostrom, Gardner and Walker, 1994). Therefore, existing collective action and property rights institutional arrangements are important in determining their impact on poverty.

Linkages

The semi-arid regions are characterised with low resource endowments and high risk or vulnerable environment. Resource vulnerability is mainly attributed to low rainfall, poor soils with no or less water. Resource endowments are limited regarding all the five capitals, except perhaps the social capital. These regions are often termed as better endowed in terms of social cohesion and networks. But, asset base of the households determines the effectiveness of these networks in reducing vulnerabilities. That is, social capital *per se* does not mean much unless it is viewed in the context of socio-economic and political dimensions (Harris, 2003). Socio-economic and political dimensions are often inter-linked. Though political power is captured by the dominant social class, economically powerful groups tend to control the power, as they get the political support from the higher level of the political pyramid, i.e., mandal, constituency, district, etc. This is true even in the case of reservations in political representation. Elite or political capture tends to get diluted in the context of competitive politics, i.e., co-existence to two political groups (see Chapter 9). On the other hand, economic and social concentration could increase the chances of elite capture. Evidence shows that elite capture is widespread, especially in the context of new institutional arrangements, like watershed committees that are created for pro-poor delivery.

The dynamics and interactions between these four aspects, viz., resource vulnerability, social structure, economic structure and political structure, determine the evolution and effectiveness of property rights and collective action institutions at the community or village level (Fig. 4.1). The relationship between property rights and collective action is neither automatic nor consistent. The linkages between these two depend on the nature of the resource and existing or accepted property rights. Collective action can lead to establishment or changes in the existing property rights. On the other hand, new property rights regimes may also create the environment for collective action. But, collective action may not take place if there are conflicting interests in the group. More importantly, it depends on the strength (socio-economic and political) of the losing group. This can be

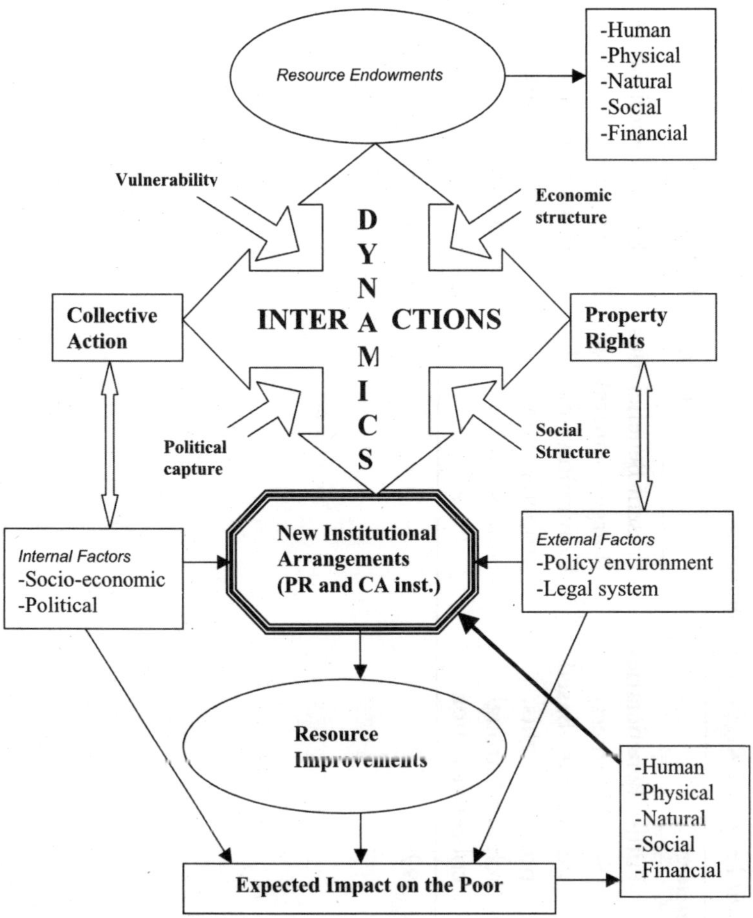

Figure 4.1 Linkages between Property Rights and Collective Action for Poverty Alleviation

illustrated with a real-life situation in the context of groundwater and grazing lands (Reddy, 1999). Groundwater is a common resource but controlled privately.

With the establishment of well-defined property rights, as in the case of land, groundwater can be converted into a com-

Table 4.1 *Perceptions about Property Rights in Commons*

Groundwater		*Grazing Lands*	
Present Beneficiaries (Large Farmers)	Future Beneficiaries (Small Farmers)	Present Beneficiaries (Large Farmers)	Future Beneficiaries (Small Farmers)
Private property rights (status quo)	Community-based property rights. (change through collective action)	Community-based property rights (status quo)	Private property rights (change through legal action)

Source: Adopted from Reddy (1999).

mon resource – *de jure* as well as *de facto*. Collective action arrangements could help in managing groundwater on a community basis. Presently, only a few rich farmers are having access to groundwater due to the availability of groundwater aquifers at greater depth, which is increasing over time. While majority of the farmers (small and marginal) show interest in groundwater management on a community basis with little help from government, large farmers prefer the present system of private management (Table 4.1). The persistence of diagonally opposite perceptions between present and future beneficiaries makes the promotion of collective action and making it effective an onerous task. Same groups react differently in the case of grazing lands.

Households use common grazing lands for various purposes and feel that these lands are important livelihood supportive mechanisms and hence needs to be protected. Though almost all the households depend on the grazing lands for their fodder and fuelwood needs, benefits derived differ across households, in relative and absolute terms. Small farmers and landless households depend more on the grazing lands in terms of relative share, i.e., greater proportion of their household needs (fodder and fuel) are met from the common grazing lands. On the other hand, large farmers extract more fodder and fuelwood in absolute terms, as they own more cattle. These variations in the dependency are reflected in the perceptions of these groups regarding the management of the grazing lands. Here, the group perceptions are diagonally opposite to that of groundwater. Small and landless demand privatisation of grazing lands so that they can get a legitimate share in the land. Large farmers support the present arrangement of treating it as a common grazing land.

In both the cases, the existing property rights are biased against the poor. The reason being that the existing property rights do not address the equity issues. As a result, short-term individual economic interests cloud over the long-term social or community interests. Here, there is a clear dichotomy as far as the linkages between property rights and collective action are concerned. In the case of groundwater, collective action is a prerequisite to change and enforce the property rights, while in the case of grazing lands clearly defined private property rights would replace the collective action institutions. In both the cases poor tend to benefit. Another alternative would be to incorporate equity principles into the management of grazing lands through user charges and incentives for non-users. This brings out clearly that in the absence of equity concerns either or both collective action and property rights could not necessarily lead to poverty alleviation. Bringing the equity concerns, to the centre stage is the crux of the problem. Equity cannot be brought in mechanically or imposed, as it is linked to numerous factors.[3] These include changes in economic structure, policy and legal support systems. Poor are keen to change the existing property rights and ready to act collectively. But, the existing socio-economic and political structures constrain them in doing so, despite the fact that they are in majority.

What causes collective action and changes in property rights is difficult to pinpoint? They are intricately interlinked. In some cases it is the internal factors like political leadership or existing socio-economic conditions that prompt collective action, while in others external forces like changes in policy and legal structures impose or ignite collective action that could alter the internal factors. Similarly, successful resource management strategies, prompted by individuals or NGOs, could lead to policy changes and legal provisions.[4] These aspects are elaborated in the next section. The new institutional arrangements, whichever way they take place, with any improvement over the existing ones would lead to resource improvements. These improvements could have an impact on poverty provided the new institutional arrangement incorporate the equity concerns effectively. In fact, the effective reduction in poverty would help in sustaining the new regimes of collective action and property rights arrangements. While the expected impacts on poor are influenced by the external and internal, especially structural, factors, the expectations on the part of poor also helps in evolving new property rights regimes and collective action strategies. Poor would have incentive to participate if their expected benefits are positive and substantial.

Thus, collective action and property rights though are necessary but not sufficient to alleviate poverty as long as equity concerns are not integrated. In the absence of equity collective action strategies always tend to be a 'zero sum' game, as the existing socio-economic and political structures always go against the poor. While collective action appears to be the most needed to bring in equity in the case of certain resources like water, especially groundwater, without changing the existing property rights. Equity issues can be integrated into the existing collective action strategies without altering the property rights regime, as in the case of grazing lands. But, in both the cases, there is need for broader consensus involving all the stakeholders (entire community). Changes in property rights regimes (individual or community) should be resource-specific. Collective action and property rights are closely linked, but their order of importance (which is necessary and which is sufficient condition?) depends on the type of resources and the nature of existing property rights. The high transaction costs involved in addressing the equity issues in property rights deter the required changes, thus allowing the persistence of inefficient property rights regimes (Libecap, 2002).

Institutional Models for Watershed Management in Andhra Pradesh

Participatory watershed management is found to be effective (especially NGO-managed) but most of them are small in scale and can only be expanded by repeating the same slow, costly, in-depth techniques (Farrington and Lobo, 1997; Knox, Swallow and Johnson, 2001). This process has become the main bottleneck for scaling up of the programme. Scaling up gets further complicated when sustainable rural livelihoods issues are integrated into watershed development approach. At the same time, ad-hoc scaling up in a targeted fashion is neither effective nor sustainable. Hence, attempts should be made to achieve effective scaling up through appropriate policy designing, which is tuned to the demands of the community and enhance the potential of the implementing agencies in a dynamic process. In AP watershed policies were driven by the need for scaling up the programme. Political interests, such as covering of all political constuencies and availability of funds, both from the central government and donors, necessitated scaling up of watershed development in AP. While there was clear emphasis and participatory approach, means to achieve and sustain collective action institutions were not given due importance. For instance, while giving importance to community-based decentralisation approach, constitutional bodies like PRIs or property rights institutions are not given due importance.

Of late, much emphasis has been placed on the decentralisation strategy on the notion that decentralisation of powers to the local units of government and management is one of the better ways of empowering people, promoting public participation and increasing efficiency. Institutions, both formal and informal, play a crucial role in strengthening the decentralisation process at the cutting-edge level. Panchayats, cooperatives, watershed associations, water users associations (WUAs), Vana Samrakshana Samithis (VSSs), etc., constitute formal institutions, while institutions like people's collectives and Self-Help Groups (SHGs), supported by various NGOs, come under the rubric of the informal system (Oliver et al., 2001). However, different approaches are used to explain various institutional arrangements operating in rural areas. These institutions are termed as democratic/participatory and constitutional/parallel. While PRIs are the constitutional democratic bodies, all other institutions are not constitutional and fall under the generic term of community-based organisations (CBOs).

PRIs, as statutorily established institutions, possess legal and constitutional rights and mandate for natural resource planning. Baumann (2000) identifies several positive aspects of PRIs for handling, planning and implementation of CPR activities. According to him, panchayats have the potential to integrate watershed management into wider development activities. Further, they have the capacity to draw the services of line departments, powers to levy and collect taxes and, more importantly, powers to prepare development plans according to people's wishes. All these attributes make a strong case for the intervention of panchayats in planning and implementing schemes for natural resources and particularly watershed development programme. This is despite the fact that the panchayat's rights over natural resources are inconsistent with the rights granted to other bodies. Domination of party politics controlled by elite farmers, corruption, lack of downward accountability, lack of technical expertise and panchayat's territorial jurisdiction seldom corresponds with their natural resource boundaries. The cumulative effect of all this has been rather incoherent management of natural resources.

However, this cannot be an excuse for not involving panchayats in the management of natural resources. In fact, the recent move of the Central Government, entrusting responsibility of watershed development programme to gram panchayats through Haryali Guidelines, has very much favoured. The Haryali Guidelines, issued in March 2003, aimed at empowering PRIs in planning, executing and managing the watershed development activities. Under this new initiative, all watershed development activities would be implemented through the PRIs by providing them with necessary administrative, technical and financial support. The gram sabha will work as watershed committee and gram panchayats will be supported either by the block/zilla panchayats or the line departments or a reputed NGO in the matters of technical aspects. For implementing all watershed projects, zilla panchayat will work as project implementing agency (PIA). With the passing of responsibilities to panchayats, the existing organisations and institutions will cease to have any role in watershed development activities. As a result, gram panchayats are now expected to perform both executive as well as governance functions.

In spite of provisions of the watershed guidelines, there are little efforts on the ground to give a meaningful role to panchayats. Involving PRIs in the whole process needs to be looked into afresh. They could play an important role as PIAs besides playing a catalytic role in those NGOs performing as PIAs. They need to be given a fair trial before discarding them (Reddy et al., 2001). NGO-managed watersheds are found to be performing better in general, although, there are wide variations across the NGO-managed watersheds. In fact, some of the NGOs had abandoned the watersheds after receiving the initial funding, which were later taken up by the government agencies in order to continue their implementation. Perhaps, this is one of the important reasons for the poor performance of watersheds managed by the government agencies (Reddy et al., 2001). In the case of watershed development the self-help and user groups, formed by the residents of the watershed area, are found to be the beginning as well as the end point for the programme. The programmes success depends upon consensus among a large number of users. Moreover, collective capability and collective action are required to successfully manage existing structures as well as new ones created by the programme (D'silva and Pai, 2003). What is important is the formation of beneficiary groups/community organisations in the large number of villages, especially where NGOs are operating. And, all the more significant is the awareness that has been generated about the need for as well as the potential benefits that may accrue from watershed development programmes (Shah, 2000).

PRIs and watershed institutions have different objectives, different visions of the community, and different perspectives on the process of collective action. However, these differences need not be a point of conflict, as long as watershed management policies honour the designated roles of these two systems

(Baumann, 1999). One of the defining differences between PRIs and watershed institutions is the principle of accountability. PRIs are accountable to the electorate and can be voted out, whereas watershed institutions are accountable to the government, which can stop funds and disband committees, if specified procedures are breached (Baumann, 1999).

There are several provisions in the watershed guidelines for convergence. The programme starts with the consent of gram panchayat in terms of a resolution that the panchayat will ensure maintenance of assets created and would actively participate in programmes in the areas of planning, monitoring and reviewing of progress. Panchayat Raj and its guidelines are both instrumentalities that aim to devolve development initiatives to local communities. The former is a constitutional part of Indian democracy and the latter an executive order of a Ministry. Apart from the fact that both aim to decentralise, they differ in their legislative status, objectives and approach (Baumann, 1999). Further, they also differ in their conceptualisation of the community and of empowerment. The community in Panchayat Raj parlance is treated as an integral part of the wider social, economic and political system. The three-tier structure network—gram sabha to village, block, and district levels—ultimately provides an avenue for the representation of local needs in the national governance. The community, in the guidelines, is atomistic; watershed projects do not address external influences on the local community; and there is no system whereby local communities can decide on their needs and express these at higher decision-making levels (Baumann, 1999).

Notwithstanding the above, there are differences of opinions amongst both researchers and practitioners with regard to the role of panchayats in watershed development (Joy and Paranjape, 2003). The point of contention is whether or not to involve panchayats in water management or to link them with the CBOs. Those who are in favour of such linkages opine that panchayats being elected bodies, by design, are accountable, and more specifically, have the provision to constitute sub-committees. On the other hand, those who favour CBOs argue that the panchayats are afflicted by politics and CBOs being autonomous organisations are free from political pressures. Arguments of this nature have, in fact, made it difficult to generalise whether CBOs or PRIs should be assigned the responsibility of managing the watershed management. But the point is, whether there is any need to treat them separately? The answer is they need to be linked together for the effective implementation of watershed management.

APRLP Model

In order to address some of the institutional and livelihood issues, the Andhra Pradesh Rural Livelihoods Project (APRLP) was initiated in partnership and support of DFID, UK, with an aim to reduce poverty through effective and sustainable rural livelihoods (SRL) strategy in five drought-prone districts of Andhra Pradesh (Anantapur, Kurnool, Mahabubnagar, Nalgonda and Prakasam). In the APRLP model the SRL strategy is being integrated with the scaling up of watershed activity by supporting capacity building, livelihood support, and convergence of other schemes and services (collectively called "watershed-plus") (GoAP, 1999). The structure of the APRLP is presented in Figure 4.2. In this the capacity building programme is emphasised. Though this project clearly spells out the key features, components and impacts, it deliberately avoid any details on the implementation process.[5] For, the implementation is expected to be dynamic and a learning experience in itself, as it is area-specific. Implementation of the programme is expected to be evolving continuously through learning and correcting. The APRLP has seven components, viz., (i) capacity building for primary and secondary stakeholders, (ii) innovation to enhance the impact of watershed works, (iii) lesson learning and policy influence, (iv) convergence, (v) gender and equity, (vi) watershed and watershed-plus SRL initiatives, and (vii) participatory technology development (GoAP, 1999). Various institutional

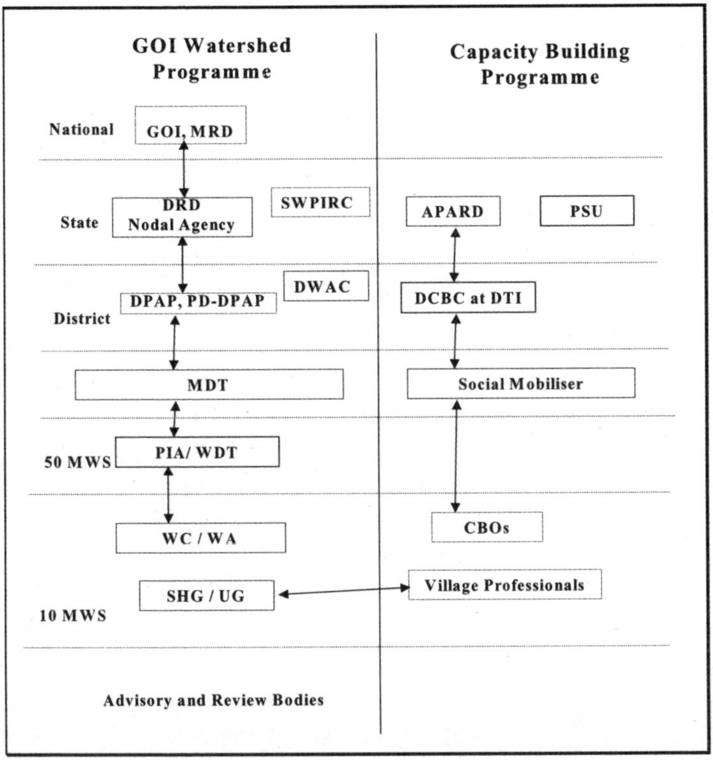

Figure 4.2 Structure of APRLP

arrangements are specified to take care of these components at micro, meso and macro levels.

At the state level Commissioner of Rural Development (CRD) is the nodal agency. Two separate units, namely, project monitoring unit (PMU) and project support unit (PSU) support the programme. While PMU is the main implementing agency, PSU supports in research, development and policy guidance. PSU was institutionally under the CRD and managed by the Special Commissioner, APRLP. PSU was closed in 2003. The role of the PMU is to supervise and monitor APRLP in five districts. The ultimate goal of strengthening the CRD's office is to achieve the effective implementation of APRLP. PMU is primarily responsible for the implementation of project and has a strategic role in watershed programme management in project districts with appropriate links with other APRLP structure.

The PMU, being the state level management unit, is supervising the project for its smooth and effective implementation. It is providing all necessary logistic, technical and administrative support to the APRLP districts in adopting APRLP approaches and implementing various activities of the project. The PMU focuses on seven core areas viz., (a) capacity building, (b) social mobilisation, (c) gender, (d) natural resource management, (e) productivity enhancement, (f) livelihoods, and (g) monitoring and evaluation. Each of these core areas is being managed by subject specialists working as the Assistant Project Coordinators (APCs) in the PMU.

APRLP has strengthened existing structures (as well as created new management structures) within the ongoing programme, in order to further develop the system's capacities in line with the new priorities of the programme. Initially, the Project Director, Drought Prone Area Programme (DPAP) was in charge of the programme at the district level. Later, DRDA was replaced with District Water Management Agency (DWMA) (Fig. 4.3). The earlier multidisciplinary development teams (MDTs) consisted mostly of technical personnel. However, given APRLP's priorities (and in order to bring about a shift in the ongoing programme), the specialist capacities of the MDT structure have been strengthened. MDTs working with APRLP will specialise in social mobilisation, agriculture, livestock and watersheds. In each MDT, one member will be identified as a coordinator for APRLP activities. PIAs will also need to appoint a full-time coordinator and have specialists in social mobilisation, agriculture, livestock and watersheds.

The district level structure includes a special project directorate created by the AP government for implementation

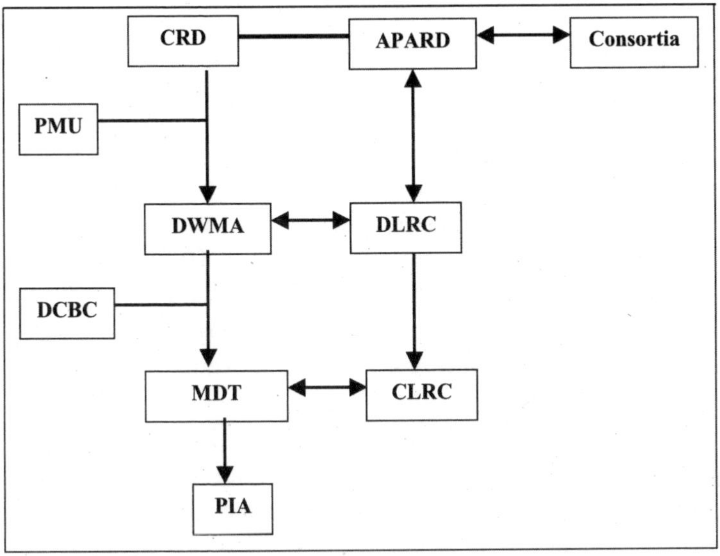

Figure 4.3 Revised ARLP Structure

of watershed programmes. Staff is drawn on deputation from parent technical departments (forestry, agriculture, soil conservation and animal husbandry). However, the tenure of these officials does not continue throughout the programme. Also, double task obligation to the parent department and the watershed development leads to conflict in priorities and restricts them to contribute to the optimum extent. APRLP had taken an initiative to study the current status of these MDT members. The study also brought out the coordination needs among the team members and fixed responsibility allocation. Many of the MDT members also performed the roles of part-time PIAs with a result that proper justice could not be done to both responsibilities. As part of APRLP, it has been decided that the watershed should have a full-time PIA coordinator for about 10 watersheds and the respective MDT should also have co-coordinator for about 60–70 watersheds.

Districts have finalised these arrangements so far and others are in progress. It has also been decided that MDT co-coordinators will be provided additional support in terms of office automation, staff and new tools and systems. They will be responsible for monitoring the overall programme within the specified watersheds and provide feedback to the Project Directors. This arrangement will ease their burden and they will be able to spare time for introduction of newer initiatives, learning from experiences and documentation. Gaps in the positions of social mobilizers at WDT and MDT levels are being filled to give thrust to community mobilisation work, which is an important component of APRLP initiatives.

District Capacity Building Centres (DCBCs) were established in order to strengthen the capacity building process. DCBC members have come together to work under AP Directorate of Training, which will coordinate the work. This arrangement will also relieve the DCBC members from engaging themselves in administrative, planning and coordination work so that they can focus on developing newer approaches, strategies for district level innovations and experiential learning. Similarly, District Livelihood Resource Centres (DLRCs) and Cluster Livelihood Resource Centres (CLRCs) were established for addressing the livelihood issues.

APRLP recognises that women's SHGs are an important vehicle for development and achievement of sustainable livelihoods. APRLP seeks to draw upon their existing strengths (social, human and financial) and further build upon to develop the scope of their activities beyond thrift and credit to livelihood promotion. Existing SHGs will be strengthened through appropriate capacity building inputs (e.g., exposure visits, etc.) and encourage them to form a village organisation and include the leftout poor.

User groups will be formed on the basis of watershed treatment plan. These will be groomed as production groups (e.g., farmers, livestock, producers, etc.). They will develop plans based on group discussions supported by PIAs' technical inputs where appropriate and transect walks. These plans will be submitted to the watershed association for approval. The work begins as soon as the concerned user group contributes its share in cash. Watershed associations and committees will not be elected. Eligibility will be based on the contribution and interest shown by different members during the probation phase.

NGO Model

Accion Fraterna (AF), a non-governmental organisation, established in 1982, has played a leading role in watershed development in the Anantapur district of Andhra Pradesh, by taking up several programmes to strengthen watershed development. In fact, some of its learnings were incorporated into 1994 watershed guidelines. AF has been engaged in institutional development at the village level in order to make watershed programmes self-sustained in the future too. It has evolved social accounting/auditing procedures and also detailed village selection/de-selection criteria for watershed development. Its emphasis on the constitution of village-based organisations (VBOs) and facilitating their effective functioning for participatory watershed development and its sustainability are both innovative and unique. It has also been taking care of the gender aspects and also giving stress on due representation for all sections of the society, particularly disadvantageous groups, while forming collectives to implement the watershed programmes. AF has recently adopted the participatory approach of the inclusion of the institutions that matter in the implementation of watershed development programmes (Fig. 4.4).

The Gram Sabha—as general assembly of the village—is recognised as an important VBO responsible for general policy direction and decisions of social binding. All other institutions are answerable and accountable to it. These institutions include Watershed Development Committee (WDC) to work as an executive body of Gram Sabha; Village Development Council (VDC)

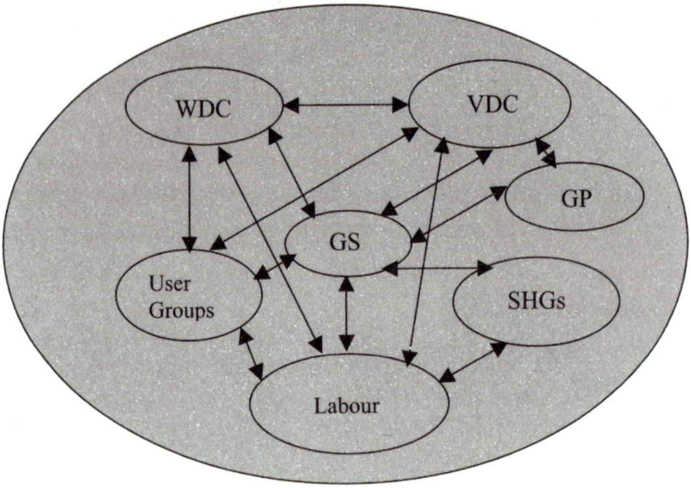

Figure 4.4 Linkages among Village Institutions—AF model

is established with village elders and other influential people as a forum for collective action and synergy for integrated village development; Gram Panchayats, an elected body of the village; user groups for each activity; women SHGs to focus on basic services and alternative income opportunities; and labour groups to enhance collective bargaining and avail government anti-poverty programmes.

Social audit, transparency and accountability mechanisms adopted by the AF in watershed development programmes include:

- Funds are transferred to WDC account, jointly operated.
- All payments are made by cheque after approval by WDC.
- All details are made available in watershed office and displayed prominently.
- Details of income-expenditure to be displayed at intervals of six months in a prominent and central place in the village.

- A watershed map with all the activities is drawn and displayed at a prominent and central place in a village.
- Every family to be given a detailed half-yearly report at least three days before Gram Sabha.
- Anybody in the village can verify the books of accounts at any time.

The criteria, followed for selection of villages for watershed programme under the AF, included biophysical indicators in conjunction with some social indicators such as literacy, landlessness, and access to drinking water. The deciding factor would be the urgency with which watershed development was needed in a given village. The biophysical indicators (rainfall, sediment yield, vegetation, groundwater level, etc.) were taken from the Andhra Pradesh Remote Sensing Agency's data. Same criteria are used in the APRLP and other government watershed development programmes.

At the implementation stage of participatory watershed development programme, the 'success factors' in the village become critically important and the choice of village necessarily be based on the 'success criteria' in conjunction with the biophysical needs of the village. Past experience suggests that unity and collective leadership in a village are crucial to effective watershed development. A village's need for watershed development apart, an important criterion would be the unwillingness of the people to take initiative and leadership in a participatory approach. In the first-generation phase of a participatory watershed development programme, villages need to be identified where a participatory approach can be successfully demonstrated. This would have a motivating effect on neighbouring villages and create demand for replication of the programme in neighbouring villages. This has the potential to foster social equity and harmony in place of factionalism and bloodshed in conflict-ridden villages and may see their transformation from 'bloodshed' to 'watershed' development. Thus, watershed development needs to be turned into a social movement. The operationalisation of a fully participatory approach for watershed development in 'socially feasible' villages can slowly reverse the conventional 'top-down' approach of government, and even other government development programmes could benefit by emulation.

Although remote sensing data (focusing physical parameters of soil, water, vegetation) on a village is generally taken into account while selecting a village for watershed development programme, initiative in this regard should come from the villagers showing interest in implementing this programme in the village. If a Gram Sabha convened by the Gram Panchayat or by informal leaders, with at least two-third of the voters present, and unanimously resolves to execute the programme, then, the village may formally request AF to include it in the said programme. Willingness of the villagers to actively participate and contribute wherever necessary (10 percent or 5 percent of cost as the case may be) is also one of the important criteria for the selection. The villagers should follow the watershed guidelines in regard to the necessary institutional arrangements for the purpose of implementation (i.e., formation of watershed associations, watershed committees, user groups, and SHGs) and monitoring of the programme. The process of selecting a village for watershed development is essentially a community mobilisation process of involving, facilitating, organising, enabling and empowering the whole village. Many villages are still not in a position to self-motivate and participate actively, but will do so gradually, especially if they can visit successful models in neighbouring villages. But, for any reason, if a village fails to satisfy these conditions or any case of misappropriation of finances is noticed at any stage of the programme, then, the village stands the risk of de-selection from the watershed development programme and punitive (criminal prosecution) action against it. Important preconditions for selecting watershed villages include:

- At least 75 percent of the land should follow non-expensive agricultural methods such as ploughing across the slope, use of manures as per soil testing reports, seed treatment, maintain recommended population of plants, sowing across the slope, inter-cropping and dead furrow.

- At least 50 percent of the farmers, who get benefited under bunding programme, should take up crop rotation, at least in one acre of land, each year.
- At least 75 percent of the families in the watershed villages should take up horticulture, which should be taken up in the name of either girl children of the family or female head (wife) in the family. To the extent possible, the villagers should support the landless farmers in taking up horticulture by availing them with some village land.
- Tree planting should be taken up in villages, where there are hills or hillocks. At least 30 percent survival rate should be ensured for planted saplings.
- At least 90 percent farmers, who have taken up horticulture, should take up vermiculture/and use vermi compost.
- Combined efforts should be made by the villagers to eradicate the weed plant 'Vayyaribhamalu' (alternate host parthineum).
- Social restrictions should be implemented on cutting and felling of trees. Permission of VDC should be insisted for cutting trees under inevitable circumstances. And, as a compensatory method, five new trees should be planted per each tree cut.
- Efforts should be made for the successful maintenance of contour bunds, water bodies, survival of plants, bio-gas units, kitchen gardens etc. 'Sri' (low water intensive method of paddy cultivation) method should be practised in at least 25 percent of the land in case of paddy cultivation.
- Dairy farming should be taken up as an activity to supplement agriculture. Farmers having irrigation facilities should take up pasture development and improve dairy.
- Villagers should also abide by certain programmes like *shramadan* (voluntary labour), family planning, 100 percent immunisation/vaccinations, prevention of wastage of water

and ensuring safe drinking water, maximum enrolment of children in primary schools (at least 90 percent children) and to prevent dropout till primary schooling is over.

- Moreover, the villagers are expected to discourage the sale and consumption of alcoholic beverages in the village, take proper care of the orphans (providing food, shelter, etc.), and maintain better sanitary condition in the village.

Institutional Imperatives

The models discussed above are among some of the best in watershed implementation in the country. As mentioned earlier, some aspects from these models like livelihoods, village development council, etc., are incorporated into the national watershed guidelines. There is clear emphasis on participation in Andhra Pradesh Rural Livelihood Programme (APRLP) as well as NGO models, as participation is now recognised as key to the effective implementation and management of watersheds. Both the models try to bring in participation through capacity building and incentive/disincentive structures of providing livelihood support systems. Even, the proposed guidelines seem to adopt similar approach to participation. While these approaches go a long way in enhancing participation and collective action in watershed management, the issue of sustaining collective action is not squarely addressed. For, property rights issues are not considered while emphasising participation. The linkages between property rights and collective action are not taken into account while designing the participatory guidelines.

Social organisation and its sustainability is linked to the allocation of property rights and the distribution of benefits across different sections of the community. In other words, whether property rights are defined clearly and equitably, rather than who has the rights—individuals or groups. Unless property rights are defined clearly and equitably it is difficult to ensure sustainable resource management even under community management. Allocation of rights and distribution of costs and benefits are the most important among the rules and regulations in managing the commons. These distributional aspects are important and affect the monitoring costs to a large extent. If solved to the satisfaction of all socio-economic communities in the group, they would reduce the costs of monitoring. For, free rider attitudes are more prevalent under institutional arrangements where costs and benefits are distributed unequally across households.

Equity and property rights in access to natural resources are crucial for sustaining livelihoods in rainfed and resource-poor regions. Equity in the distribution of economic gains among the community members is as important as the equity in coverage. While the former is concerned with the equity in access, the latter pertains to equity in outcomes. Equity issues pertain to the neutrality of technology in terms of location (different geographic locations of the watershed) and well-being (economic status) of the participants. Inequity in the former case is purely technical while the latter is structural and institutional. For, no technology has an in-built bias towards a particular class/caste. The bias is always due to the existing institutional structure (agrarian structure, water markets, credit markets, social structure, etc.). In both the cases, inequalities could be minimised through institutional arrangements. In other words, technical inequalities can be corrected though compensating the participants of the disadvantaged locations. And, distributional bias needs correcting of distortions in land, labour, water and credit markets. Failure to recognise the problems of inequity, especially in water, is fatal in understanding the process of watershed management. The water and livelihood linkages are stronger in rainfed regions. Equity aspects are also important from the collective action point of view. In this context, access to water by the poor can only be guaranteed if property rights in groundwater are clearly and equitably defined. There is also need for delinking water and land rights. The issue of groundwater management is often evaded due to its political sensitivity, though high transaction costs are given as an excuse. The experience of *Pani Panchayats* (Maharashtra) in India and in South Africa shows that how the changes in property rights institutions could bring in equity in access to water resources (Reddy, 2002). The missing link is the political willingness to take hard decisions. Such decisions are hard to come as long as 'elite capture' is predominant in the political equations.

Notes

1. This can be observed in general across number of donor-supported (driven) programmes across the states.
2. The characteristics of these models include: nominal = membership of groups with or without payment; passive = silent participation in meetings or getting information on decisions after the meetings; consultative = being asked for opinions without necessarily being able to influence decisions; active-specific = volunteering to undertake specific tasks; active = pro-actively expressing view, taking other initiatives; interactive (empowering) = with voice and influence on decisions; and informed (empowered) = being able to take into account information and opinions of external agents (experts) and make considered decisions.
3. Due to this reason, we have not introduced equity as an explicit factor in Figure 4.1.
4. A case in point is the 1994 watershed guidelines, which have incorporated a number of principles that were in practice in successful watersheds across the country (GoI, 1994). Similarly, the proposed Neeranchal Guidelines (GoI, 2006) have addressed the concerns raised from the implementation of the earlier Haryali Guidelines (GoI, 2003).
5. The key features, components and expected benefits are discussed in GoAP (1999).

5

Implementation and Sustainability

A number of watershed-based programmes have been promoted under the administrative control of Ministry of Rural Development, Government of India. The Task Force on Integrated Agriculture Development in Drought-Prone Areas strongly emphasised the adoption of watershed approach while implementing the Drought-Prone Areas Programme (DPAP) during the Fifth Five-Year Plan (1974–79). The approach was also adopted for the implementation of Desert Development Programme (1977–78), which concentrates on the reforestation activities to prevent the expansion of hot and cold deserts. The National Wasteland Development Board also advocated the watershed approach in the implementation of Integrated Wasteland Development Projects (1987). The Ministry of Agriculture, Government of India has been implementing the National Watershed Development Programme in Rainfed Areas since 1990, with the aim of improving production potential in rainfed areas. The Indian Council of Agricultural Research (ICAR) has also launched several pilot watershed projects in different agro-climatic zones of the country. Similarly, while the Integrated Watershed Development Project (IWDP) emphasises the development of non-forest wastelands through silvipasture and soil and water conservation measures, the National Watershed Development Programme in Rainfed Areas (NWDPRA) concentrates on the development of arable lands for improving their production potential. Watershed projects managed by NGOs and international funding agencies often combine these features.

The Ministry of Rural Development adopted the participatory watershed guidelines strictly from 1995–96 onwards. These new guidelines are specific about various aspects of participatory watershed management and provide a definite design for participatory approach. More importantly, many state governments, since 1995 have adopted these guidelines. The state of Andhra Pradesh is in the forefront so far as implementation of watershed development programme in recent years is concerned. This chapter is an attempt to examine the implementation of watershed development programme under the new guidelines in Andhra Pradesh. The focus here is on the post-1995–96 guidelines phase of implementation for the reason that our sample watersheds pertain to this phase. Though there were some changes to the guidelines during 2001, they were not substantive in nature.

Watershed Management: Process of Implementation

In the light of successful experiments the watershed development model has gained currency. The logic runs as follows: In rainfed farming areas, a comprehensive land improvement programme at the watershed and micro-watershed level, through emphasising improved water harvesting and soil conservation, will lead to the sort of agricultural productivity benefits associated with irrigated areas, as well as securing drinking water supplies. The main approach has been through land improvement structures such as check dams, infiltration dams, contour trenching amongst others. Traditional structures, plantations, etc., may also play a role. From the initial conditions, with these land improvement structures, and given sufficient rain over a number of years, it is anticipated that the ground and surface water will recharge giving an improved hydrological regime. This in turn will allow more ground and surface water extraction, an extension of irrigated area, double and even triple cropping, and so higher land productivity. This should lead to a more dynamic village economy and diversified livelihood opportunities. It is also hoped that agricultural practices may move onto a more sustainable basis—with less water-demanding crops.

The watershed implementation, as it has become manifest in the most recent DPAP approach, has six technical elements. These include: (a) regenerates, preserves and utilises natural resources (i.e., water, soils and vegetation) sustainably; (b) improves the catchment protection, reduces erosion, improves moisture in priority catchments retention; (c) ensures community participation throughout the project cycle; (d) establish and strengthens local institutions so that they are able to support the local population; (e) increases employment opportunities and level and security of incomes, including those of poor families and landless and women; and (f) increases alternate livelihood opportunities with specific focus on women, poor and landless.

Implementation Approaches

The respective ministries at the central and state levels have laid down guidelines regarding the norms, funding patterns, technical components, organisational arrangements and so on. The guidelines developed at the central level are applicable to the watershed programmes being implemented throughout the country. These are:

- Ministry of Rural Development, Government of India framed the guidelines for implementation of the Drought-Prone Areas Programme (DPAP) through watershed approach (1978).
- Ministry of Agriculture prescribed the WARASA guidelines (1990) for the execution of National Watershed Development Programme for Rainfed Areas (NWDPRA) in the country.
- Ministry of Rural Development, also developed a manual for DPAP and Desert Development Programme (DDP) in 1992.
- National Institute of Rural Development (NIRD), with its 3-year-long action research project in the drought-prone district of Andhra Pradesh developed a set of guidelines for the preparation of watershed projects.
- Council for Advancement of People's Action in Rural Technology (CAPART) also prescribed the guidelines (1994) for smooth implementation of watershed projects by the non-governmental organisations (NGOs).
- National Wastelands Development Board (NWDB) stipulated guidelines for the execution of Integrated Wastelands Development Projects (IWDPs) throughout the country.
- National Remote Sensing Agency, Department of Space has also developed an Integrated Mission for Sustainable Development (IMSD) by using satellite remote sensing and geographic information system for preparation of natural resources data base, generation of action plans for sustainable development of land and water resources, identification of wastelands and watersheds in the country from 1987 onwards.

The following committees set up by the central government reviewed the implementation of DPAP and DDP from time to time:

- Inter-departmental Group on DPAP and DDP (1984)
- National Committee on DPAP and DDP (Y.K. Alagh and L.C. Jain Committee, 1988).

- Task Force on DPAP and DDP (Swaminathan Committee, 1992)
- Technical Committee on DPAP and DDP (Hanumantha Rao Committee, 1994). Recommendations of this committee were known as participatory watershed guidelines and adopted for implementing watershed development programmes since 1995–96 at the national level.

Field Implementation of Guidelines

The guidelines provided a detailed outline of the implementation process from the apex level to micro-watershed level (Fig. 5.1). The size of the watershed is limited to 500 hectares uniformly across the regions. The micro size of the watershed is convenient for administrative purposes, especially to encourage participatory approaches. Detailed implementation process is presented below:

1. *Selection of districts:* The watershed programmes are being implemented in 337 districts of India under DPAP, DDP and IWDP under guidelines suggested by Hanumantha Rao Committee in 1994. These districts were categorised by Government of India by environmental, social and developmental indicators. High priority is accorded to low-rainfall regions with concentration of SCs/STs and low literacy rates.
2. *Organisational structure:* The Ministry of Rural Development at central level releases funds to the concerned state governments to implement the watershed programme at state level according to its guidelines. In the state, the Watershed Programme Implementation and Review Committee (SWPIRC) is constituted under the chairmanship of the Chief Secretary/Additional Chief Secretary/Agricultural Production Commissioner/Development Commissioner. Secretaries/heads of related departments, Vice Chancellors of the state

agricultural universities, directors of a few state level training institutes like SIRD, ATI and 5–6 representatives of important NGOs/VAs are taken as the members of this committee. The Department of Rural Development is the nodal agency. (Fig. 5.1).

At district level the Zilla Parishad (ZP)/DRDA is responsible for administration and implementation of watershed development

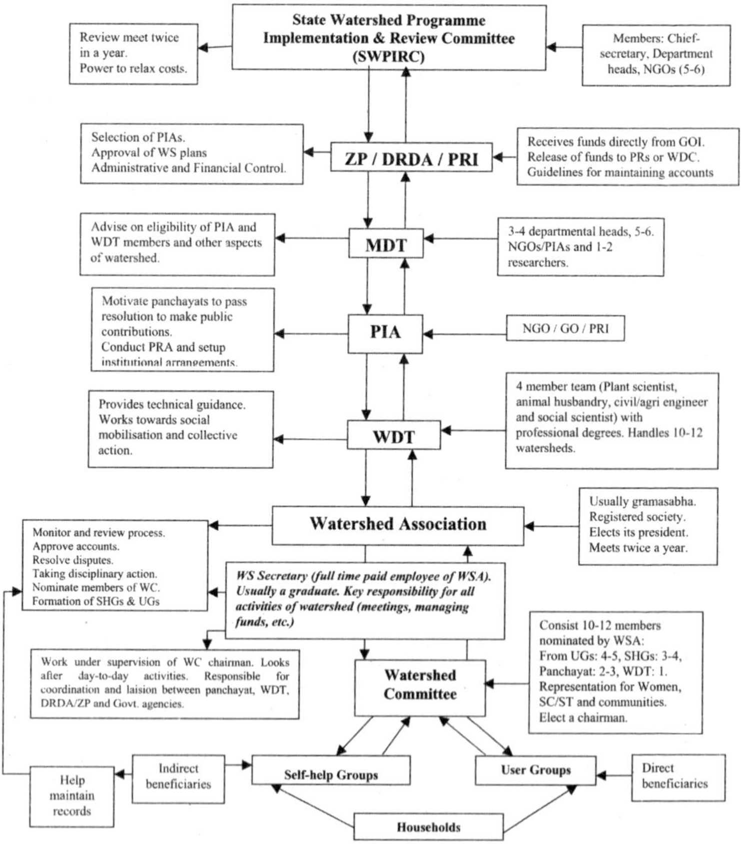

Figure 5.1 Institutional Structure of Watershed Implementation

projects. They receive the funds directly from the Government of India. They select the PIAs and approve the watershed plans. They hold the ultimate power of administrative and financial control over PIAs, releasing the funds to PIAs, lay down the guidelines for managing the accounts, etc. They also establish the Multi-Disciplinary Team (MDT) or watershed development advisory committee at the district level. MDT consists of 3–4 departmental heads from different disciplines of the government in ZP/DRDA, 5–6 members of voluntary agencies and 1–2 members from the research and training institutions at the district level. MDT advises on the selection of PIAs and members of the Watershed Development Team (WDT) and various other aspects.

The government departments, PRIs, universities, voluntary agencies and research institutes would be involved as PIA for implementing the programme. Ultimately, as per the 1994 guidelines, the role of PIA should be shifted to PRIs once 73rd constitutional amendment comes into force. The Haryali Guidelines of 2003 attempted to do this in a superficial manner (see for details Chapter 3). To secure government funding, as per the 1994 guidelines, local communities have to form a Watershed Committee (WC). These WCs get technical support from a four-member Watershed Development Team (WDT), which in turn is employed by the PIA. The Haryali Guidelines have replaced WC with the PRIs. The PIA may be a local government agency or an NGO (NGOs are preferred), and has a mandate to work with a community for four to six years. During that time community resources are expected to build up, through saving schemes, to pay for long-term maintenance. This is one way of ensuring sustainability of the watershed management. But, the role of NGOs, as PIAs, is reduced substantially in the Haryali Guidelines, make the line departments the sole implementing agencies with the excuse that PRIs have enough capacities. However, the proposed Neeranchal Guidelines are reinstating the WC.

Each PIA is expected to handle 10–12 micro-watersheds, each covering about 500 hectares. PRIs at district, Samiti/mandal and village levels can monitor and review the implementation of programme and give suggestions and guidance for improvements in administrative arrangements and for ensuring convergence of other developmental programmes to supplement and complement the watershed programmes. The Gram Panchayat shall be involved in community organisation, training programmes, formation of SHG/UGs, development and sharing of common property resources, and operation and maintenance of existing and created community assets. The PIA will appoint the WDT comprising four members, one each from the disciplines of plant sciences, animal sciences, civil/agricultural engineering and social sciences for implementation. WDT is responsible for technical matters while planning and implementing the watershed apart from mobilising and organising people for collective action.

At watershed level, an association of all the members of village community, who directly or indirectly depend upon the watershed area for their livelihood, is formed and registered as Watershed Association (WA), under the Registration of Societies Act. It elects its own President and office bearers. There is a demand that 'consensus' must be reached rather than going through election process. This is the responsibility of the WDT, especially the social organiser. The WA, in its first General Body meeting, nominates 3–4 representatives from self-help groups (SHGs) and 4–5 from user groups (UGs) as its members, with adequate representation of women, SCs/STs. The Gram Panchayat nominates 2–3 members and the WDT is requested to nominate one of its members for the WC. The WA meets as frequently as necessary, but not less than twice in a year, to finalise and improve the projects and annual action plans. It monitors and reviews the implementation of watershed development plans, resolve the disputes and lay down procedures for the operation and maintenance of community assets. In other words, it exercises overall supervision and control over planning, implementation and maintenance of watershed development works and activities.

The WC elects one chairman from its members and carries out day-to-day activities of the watershed development projects as assigned by the WA. The WC is also responsible for coordination and liaisoning with the Gram Panchayat, WDT, ZP/DRDA and the government departments for the smooth implementation of watershed development plans. It appoints a qualified local person as secretary and three volunteers (one woman, one SC/ST and one from any community) to assist the committee in programme implementation and to maintain the records and accounts.

Formation of self-help groups and user groups is vital in the institutional dynamics of watershed management. They provide the basis for collective action. Broadly, the households in a village can be grouped under watershed (direct) beneficiaries and (indirect) non-beneficiaries. Direct beneficiaries will be organised into user groups by the WDT members. These groups are formed on the basis of a common activity in the watershed. Similarly, indirect beneficiaries are grouped into 10–15 member groups and formed as credit and thrift societies or to start a livelihood activity.

Implementation of the Programme in Andhra Pradesh

Andhra Pradesh (AP) is one of the states that followed the central guidelines in totality. At the same time it has taken the advantage of the flexibility provided in the guidelines to adapt to the local specifications at the implementation level. Three important improvisations could be noted (Table 5.1). Priority is given to the villages adjacent to the existing watersheds in selecting the watersheds. This would enhance the environmental benefits and the associated economic benefits from the programme. At the district level Project Director, DPAP has been in-charge of watershed implementation making it more focused and

Table 5.1 *Summary of MoRD Watershed Treatment Guidelines and their Adoption in Andhra Pradesh*

Item	*MoRD Guidelines*	*Variations in AP Guidelines*
1. Objectives	Economic development through regeneration of natural resources in drought-prone areas.	Economic development through regeneration of natural resources in drought-prone areas.
2. Approach to watershed treatment	Integrated treatment of both non-arable and arable lands on watershed basis.	Integrated treatment of both non-arable and arable lands on watershed basis.
3. Selection of watersheds	On the basis of drought conditions in the area and a number of indicators which signify backwardness.	Villages selected based on certain parameters and weightages.
4. Size of the watersheds	Only MWs of 500 ha each are selected. In case of more than one MWs in a block, these need not be contiguous.	Contiguity with existing watersheds is favoured (and is one of the criteria used for watershed selection).
5. Time period	Four years.	Four years.
6. Selection of villages	Where people's participation and voluntary contributions are forthcoming. The area should have acute shortage of drinking water, preponderance of SC/ST population and wastelands.	Villages selected based on certain parameters and weightages given to each parameter.
7. Role of NGOs	Can be one of the implementing agencies for a group of 10 or 12 MWs.	Can be one of the implementing agencies for a group of 10 or 12 MWs.

8. Institutional arrangement (a) State level	A Watershed Development Programme Implementation and Review Committee under the chairmanship of the Chief Secretary.	A Watershed Development Programme Implementation and Review Committee under the chairmanship of the Chief Secretary.
(b) District level	Usually, either the DRDA or ZP is responsible for implementing programmes at district level. A District Watershed Advisory Committee, which offers guidance on issues of implementation, including PIA selection	In AP, a PD, DPAP has been sanctioned in DPAP districts who has responsibility for all watershed works. The PD, DPAP is the chairperson of the DWAC, which also has PIA representation.
(c) Watershed level	One of the following can be selected as the PIA at the watershed level: 1. The voluntary agencies (NGOs) 2. Agricultural universities 3. Agricultural research institutions 4. Training institutions 5. Corporations 6. Co-operatives 7. Banks 8. Public and commercial organisations 9. PRIs	A multidisciplinary team to cover 50 watersheds (roughly division level) comprised of three seniors and three assistant line department functionaries (forestry, engineering, agriculture). Each PIA to field one multi-disciplinary WDT, which covers up to 10 watersheds.

Table 5.1 (*contd.*)

Table 5.1 (*contd.*)

Item	*MoRD Guidelines*	*Variations in AP Guidelines*
	10. Government departments A multidisciplinary watershed development team to assist the PIA.	
(d) MWs level	A micro-watershed association, which shall be a registered body. This will be supported by a micro watershed committee with representatives from self-help groups (SHGs), user groups (UGs), women etc.	A micro-watershed association, which shall be a registered body. This will be supported by a micro watershed committee with representatives from self-help groups (SHGs), user groups (UGs), women etc.
9. Agency for planning and execution of MWs plans	Watershed Committee through the SHGs and UGs. The Gram Panchayat links critical	The link with Gram Panchayat is not critical.
10. Approval of MWs plans	PD, DRDA and PIA	PD, DRDA and PIA
11. Flow of funds	GoI, MRD to DRDA	GOI to PD, DRDA to PD, DPAP to IA/WC
12. Cost norms/ha		-do-
RNR cost / ha	Rs. 6,000	
HRD	5%	

NLBAs	No provision	
NGO	Significant	
13. Concept of cost and benefit sharing (a) Cost sharing	Compulsory, 5% in respect of CPR and 10% in respect of private lands.	Compulsory, 5% in respect of CPR and 10% in respect of private lands.
(b) Benefit sharing	Not well defined.	Not well defined.
14. Maintenance of assets during post project period	Concerned WDT to take care with the help of the micro watershed committee. To support this activity, a micro-watershed development fund is proposed to be created and cost contributions will go to this fund.	Concerned WDT to take care with the help of the micro watershed committee. To support this activity, a micro-watershed development fund is proposed to be created and cost contributions will go to this fund.
15. HRD	A provision of 5% of the total funds is made.	A provision of 5% of the total funds is made.
16. Gender	This question is addressed in the guidelines, but strategy has not been spelt out clearly.	Experimentation with involvement of women-only. SHGs representatives in WC beginning.
17. Equity	This question has been addressed but the strategy is not well defined.	This question has been addressed but the strategy is not well defined.
18. NLBAs	No provision.	No provision.
19. M&E	Financial spending targets.	Financial spending targets.

accountable. Funds also will flow to PD, DPAP and then to the PIA and downwards. Representation of women SHGs in the WCs at the village level is encouraged. This is expected to widen the scope of watershed benefits beyond land and crops and to drinking water, fuelwood, etc. Another interesting innovation in AP is the inter-departmental coordination between rural development and forest departments. On the other hand, the linkages between PRIs and WCs remained weak in AP when compared to states like Madhya Pradesh. This has repercussions to the sustainability of the watershed development in the long run (more on this in Chapter 9). More importantly, the focus in AP is more on extentensive implementation rather than intensive approach. This has a negative bearing on the participatory dimension of the implementation and sustainability of the programme.

The DPAP has mainly used funds allocated from central government sources. Private land, forestland, community land and other CPRs are considered for watershed treatment. Whilst the government provides the major part of funding for the works, individuals within the community are also expected to contribute towards the cost of works (about 10 percent). From these funds a part is set aside for maintenance once the four-year implementation phase is completed. The main activities taken up under the watershed development programme include:

- Entry point activities (e.g., building bus shelter or approach road or water tank).
- Soil and moisture conservation (contour-bunding, rock-filled dams, brushwood dams, gully control structures).
- Water harvesting structures (continuous contour-trenching, check-dams, percolation tanks, farm ponds).
- Horticulture (plantation of appropriate species).
- Social/agro-forestry.
- Pasture development.
- Distribution of bio-gas and smokeless *chullahs* (stoves).
- Self-employment revolving fund for thrift groups.

The watershed development policy seeks to improve the productivity of land resources and to this end both private and village common (revenue) lands are treated. However, one of the major categories of landownership in India—forestland—is so far not directly addressed. The potential linkages between these two are being explored in AP. After policy level discussions at the state level, it was decided that funding for Joint Forest Management (JFM) programme should be linked to the Watershed Development Programme. The funding for JFM programme would be done on the same basis as per the watershed programme following the Hanumantha Rao Committee guidelines. Forest Range Officers (FROs) will act as PIA.

Water conservation has been accorded the status of core activity under the JFM programme. Forest conservation is undertaken along with watershed activities, unlike the usual practice of protecting a demarcated patch of forest. So wherever the Vana Surakshaka Samiti (VSS) is protecting the forest, water-harvesting structures are being built and watershed development activities are also taken up. The guiding principle is: "once you catch water, the forest would grow automatically". As watershed activities become the priority in this programme, the state government is also funding the programme under watershed development activities. It is also channelling funds from the employment assurance scheme (EAS) and other union government sponsored schemes like the integrated watershed development programmes for this programme. Spending money from development programmes like the EAS on forestry has the approval of the Planning Commission, which has now issued guidelines to all states to earmark funds for forestry projects under the EAS and Jawahar Rojgar Yojana. This may represent a radical move towards intersectoral coordination, although results on the ground will need careful assessment.

As mentioned earlier, the conflict between intensive and extensive approaches to watershed development is not well understood at the policy level in AP. Obviously, policy makers assume that participatory development might come easily in a society with proud traditions of collective resource management and maintenance. Moreover, participatory watershed development is misunderstood as a technology package and hence can be implemented easily with appropriate incentive structure on a large scale. While, the substantial incentive package (money) has created a lot of interest, it failed to translate the interest into effective implementation due to thin spread of human efforts. In the absence of intensive and concentrated efforts bringing awareness and mobilising local communities, watershed management is understood and treated as one of the many developmental programmes that demand little of communities involvement. As a result, sustainability of the technology on a large scale remained a question mark. Communities, which are used to state subsidies, are treating the watershed development as one such programme. Being a long gestation programme impact of the watershed technology is neither immediate nor dramatic. Moreover, watershed technology in AP is focused mainly to improve the productivity of rainfed agriculture, rather than creating irrigation facilities, though creating or improving irrigation facilities is possible in the regions with above 700 mm rainfall. This further dampens the community initiatives, as creating irrigation facilities is believed as the panacea for all (agricultural) problems.

The nature of watershed technology calls for an intensive approach where efforts need to be diverted towards mobilising people, explaining and convincing them about the merits of the technology. There is also need to recognise watershed technology as a common good, which needs participatory development. Hitherto the watershed development programmes are treated like any other programmes, emphasising on the spread rather than sustainability. Unlike in the case of individual-based technologies like HYV the watershed technology is subject to the collective action constraints and hence the adoption and owning of the programme is slow. Unless this constraint is recognised and given due importance, it is highly unlikely to achieve the desired objectives.

The approach in this regard is to recognise community action as a primary objective in watershed development programmes. Given the fact that watershed development and community action are mutually inclusive, there is need for interdisciplinary approach of integrating technology and philosophy. This calls for an attitudinal change on the part of implementing agencies. The state should create congenial policy environment for promoting community action institutions. However, the present trend does not seem to be in this direction. While participatory development is propagated on a large scale, one hardly finds any legislative, policy or political support for it. The analyses in the following chapters prove that under the circumstances that are conducive to community action the watershed programme has great potential to enhance the livelihoods of the communities in a sustainable fashion.

Implementing the Watersheds: Field Observations

Prior to getting into impact assessment in the following chapters, this section looks into the process of implementation at the cutting-edge level and its possible impacts on livelihoods and sustainability of the programme. As mentioned earlier, it is the process of implementation rather than the technology *per se* that determines the sustainability of the programme. For, technology is reasonably reliable (Chapter 2), but its impact on livelihoods is contingent upon maintenance of structures over longer periods, which in turn depends on the strength and sustainability of the social capital built in the process of implementation. Technically, the key to success is ensuring the appropriateness of the physical works to the hydrological regime. Socially, the key to success is ensuring community planning functions in a way that ensures a long-term vision of local watershed development prevails over short-term sectional/factional opportunism. Our field observations, therefore, mainly focus on the process of implementation, rather than the economic impact.

From the field it appears that the impact—social and economic—is critically dependent on a number of key factors, chiefly the sensitivity and appropriateness of implementation activities to the actual village circumstances and needs. Where there is a good fit, we have seen that there appears to be significant medium term benefits (and probably sustainable in the long term). This appears to be occurring mainly where the PIA is an NGO with a long term prior presence in the village. On the other hand, government PIAs have less time, personal identification and linkages with the villages in which they are working, as they are only partially involved. They are also less likely to have facilitation skills necessary for group discussion. Hence, it appears that implementation by government PIAs is poorer. As a result, the main victim is the security of the improvements to the hydrological regime.

Our observations are based on our visits to a number of villages in six districts of Andhra Pradesh, transect walks, group discussions and peer group interactions with farmers, beneficiaries and non-beneficiaries, office bearers of the watershed associations, PIA and members of the WDTs:

1. The new guidelines for watershed development are mostly adhered to, at least in design, while implementing the watersheds. In some cases, these are strictly adhered to even at the cost of poor results. In a number of locations the priorities of the people are not strictly related to watershed development. The most common demand relates to the repairing of the feeding channels to the existing tanks. Spending of money for this purpose from watershed funds is not allowed. As a result, funds are returned unspent despite the fact repairing these channels would be more beneficial to the community. This inflexibility is causing bitterness among the communities. This problem, in fact, is recognised by some of the project directors who are trying to facilitate the use of watershed funds for other important requirements.[1] Similarly, selection of WA president on consensus basis is often stretched too far.

There are instances where an election to the post would have facilitated the smooth implementation of the programme.

2. Selection of PIA appears to be critical in the whole process. For, success of the watershed programme depends on commitment and honesty of the PIA. In fact, impact of the programme is conspicuous in the watersheds managed by some the credible NGOs. Unfortunately, of late, the selection of PIA is taken lightly with some measure of ad-hocism. As a result, there are number of instances where PIAs have abandoned the works after receiving the initial payment. Besides, some of the established NGO PIAs, such as Deccan Development Society (DDS) in Medak and Rayalaseema Development Trust (RDT) in Ananthapur, are not keen to continue due to bureaucratic hassles and inflexibility in the implementation process.
3. Though new guidelines, which emphasise the social aspects, are followed, technical aspects still seem to override the social aspects in the whole process. For, there is little time allotted for social development works. WDT, consisting of one social organiser and three technical people gets about three months to organise people, in 12 watersheds. As a result, the WDTs are resorting to 'carrot and stick' strategies to bring about collective action. It was pointed out in most of the cases an anonymity in selecting the office bearers of the WAs. The initial community meetings usually are marred by groupism and often end with a tussle for the positions. After two such meetings WDT issues a warning that unless there is some consensus in selecting the leader, the programme will be shifted to the neighbouring villages. The amount of money being huge (about Rs. 14 lakh at that time), this trick seems to be effective and hence widely used. The main reason being that the WDT does not have enough time to interact with local communities in order to explain and convince them to work towards a common good.

4. The process of project implementation goes on smoothly if the elected (selected) leaders are influential and sincere. In case of weak leadership there are complaints and allegations, especially on the secretary, who is the key person. For instance, in one watershed, where the secretary is weak, farmers complained that they were not consulted while deciding the location of the check-dams. On the contrary, in another watershed where the secretary has a following, are impressive. These differences are not due to the power equations in the village but mainly due to the enlightened leadership. Incidentally, in both the villages, the secretaries belong to the minority community (Muslim), but in the latter case the secretary has lot of experience in developmental works, as he was involved in the activities of the local Krishi Vigyan Kendra (KVK). The secretary in the former case, on the other hand, is a complete novice in this regard.
5. The salary of the secretary does matter which motivates him to work sincerely and honestly. The present salary of the secretary is very meagre (Rs. 600 per month) in comparison to a daily labourer who gets more than double. This discourages the secretary to devote his time to monitor the work. As a result, user groups are not formed in majority of the watersheds.
6. The transparency in terms of maintenance of records of day-to-day activities and payments made for the works is very much important in order to avoid any sort of confusion or allegation and counter-allegation between the secretary and beneficiaries of the watershed programme. This is clearly reflected in a number of watersheds. In some cases, the maintenance of records is not at all done; as a result, people make allegations against the secretary and chairman. Maintaining records depends on the educational level of the secretary. Though getting a graduate as secretary (as prescribed in the guidelines) is difficult at Rs. 600 per month, the PIA need to keep in mind the educational status of the secretary.

7. The concept of user contribution and stake in the programme is hardly followed. In almost all the cases the user contribution—kind (labour) or cash—is marginal or nil. Users participation is usually limited to supervising the works in their fields. In some cases contributions are accounted by cutting the wages of the labourers. In other words, labourers were paid lower than standard wage rate and the difference between the standard rate and actually paid is used to pay the farmers contribution. This practice seems to be very common. Recent field visits suggest that this practice has become frequent further with the increased allocation of funds for watershed development. This indicates that the short-run indirect beneficiaries are being exploited. On the contrary, they are not interested in safeguarding the plantations carried out by the programme on their (uncultivable) lands. In fact, in one of the villages, employing a guard with the programme funds protected these plantations. But, once the programme was over and the guards have left, nobody (including the landowner) took care of the plantations. During our visit (six months after the programme was completed) we could only see some traces of the plantations. When enquired with the farmers, it appeared that they are not interested, as they do not see any benefit from them, at least in the immediate future. Similar is the attitude regarding repairing of the structures. Farmers expect that PIA should take the responsibility of carrying out these repairs.
8. More importantly, the concept of revolving fund is not properly evolved. There is no mechanism to continue this fund through user contributions. During the course of the programme, some money is pooled, which is used for repairs and maintenance works. At this stage, there is no procedure to collect the user contributions. As a result, the revolving fund would evaporate after a few repairs and the structures would degenerate in the long run.

9. Another related aspect is the fallow-up action after the withdrawal of the PIA. PIAs do not have role in the watershed after they complete their work in six years. In most of the sustainable/successful NGO-run watersheds the NGOs are rarely withdrawn from the scene. As per the guidelines, the WA (a registered society) is supposed to take care of the post-implementation process. But, as our experience shows, this is hardly the case. Our discussions with the WA members in this regard drew a blank. It appears they are neither familiar nor educated in this matter. Some of them are not even sure how to utilise the revolving fund they have generated. In the absence of a smooth process of PIA withdrawal and preparing the community (WA) for taking over the watershed after six years, there is void in the process of watershed management, which could hinder the sustainability of the programme.
10. On the whole, the demand-driven approach is missing in the whole process. There is a need to gauge the potential of the technical package before luring the communities with the money packets. As a result, we apprehend that this programme, if corrective measures are not taken, may end up as another subsidy (big) programme.

As far as the overall economic impact is concerned, it is somewhat visible, in terms of availability of *in situ* moisture and water for longer periods in the vicinity of check-dams. In fact, some of the enterprising farmers are making use of it by planting horticultural crops in the, hitherto, degraded lands. However, our data may reveal some of the finer aspects (in following two chapters), such as groundwater improvement, availability of water and fodder for livestock, etc., of this impact. Where water harvesting is improved, the question of how the potential benefits will be shared, arises. From the field visits it is clear that bore-wells are proliferating rapidly, particularly on the lands of middle and wealthier farmers. Many landowners are sinking bore-wells adjacent to the new dams and tanks to take advantage of whatever increased water harvesting has occurred. In many cases groundwater levels are declining. However, there is no sign at present of any attempts to harmonise the level of extraction with the level of recharge.

Implementation and Sustainability

As we have seen, there are shortcomings in the implementation of the programme. We now turn to causal explanations beyond the micro-level details. For, the attitude, philosophy and ideology of the policy makers are crucial in determining the development path. Here, we focus our attention on three important issues, which have political undertones. These include (a) extensive coverage of watershed programme, (b) adhering to the basic philosophy (guidelines) of participatory approach, and (c) involvement of PRIs in the implementation of watersheds.

The core philosophy of the policy makers dealing with natural resources has not altered despite numerous changes at the macro level, specifically after the restructuring of the watershed guidelines. The philosophy towards development programmes continues to be supply-sided or target-oriented to the neglect of demand side. The focus is mainly on extensive coverage by number of watersheds rather than concentrating on exploiting the full potential of the technology, which requires an intensive approach. The state's experiments with watershed development are laudable. For the first time the participatory approach is being implemented from above at the macro level. Unfortunately, the grandeur belies the effectiveness of the programme. More importance is given to spread than intensity in order to cover more people (pressure from local politicians?). As a result, the long-run sustainability of the programme is at stake.

The problems here are practical. For, more number of PIAs is required to implement the programme on a large scale. Given the critical link between the quality of PIA and the impact of the programme, it is necessary to identify good PIAs, which are in short supply. Our field experience clearly indicates that there are only 2–3 good PIAs (NGOs) in each district, which can handle at the most 36 watersheds. But, the number of watersheds runs into hundreds in each district. In order to cover this many watersheds DRDA is opting for lesser-known NGOs as PIAs or entrusting the work to various departmental officials. This approach is not only resulting in proliferation of dubious NGOs but also affecting the quality of work, as most of the officials' work as part-time PIAs. In fact, in some cases, the implementation of watersheds is thrusted upon the government officials[2] due to abandoning of watersheds by NGOs after getting the initial money. Now, people are aware that becoming a PIA is a profitable venture with lots for money available for it.

Despite the emphasis on participatory process and building up social capital in the guidelines, only cursive attention is paid to this aspect. For, it is widely acknowledged that participation ensures better performance (Reddy, 2000; Kerr et al., 2000). Often participation is defined as per the convenience of the implementing agencies. Some define it as voluntary participation of labour, cash or involvement in post-implementation maintenance. Few NGO-led projects have a comprehensive participation in terms of community involvement while designing, executing, contributing—cash or/and kind—taking over of the maintenance, etc. Only in the case of comprehensive involvement the impact is sustainable (Kerr et al., 2000). Most of watersheds under the new guidelines also fall under the earlier category. Strengthening the social capital base and ensuring community participation is a difficult job demanding lot of time and efforts from the implementing agencies. Only the best projects are found to have devoted substantial time towards social organisation when compared to 2–3 months in others. This is no different from the earlier approach where they found that while the projects with NGO component devoted one year to organising people prior to making watershed investments, the government-implemented projects devoted only a few weeks (Kerr et al., 2000). More importantly, scrutinising the villages for potential, especially social, to receive and absorb the technology is a prerequisite for watershed technology to sustain. As mentioned earlier, in majority of the cases, three months time is given to a team of four (WDT), with one social organiser, to cover 12 watersheds.

Apparently, there is a conflict between extensive and intensive approach to watershed development. While the nature of watershed development technology requires intensive approach, the state is interested in scaling up of the programme due to political obligations. Intensive approach is followed by the established NGOs (PIAs) by devoting more time towards social development. For instance, in some of the villages, where Rayalaseema Development Trust (RDT) is implementing the watersheds beneficiaries contribute up to 30 percent of the costs as against the mandatory 10 percent. It is apprehended that watershed programmes in Andhra Pradesh will meet with same success as that of earlier watershed programmes despite the new guidelines. This is mainly due to the scaling up of the programme and poor implementation.

In recent times a lot of emphasis is placed on the decentralisation strategy as it is believed that decentralisation of powers to the local units of government and management is one of the best ways of empowering people, promoting public participation and increasing efficiency. Institutions, both formal and informal, play crucial role in strengthening the decentralisation process at the cutting-edge level. Panchayats, cooperatives, water users associations and Van Samarakshna Samithis (VSSs) form part of formal institutions while institutions like people's collectives and SHGs come under the rubric of informal system. Several authors have documented the case studies of CPRs and other rural institutions. Different approaches are used to explain various institutional arrangements existing in rural areas (for a review, see Reddy, 2000). However, most of these studies pertain to informal institutions at the local level. There are few studies that deal with the role of formal or legal institutions such as PRIs and JFM in CPR management. This aspect assumes importance in the light of the enhanced powers to PRIs after the 73rd constitutional amendment.

The 73rd amendment and Extension of Panchayat Act for the Scheduled Areas had brought panchayats to centre stage as a potential key player in the area of natural resource management. The functions of the panchayats have been suggested in the eleventh schedule to the Constitution, which includes agriculture, soil conservation, watershed development, social forestry and farm forestry, fuel and fodder and maintenance of community assets. Thus, there is legal framework available to the panchayats to work on natural resource management, such as watersheds. The 1994 watershed guidelines have also clearly spelled out that the responsibility of watershed management should be shifted to village panchayats once the 73rd amendment comes into force. However, not many states have delegated the authority to them. Some state governments have made considerable progress down the road while others have yet to make a beginning. Andhra Pradesh is silent on this issue. On the other hand, it is spearheading the spread of watersheds through a framework that ensures the control and command mechanisms in the hands of the state.

A key issue is the institutional basis and sustainability of the DPAP interventions. The DPAP scheme is generally weakening and subverting the panchayat structure by creating parallel ad-hoc and temporary village institutions (that are not constitutionally based), which are receiving much more significant funds than the village panchayat. They are actually replicating the line agencies and their authority structure at the village level, rather than handing authority to the panchayats (on this basis the line agencies could become accountable service providers responding to village demand).

It is clear that the political dimension is casting a long shadow over the potential developmental benefits. The extent of this is as yet very hard to judge, but it has become very clear from our field visits that the rosy narratives about straightforward agriculture and livelihood improvements from land treatment are highly misleading. This ostensibly technical resource improvement programme is being opportunistically used to a greater or lesser extent in different locations by the prevailing political interests to promote the co-dependency and co-option of the village through financial patronage to particular political factions. Even some NGOs are getting co-opted—and are sometimes resistant to the idea of strengthened village panchayats, which might disrupt the cosy co-dependence they have established with villages on the basis of cash-based activities. Many of the shortcomings of the DPAP implementation in Andhra Pradesh reflect the political economy of power alliances both within the village and the various government structures.

Notes

1. However, the flexibility to take tank repairs is given to project directors later. In fact, in some districts like Anantapur, revival of water bodies was taken up on priority under watershed development programme.
2. This is being institutionalised with the advent of Haryali Guidelines. Though Haryali Guidelines say that PRIs should be the PIAs, line departments carry out most of the implementation, as the PRIs do not have the required capacities. And, NGOs are more or less sidelined.

6

Watershed Management and Rural Livelihoods

In an agrarian economy rural livelihoods are intricately linked with the access of rural people to natural resources such as land, water and biotic resources. In recent years, watershed management has been viewed as a vehicle to improve the livelihood security of rural people in many parts of the world where water scarcity is a critical constraint upon local level development. However, there is an in-built limiting factor in watershed management, as the direct benefits flow to landed households only, whether poor or rich. There are major doubts over whether households without land will benefit from this type of development. On the other hand, while the externalities[1] arising from watershed management complicate the specification of benefits that are due to the watershed management, they may result in wider spread of enhanced livelihood security including that of landless households. This chapter attempts to understand and assess the impact of watershed management in enhancing the livelihood security of the rural households in Andhra Pradesh (AP).

The new guidelines of the Ministry of Rural Development, Government of India, with its definite focus on a people-centred approach, brings the watershed development programme closer to a Sustainable Rural Livelihoods (SRL) framework (Turton, 2000; Baumann, 2000). The SRL framework allows one to 'map' the consequences of specific changes, including changes brought about through external interventions intended to improve people's lives (Soussan et al., 2000; Ellis, 2000). It provides new ways to address poverty issues beyond the traditional methods of employment generation and target group programmes. SRL framework helps us examine the poverty issues in relation to five 'capital assets' (physical, financial, natural, human and social) identified in the framework (see Chapter 1). The participatory initiatives, such as watershed management or joint forest management (JFM), typify this approach. The points of intervention and impact of such programmes can be 'mapped' on the livelihoods model, which is a core objective of this chapter.

Interventions can aim to strengthen different capital assets depending on the needs of local communities, including food security, drinking water supply, savings and credit, etc. It provides a coherent framework within which multi-sectoral activities can be placed. The SRL approach ties in closely with the thinking in the Ministry of Rural Development about how to improve the effectiveness of government poverty reduction schemes. Though there are some early impressions of the impact of the watershed management programme under the new guidelines (Rao, 2000a), this is among the first systematic studies from the sustainable livelihoods angle of how watershed development affects the recipient communities.[2] The main objectives of this chapter are: (a) an assessment of linkages and impact of watershed management on livelihoods across socio-economic groups of the community, beneficiary as well as non-beneficiary households, and (b) the identification of a number of issues that need to be taken into account in the future development of policies for sustainable rural livelihoods through watershed management. AP is among the frontrunners in implementing the watershed development programme in India. It was the first state to take advantage of the huge allocations available for watershed development programmes and has been influential in defining the direction that the new national guidelines should take. About 4.5 million hectares have already been covered under 10,000 watersheds with an expenditure of Rs. 2,000 million (US$45 million). As such, the watershed management programme in AP needs to be judged within a context of large-scale implementation, with all the limitations this entails.

Conceptual Framework and Approach

The concept of sustainable livelihood is increasingly being accepted as providing both a basis for understanding the nature of poverty and for identifying the types of strategies that can reduce poverty in an effective and sustainable manner. This approach reflects the now accepted understanding that poverty itself is a complex, multi-dimensional experience that includes both material and non-material aspects of life (Soussan and Lincklaen, 2003; UNDP, 2003). It lays stress on livelihood assets, or capitals, as the basis for the sustainable improvement of people's livelihoods. This is seen as a more effective reflection of development than income as it reflects both the ability to accumulate wealth and the capabilities (or assets) that households can deploy to secure a living. These assets are also under the control of the households and are the basis for giving people greater choice over the directions that their livelihoods take.

The impact of any programme on rural livelihoods can be assessed from many angles. As mentioned earlier (Chapter 1), the five capitals framework of SRL is adopted here.[3] These capitals include natural, financial, physical, social and human (Carney, 1998; Davies, 1996; Soussan et al., 2000). Sustainable rural livelihoods are critically linked to the enhancement of these five capitals. There is a need to clarify the meaning of 'assets' or 'capitals' in livelihoods analysis. These terms are conventionally associated with a stock, whereas in the dynamics of livelihood operations there are many aspects of the five assets that are akin to flows. A better understanding of these concepts can be gained by looking at them in relation to entitlements theory (Sen, 1982, 1985; Scoones, 1999). With this perspective, the livelihoods assets can be seen as a capability or a potential that can be deployed to undertake, or 'invested in', livelihood activities. They are not uniform in character; for example, under natural capital, access to water resources is contingent upon the flow of water through the hydrological cycle, whereas social capital can take the form of the network of social relationships that households possess and have potential to influence the viability of livelihood activities. From this perspective, livelihood capitals will accumulate where the potential to which the household has an entitlement increases.

Improvement in all the five capitals and less dependence on vulnerable (less resilient) activities or strategies could be termed as 'strong SRL' while improvement in some of the capitals should at least compensate any decline in other capitals and high dependency on vulnerable strategies could be termed as 'weak SRL'. These five capitals are complementary to one another, and especially to natural capital, which has a pivotal role in the livelihoods of rural people: "Predominantly, the poor of the world depend directly on natural resources, through cultivation, herding, collecting or hunting for their livelihoods. Therefore, for the livelihoods to be sustainable, the natural resources must be sustained" (Rennie and Singh, 1996: 16). Improvements in each of these capitals are in turn dependent on various indicators. These linkages can be expressed in the following functional forms:

$$SSRL = f(\Delta FC; \Delta PC; \Delta NC; \Delta SC; \Delta HC; \Delta\%Y_{VA})$$

where

SSRL = Strong sustainable rural livelihoods

ΔPC = Change in physical capital
ΔNC = Change in natural capital
ΔSC = Change in social capital
ΔHC = Change in human capital

ΔFC = Change in financial capital
$\Delta \% Y_{VA}$= Change in the share of income from vulnerable activities

SRL is defined as strong SRL (SSRL) if
$\Delta PC>0$
$\Delta NC>0$
$\Delta SC>0$
$\Delta HC>0$
$\Delta FC>0$
$\Delta \% Y_{VA} \leq 0$

SRL is defined as weak SRL (WSRL) if
$(\Delta PC + \Delta NC + \Delta SC + \Delta HC + \Delta FC) > 0$

and

$\Delta \% Y_{VA} \geq 0$

where

PC = f (A, WSS, Inf...)
NC = f (W, L, CPR...)
SC = f (M, Ca, Ins, Eq, G...)
HC = f (H, Ed., Sk...)
FC = f (S...)

where

A = assets of the households (non-productive); WSS = watershed structures; Inf = common or community infrastructure.
W = water; L = land; CPR = common pool resources other than water.
Ca = collective action; Ins = institutional strength; Eq = equity; G = gender.
H = health; Ed = education (literacy); Sk = skills.
S = savings. And, income (Y); employment (E); etc., could be termed as strategies that boost the savings. Though migration (M) is also a strategy, it is included in social capital due to its social implications. Migration plays an

important role in developing social networks as well. These strategies would reflect in the livelihood activities.

Measurement of Variables and Limitations

In the present context, physical capital is measured in terms of household's possession of durable assets (excluding land) like, house, durables, etc. Watershed-related structures reflect the physical capital created at the village level under the watershed programme. Increases in natural capital are measured in terms of changes in access to or improvements in land, water and other CPRs. It is essentially a flow: the availability of productive potentials as inputs into livelihood activities that come from the dynamics of ecosystems functioning. Of course, natural capital can be treated as a stock in the short term: for example, by felling trees in a forest or over-fishing a lake, but this is not sustainable and is at odds with the concept of sustainable livelihoods. Changes in land values over the period are taken as a proxy for land quality, as land prices are often directly linked with land quality (Reddy, 2001). Changes in availability of drinking water are measured in terms of quantities consumed and time spent in fetching water at the household level. In the case of irrigation water, changes in area under irrigation, number of wells and the depth of the water tables are taken as indicators. The changes are taken over a period of five years and seasonal variations, especially during summer, are also elicited. Use of fodder from common pool resources (CPRs) and time spent in fetching it is taken as a measure of improvements in CPRs other than water bodies.

Eduacation, skills and health are the main elements of human capital. Changes in human capital are measured through changes in education and medical expenditure, as this can best capture variations within communities.[4] These can be measured directly. And, changes in the migration pattern at the household level, the status of women in the decision-making process at the household level as well as women's participation in SHGs, active participation of the community in the watershed activities and the equity in terms of beneficiary coverage and benefit flows represent social capital. These measures are ones that can be more easily assessed than the social networks that are referred to in the literature (Putnam, 1993) and, more pertinently, they are directly linked to watershed management: either as part of the process (such as women's participation in decision-making) or as a factor that watershed management seeks to influence (equity in benefit flows). As such, this approach to social capital means that the direct influence of watershed development on it can be assessed. Moreover, changes in social networks are of long-term nature.

Financial capital is measured in terms of income and savings: that part of cash income that is not used for consumption or social payments. The income can be derived from various livelihood activities, such as agriculture, wage labour, livestock, non-farm activities, returns on investments, etc., at the household level. Stability in livelihoods is assessed in terms of the security of the income sources and diversification of income-generating activities.

The major problem in measuring these indicators is that some of them are measured at the household level and some or at the village or community or group level. Synthesising these levels in a coherent manner is difficult, though SRL framework is capable of integrating local and global aspects of change. Similarly, integrating quantitative and qualitative aspects is also difficult, as quantification is not possible in all the cases. While measurement of changes in some of the variables, such as income, employment, assets, savings, etc., is straightforward, measurement of change in variables like water, CPRs and migration is rather tricky. On the other hand, measurement of change in some of the variables like collective action and gender is difficult, as these variables are qualitative in nature. Moreover, attributing the changes to a particular programme like watershed development is difficult, as there could be other variables (programmes) influencing these changes. For instance, changes in educational and health status could be due to programmes other than watershed management.

Similarly, short-term improvements in water bodies, surface and ground, could be due to medium-term rainfall fluctuations across locations (villages) rather than due to watershed management.

However, these problems or limitations can be taken care of to some extent through the adoption of appropriate techniques of data generation and estimation procedures. An appropriate baseline survey of the households would help in capturing the changes better. Often, such baseline data sets are not available. In such a case, the problem is that we cannot observe the participating households without the programme at the same time. One way of addressing this problem is to have a control group, which is similar to the participating group in all respects except the programme. Control group provides the counter factual of the participating group. But this is not straightforward, as it is difficult to find such a matching group at least in terms of observable indicators: there are many unique characteristics to each village in terms of these specific indicators. The second best solution in this regard is 'reflexive comparison' where before and after scenarios are compared for the participating households. This would provide reasonable estimates of the impact provided that there is no serious memory lapse problem among the respondents (Ravllion, 2001). Memory lapse is directly linked with the time lapsed after initiating the programme. These biases can be further minimised by using the 'double difference' method where before and after situations are examined for both control and participating groups.

We have adopted the 'double difference' method for the purpose of assessing the impact of watershed management on rural livelihoods. Before and after information is analysed for both beneficiary and non-beneficiary groups of households. Non-beneficiary households are selected from the same village of the beneficiary households. Impact assessment is carried out using the village and household level information on various socio-economic, ecological and gender aspects. The analysis is carried out between poor and non-poor (wealth rank) groups to capture the equity aspects of the programme. Statistical tests were carried to validate the impact of the watershed management. Paired 't' test was conducted between 'before' and 'after' and means test for 'with' and 'without' scenarios. Distribution of impact is validated with the help of paired 't' test between poor and non-poor groups of farmers. Qualitative information is used to strengthen the quantitative estimates. Wealth ranking is used to categorise households on their economic status.

Four watersheds in three districts of Anantapur, Kurnool and Mahabubnagar were selected for the purpose of the study. These watersheds were selected after visiting a number of watersheds in the respective districts and consultations with the district-level project directors. Only completed and successful or model watersheds in terms of implementation and impact were selected. The purpose here is that total impact can be assessed only in the technically completed watersheds. And, the selection of model or successful watersheds is not to herald the success stories but to assess the potential of watershed management in enhancing rural livelihoods when implemented under best conditions. In other words, the selection was intended to remove poor implementation as a factor, so that the potential of the watershed management guidelines could be assessed in terms of their impacts upon the livelihoods of rural communities. In these watersheds the project implementing agencies (PIAs), all of which were NGOs, were well aware of the importance of the participatory development philosophy. From each village, 30 beneficiary and 10 non-beneficiary households were interviewed with the help of a structured questionnaire. The fieldwork was carried out during the year 2001–02.

Profile of the Sample Villages

All the sample villages fall under semi-arid agro-climatic category with a rainfall of 375–750 mm though the village from Anantapur receives the lowest rainfall and the villages from Mahabubnagar receive the highest (Table 6.1). In terms of soils villages in Anantapur and Kurnool are having red soils whereas in Mahabubnagar one

Table 6.1 *Socio-economic Characteristics of the Sample Villages*

Village	*Avg. rain-fall (mm)*	*No. of HH*	*Avg. size of HH*	*Avg. size of land-holding (acres)*	*% of households belonging to (wealth ranking)*				*% of HH belonging to BC/ SC&ST*
					V. Poor	*Poor*	*Medium*	*Rich*	
Mallapuram	513	226	5.00	7.25 (16)	15 [16]	60	16	09	77/22
S. Rangapuram	665	78	4.71	4.30 (16)	17 [07]	17	21	45	69/31
Tipparaspalle	754	285	4.80	4.74 (08)	10 [08]	48	39	03	83/17
Mamidimada	749	515	4.65	4.75 (01)	08 [26]	30	48	14	46/37

Notes: HH = Households. Figures in '()' indicate percentage of area under wastelands. Wastelands include private as well as common land that are not being cultivated, forest areas, hillock areas, etc. Figures in '[]' indicate proportion of landless labour households.

village has black soils and another has mixed (black and loam) soils. Black soils are better in terms of moisture retention. Red soils, coupled with low precipitation, place Anantapur at a disadvantageous position. The impact of watershed management, therefore, needs to be assessed in the context of natural advantages/disadvantages of the watershed locations. The socio-economic profile of the sample villages is presented in Table 6.1. The proportion of landless households is relatively low in three of the villages, indicating that most of the households are potential beneficiaries from watershed management.

Agriculture is the main livelihood activity in these villages. Watershed management, therefore, is expected to have a substantive impact on the livelihoods of most households in these villages if it is any way effective in reaching its objectives. Being low rainfall regions, the livelihoods of people in these villages are critically linked with the availability of water. In most of the cases, the proportion of area under irrigation is below 10 percent. The main sources of irrigation are wells and tanks, meaning that irrigation effectiveness is contingent upon the ability to manage water within the village. Cropping patterns at the household level are linked to access to and the reliability of water. The scanty water situation is reflected in the diversified cropping pattern in the villages. Crop diversification hedges risk by spreading it across crops. Wherever assured water is available, farmers prefer to grow paddy. Extent of wastelands ranges from 16 percent in Mallapuram to 1 percent in Mamidimada. Despite being drought-prone areas, the extent of common pool resources (CPRs) is limited, as part of these wastelands is private property.

Status of Watershed Management

All the sample villages were covered under the first batch (1995–96) of watershed management programme that was developed under the (then) new guidelines. Implementation of the watersheds was initiated during 1995–96 in two watersheds (Mallapuram and S. Rangapuram) and in 1996–97 in the other two (Tipraspalle and Mamidimada) and completed by 2000 and 2001 respectively. The area covered under each watershed is about 500 hectares, except in S. Rangapuram. In most of the cases, the guidelines were closely followed in terms of implementation process.

The expenditure on watershed management ranged from Rs. 1.44 million to Rs. 2.98 million across the watersheds. On per hectare basis the expenditure ranged from Rs. 2,882 in Tipraspalle to Rs. 3,000 in S. Rangapuram. A larger proportion of expenditure was spent on technical components like soil and water conservation, horticulture and forestry (plantations on wastelands and avenues). Soil and water conservation was the single most important expenditure in all the watersheds, though there were substantial differences between the watersheds. It ranged from 39 percent in S. Rangapuram to 83 percent in Tipraspalle. These variations were due to the differences in soil and other geological conditions in the watershed that influence the number of masonry works like check-dams required. Horticulture and forestry together form the second largest expenditure component in watershed management. Two new components were included as per the new guidelines. They were entry point activity and funding of self-help groups (SHGs) that was meant for social development.

Coverage of beneficiary households under the watershed was predetermined on technical grounds, i.e., depending on the slope and terrain. However, equity in coverage is important from the social point of view, as the iniquitous distribution of benefits would thwart the collective action potential (Reddy, 1998; Hanna, 1996; Agrawal, 1994; Deshpande and Reddy, 1990). That is, when people view an established system as inequitable according to established social standards, they have incentives to undermine it (Hanna, 1996). Given the importance of social capital in the watershed management programme, some of the PIAs (e.g., RDT in Mallapuram) are adopting the full coverage of the village irrespective of the support from the DPAP/DDP. It is clear from the distribution of beneficiary households across social and economic groups that equity was not inbuilt (Table 6.2). In

Table 6.2 *Socio-economic Composition of Watershed Beneficiaries (% households)*

Village	*Proportion of Beneficiary Households Belonging to*							
	SCs	*STs*	*BCs*	*OCs*	*V. Poor*	*Poor*	*Medium*	*Rich*
Mallapuram	75	—	79	100	36	80	95	100
	(22)		(77)	(0.4)	(15)	(60)	(16)	(09)
S. Rangapuram	26	00	56	—	14	45	65	90
	(16)	(01)	(83)		(10)	(48)	(38)	(04)
Tipparaspalle	—	09	78	—	00	100	100	97
		(31)	(69)		(17)	(18)	(21)	(45)
Mamidimada	11	72	46	20	28	28	50	25
	(03)	(34)	(46)	(17)	(08)	(30)	(48)	(14)

Notes: Figures in parentheses indicate the actual percentage of households belonging to respective category. SCs = Scheduled Castes, STs = Scheduled Tribes; BCs = Backward Castes; OCs = Other Castes.

three of the four watersheds, better off households were getting disproportionately higher coverage when compared to the poor households.

Watershed Management and Rural Livelihoods

The impact of the watershed management on livelihoods in the four study villages was measured in terms of changes in various indicators. Impact was measured across different wealth ranking households in order to examine the distributional aspects of the impact. The analysis of impact indicators is presented here under the five capitals (SRL) framework along with livelihood strategies.

Physical Capital

Physical capital is defined in terms of various assets of the households, such as livestock, equipment, etc., and the assets at the community level like watershed works, infrastructure, etc. The community-based physical capital investments ranged between Rs. 2,900 to Rs. 3,000 per hectare. Majority of the households own land in the sample villages. Proportion of landless households ranges from 7 percent in S. Rangapuram to 26 percent in Mamidimada. The average per household ownership of land ranged from 7.25 acres in Mallapuram to 4.30 acres in S. Rangapuram. Availability of irrigation enhances the asset position of the households. Proportion of area irrigated is less than 25 percent in all the sample villages though it varied from 6 percent in S. Rangapuram to 25 percent in Tipraspalle. Over the period, households have also invested in irrigation equipment like borewells. There has been a substantial increase in the number of wells in all the villages (see Table 6.7), though the sustainability of these wells is questionable in the absence of replenishing mechanisms.

As far as livestock assets are concerned, size of holdings at the household level has recorded a decline over a period of five years in most of the sample villages. This is in tune with the general phenomenon across the region. The decline was prominent in the case of big cattle like cows and bullocks (Table 6.3). During the same period, there was an increase in the holdings of small ruminants. Concentration of small ruminants was quite high in S. Rangapuram and Tipraspalle in before as well as after scenarios. The shift was prominent among poor households. Often this happens due to the degradation of land—both private and common (Reddy, 2000). The prevailing drought conditions (three out of four years have experience shortage in rainfall preceding the year 2000–01) in the region might have caused the shift in favour of small ruminants. The shifts were prominent in the low rainfall villages of Mallapuram and S. Rangapuram (Table 6.3).

Natural Capital

Natural capital is the key to livelihood security in agrarian societies, especially in drought-prone areas. Here, we examine the linkages between watershed management and access to natural resources. Our focus is mainly on land assets (quality), the availability of fodder, and water, especially groundwater (drinking as well as irrigation), as these are the key forms of natural capital in the livelihoods of communities in the study area. At the household level, the value of land assets has gone up in all the villages for both dry and irrigated lands (Table 6.4). Increase in land values reflects the improved quality of land due to watershed management. This, in turn, improves the credit worthiness of the households. However, the increases, though substantial in some of the villages, are not statistically significant. The quality improvements were not limited to private lands. The improved quality of common lands was also reflected in the availability of fodder.

Fodder

Livestock rearing is an important livelihood strategy in the sample villages. The sustainability of livestock rearing depends

Table 6.3 *Changes in Size and Composition of Livestock in the Sample Households (%)*

Village/Wealth Rank	Beneficiary Households				Non-beneficiary Households			
	Buffaloes	Cows	Bullocks	Sheep & Goat	Buffaloes	Cows	Bullocks	Sheep & Goat
Mallapuram	–17	–20	–5.6	108	23	–18	–33.3	00
S. Rangapuram	24	–03	00	62	–100	–90	–50	200
Tipraspally	00	00	4.9	–9	00	–67	33.3	33
Mamidimada	00	–27	–5.6	06	00	00	–25	–33

Note: – indicates no values, the rest indicates changes from 0 to 1 or vice versa.

Table 6.4 *Changes in Land Values (Rs per acre)*

Village/Wealth Rank	Irrigated Land			Dry Land		
	Before	After	% Change	Before	After	% Change
Mallapuram	32609	35582	09	18085	20620	14
S. Rangapuram	13125	43154	229	12654	18021	42
Tipraspalle	24091	33360	38	13141	18830	43
Mamidimada	28295	39372	39	15049	21910	46

Note: The differences are not statistically significant in any of the cases.

on the availability of fodder on a sustained basis. Further, the structure of livestock holding also reflects the type of livelihood activity adopted by the households, though it mainly depends on the quantity and quality of CPRs available in the villages. It is often argued that environmental degradation results in a shift in the livestock composition towards small ruminants. On the other hand, availability of irrigation facilities often leads to a decline in the importance of livestock. This is often accompanied by the reduction in the availability of CPRs. That is, CPRs are encroached and converted into croplands with the advent of irrigation or more remunerative crops. In other words, while marginal improvements in resource conditions strengthen the livestock economy, substantial improvements in access to resources, especially water, might erode the livestock economy. It was observed that under degraded resource conditions, households are forced to shift towards small ruminants, viz., sheep and goat (Reddy, 2000).

As indicated earlier, livestock composition has changed in all the sample villages. Fodder availability is seen in terms of dependence of cattle on different sources of feed. Grazing on common lands (CPRs) was reported after the development of the watersheds, especially among beneficiary farmers. Dependence on market for fodder (purchase) was also observed but on a very limited scale. Stall-feeding was the single most important source, followed by grazing in own lands and CPRs. Per cattle availability of fodder has increased among the beneficiary households in two of the villages after the advent of watershed (Table 6.5). Availability of fodder in absolute terms has increased in three of the four sample villages in the case of beneficiary households where as it has increased in Mallapuram only as far as non-beneficiary farmers are concerned. Over a period of 4–5 years, the importance of stall-feeding and grazing on own lands has declined though they continue to be the most important sources in all the villages. In the case of beneficiary households the share of CPRs in the total fodder consumption has increased in all the

Table 6.5 *Changes in the Availability of Fodder (per standard cattle per day)*

Village	*Fodder Availability (kgs/day/standard cattle+)*					
	Beneficiary Households			*Non-beneficiary Households*		
	Before	*After*	*% Change*	*Before*	*After*	*% Change*
Mallapuram	4.7 (3.2)	6.5 (3.3)	38 (03)*	3.6 (2.5)	5.0 (2.6)	39 (04)
S. Rangapuram	3.8 (7.7)	3.2 (10.0)	–16 (30)	1.8 (3.2)	6.4 (0.7)	72 (–78)
Tipraspally	4.8 (5.3)	4.0 (5.1)	–17 (04)	8.2 (0.7)	9.1 (0.6)	11 (–14)
Mamidimada	5.9 (1.7)	8.3 (1.5)	41 (–12)	14.0 (0.4)	15.2 (0.3)	09 (–25)

Note: + standard cattle is arrived at by converting small ruminants by equating 3:1 ratio to big cattle.
Figures in parentheses indicate average number of standard cattle units per household.
* Indicates that the difference is statistically significant at 5 percent level.

four villages reflecting the overall improvement in land quality. In fact, contribution of CPRs to fodder consumption was zero prior to the advent of watershed. After the watershed its share has increased to 3 percent in S. Rangapuram and to 12 percent in Mallapuram and Tipraspalle. The decline in stall-feeding and on own lands explains, to some extent, the shift in the livestock composition in favour of small ruminants, which are the main type of livestock grazed on CPR lands.

Groundwater

Improved groundwater tables would enhance the quality and quantity of drinking water at the household level. A major impact of this would be on the time spent on fetching water apart from the impact on health and micro-environment at the household and community level. Use of drinking water has increased in all the villages after the advent of watershed though the increase was significant in only two of the sample villages (Table 6.6). The increase was more in the case of poorer households. The time spent on fetching water has also declined in three of the villages, indicating substantial improvement in the drinking water situation. The decline in time spent was as high as 82 percent in Tipraspally, though the differences in time saving were not much between rich and poor households. These changes in access to and the quality of drinking water have, of course, a significant gender dimension, as women were the main fetchers of water and the main health carers in most households. The significant decline in the time taken to fetch water in Mallapuram and S. Rangapuram in particular would bring great benefits to all women, and especially to poor women, who are less likely to have private connections in their homes.

The impact of watershed on well irrigation is assessed in terms of increased number of wells and the changes in the depth of the water table.[5] On both these accounts the impact on groundwater is positive. Number of irrigation wells has gone up substantially in most of the sample villages (Table 6.7). Both

Table 6.6 *Changes in Drinking Water Availability*

Village/Wealth Rank	*Quantity of Drinking Water Use (Liters/day/household)*			*Time Spent in Fetching Drinking Water (hours/day/household)*		
	Before	*After*	*% Change*	*Before*	*After*	*% Change*
Mallapuram	10.50	11.85	13.50	3.59	1.67	–53.50
S. Rangapuram	10.66	12.79	20.00	1.97	0.34	–82.70
Tipraspally	11.75	14.25	21.30*	1.18	1.18	00.00
Mamidimada	12.19	14.27	17.10*	1.08	0.97	–10.20

Note: * indicates that the differences are statistically significant at 1 percent level.

Table 6.7 *Details of Wells in the Sample Households*

Size-class/Village	*No. of Wells*		*Depth of Wells (ft)*		*% Change*	
	Before	*After*	*Before*	*After*	*Number*	*Depth*
Mallapuram	17	21	110 (18)	80 (16)	25	–27
Very Poor	01 (01)	01	120	80	00	–27
Poor	08 (02)	11	150	105	38	–30
Medium	05 (01)	06 (01)	110	90	20	–18
Rich	03 (01)	03	110	80	00	–27
S. Rangapuram	04 (04)	06 (05)	120 (24)	90 (22)	50	–25
Rich	04 (04)	06 (05)	120 (24)	90 (22)	50	–25
Tibraspalle	06	18	120	90	200	–25
Poor	01	04	120	90	300	–25
Medium	05	13	140	90	160	–36
Rich	00	01	120	90	@	–25
Mamidimada	06	09	120	90	50	–25
Poor	03	04	120	90	33	–25
Medium	03	05	120	90	67	–25

Note: Number of wells includes bore wells and dug (open) wells. Figures in parentheses are number of dug wells. Changes are calculated on the basis of functioning wells.
@ Indicates the absolute changes from zero to positive figure or vice versa.

Mallapuram and S. Rangapuram used to have open wells before the watershed, but most of them have dried up in Mullapuram during the last 4–5 years. Only S. Rangapuram seems to have sustained the open wells despite poor rainfall. On the other hand, S. Rangapuram does not have many borewells even after the watershed, which is reflected in the limited area under irrigation in this watershed. Borewells have increased in number in all the watersheds. The increase ranged from 25 percent in Mallpuram to 200 percent in Tipraspalle. In all the watersheds, except Mallapuram, none of the very poor households owns a well indicating the uneven distribution of access to irrigation water. In most of the cases only the rich and medium farmers own the wells.

The increase in the number of wells was accompanied by the rising of the water table, which was a clear sign of watershed impact despite the poor rainfall during the last 3–4 years. Depth of groundwater table has increased by 25 percent and there were little variations across villages though there was some variation across wealth ranks. The impact of watershed was seen even in the case of dugwells (S. Rangapuram), while most of the dug-wells were getting dried up in the region in recent years (Reddy, 2001). There were not many wells among the non-beneficiary households and in all the cases, except Tipraspalle, there was no increase in number of wells after the watershed development.

It was observed that proportion of area under irrigation has increased, though marginally, among all the households in the sample villages after the advent of watershed management (Table 6.8). The changes range from 19 (Mallapuram) to 129 percent (S. Rangapuram). S. Rangapuram has recorded highest increase though it has only 6 percent of the area under irrigation (sample households). The increase in irrigation is statistically significant in all the villages, except Mallapuram. The increase in area under irrigation in the watershed villages was substantially higher than that of their respective district averages, especially in the low rainfall regions (Table 6.8). The increase is more in the

Table 6.8 *Changes in Area under Irrigation due to Watershed Management (among sample households)*

Village/Wealth Rank	Beneficiary Households					Non-beneficiary Households		
	Area under Irrigation (acres/hh)			% Area Irrigated		Area Irrigated (acres/hh)		
	Before	After	% Change	Before	After	Before	After	% Change
Mallapuram	0.84	1.00	19 (2)	13	15	1.38	1.83	33
Very Poor	0.75	0.75	00	10	10	0.50	0.50	00
Poor	0.48	0.76	58	11	16	1.00	2.00	100
Medium	1.30	1.28	–02	16	16	3.00	3.00	00
Rich	1.81	1.81	00	14	14	—	—	—
S. Rangapuram	0.43	0.96	123* (2)	03	06	00	4.00	@
Rich	0.43	0.96	100	04	07	00	4.00	@
Tipraspalle	1.10	1.38	25* (20)	20	25	0.56	0.93	66
Poor	0.49	0.58	18	19	22	0.40	0.80	100
Medium	1.53	1.93	26	22	27	0.83	1.25	51
Rich	2.00	2.00	00	14	14	—	—	—
Mamidimada	0.65	0.83	28** (20)	12	16	1.06	1.50	42
Poor	0.58	0.83	43	24	34	00	0.67	@
Medium	0.67	0.86	28	12	16	1.13	1.63	44
Rich	0.67	0.67	00	08	08	2.50	2.50	00

Note: * and ** indicate that the difference is statistically significant at 5 and 10 per cent levels respectively. Differences are not significant in the case of with and with out scenarios and within the poor and non-poor categories.
Figures in parentheses are the changes at the district level during the same period.
@ Indicates changes from zero to positive or vice-versa.

case of rich and medium households in all the villages. In fact, very poor did not have irrigation at all in all the sample villages, except in Mallapuram. The overall impact of watershed on irrigation was positive despite the poor rainfall during the preceding three years, which was a period of unprecedented drought. Apart from the quantitative changes in the area, qualitative changes in the availability of irrigation in terms of regular and assured supplies were equally, if not more, important in improving the economic conditions of the farmers. This aspect was reflected in the changes in land values, cropping pattern, land productivity, etc.

Human Capital

As there was little or no change in the access (availability of and distance from school/hospital) indicators of human capital in the sample villages, expenditures on education and health are used to assess the impact on human capital. Expenditure on education appeared to be receiving a high priority when compared to medical expenditure in most of the cases. Only in the cases where there were some emergencies do households seem to spend more on medical treatment. All the villages have government schools up to primary level, while Mamidimada has a high school. Despite being remote and dominated by marginalised social groups, education is considered important among the sample households. Average annual expenditure on education ranged from about Rs. 1,400 in S. Rangapuram to about Rs. 5,000 in Mamidimada (Table 6.9). Obviously, the rich spend more on education. Over the period, expenditure on education has increased significantly in two of the villages. The decline in some cases is not significant. On the other hand, medical expenditure has increased significantly in all the villages over the period, reflecting the incidence of disease. On an average household's per year medical expenditure ranged from Rs. 800 in S. Rangapuram to Rs. 2,100 in Mallapuram (Table 6.9). In all the villages per household medical expenditure among

Table 6.9 *Changes in Medical and Educational Expenditure in the Sample Households*

Village/Wealth Rank	*Before (expenditure/ household/year in Rs)*		*After (expenditure/ household/year in Rs)*		*Percentage Change*	
	Medical	*Education*	*Medical*	*Education*	*Medical*	*Education*
Mallapuram	1323	3396	2096	2113	58*	–38
S. Rangapuram	522	192	808	1442	55*	651**
Tipraspalle	3646	1856	7230	1736	98**	–06
Mamidimada	501	4255	1445	5229	188*	23*

Note: * and ** indicate that the differences are significant at 1 and 10 percent levels respectively.

beneficiary households goes up along with the economic class. That is, rich households spend more on medical expenses when compared to poor households.

Social Capital

It is rather difficult to assess the social impact of any programme, especially with short study periods. Social development is a long process and to capture social changes in totality requires a rigorous approach. Our qualitative research revealed strong social networks within the villages, though there were no apparent changes in the recent years. Apart from the general support households receive from their friends and neighbours, dependency for credit on friends and relatives is quite high in these villages. Similarly, there is an increased participation in self-help groups (SHGs) in the recent years. However, there was a general feeling about the declining cohesion and supportive nature in the communities, which cannot be attributed to a specific programme like watershed management. Here, in this section an attempt is made to assess the social impact in terms of migration and gender. Migration, while having a social impact on the household, plays a vital role in developing social networks. Equity issues also fall under social capital though equity was discussed along with income strategies (financial capital, Table 6.15).

Migration

Migration in the sample villages is long term in nature in many cases. Labourers go to other villages during harvest season to work on farms, especially for paddy and groundnut harvesting. Except in Mallapuram labourers migrate to farther places, even to Mumbai, and stay longer periods away from home (Table 6.10). On an average, each person spends more that 40 days in a year outside the villages, except in Mallapuram. In Mamidimada and Tipraspalle, a number of people migrate

Table 6.10 *Pattern of Migration Among the Sample Households*

Village/Wealth Rank	*Before*			*After*		
	Number of Persons	*Number of Days*	*Distance (km)*	*Number of Persons*	*Number of Days*	*Distance (km)*
Beneficiaries (120)						
Mallapuram (30)	4	60 [2]	3	4	60 [2]	3
S. Rangapuram (30)	11	505 [17]	42–316	13	572 [19]	75–300
Tipraspalle (30)	8	535 [18]	4–700	11	1416 [47]	8–650
Mamidimada (30)	14	619 [21]	130–562	14	778 [26]	130–846
Non-beneficiaries (40)						
Mallapuram (10)	9	454 [45]	2–9	10	790 [26]	3
S. Rangapuram (10)	4	102 [10]	100–244	7	186 [19]	111–370
Tipraspalle (10)	2	90 [9]	700	2	90 [9]	700
Mamidimada (10)	8	180 [18]	700	6	165 [17]	410–700

Note: Figures in parenthesis '[]' indicate number of days per household.

to Mumbai during the lean season. The average distance travelled is above 200 km in many cases and in Tipraspalle and Mamidimada people go up to 700 km. Beneficiary and non-beneficiary comparison brought out that migration was more widespread among the non-beneficiary households only in the case of Mallapuram. This difference was visible when we examine the migration figures on per household basis. In the case of other three villages the difference was marginal, though the extent of migration was low in the case of non-beneficiary households. Among the beneficiary households the total number of days migrated in a year per household ranged from two days (Mallapuram) to 21 in Mamidimada. Whereas in the case of non-beneficiary households it ranged from nine in Tipraspalle to 45 days in Mallapuram. Our qualitative research has indicated that migration in these regions is basically distress in nature[6], though people from Mahabubnagar traditionally go to farther places like Mumbai where they get better wages. Migration was also more among the poor and medium economic classes, while only a few rich households went out in search of work. These migratory labourers were involved mainly in agriculture-related works in the irrigated regions, construction and *beedi* works. Migration was also more in the lean seasons when employment opportunities were low in the village.

There was an increase in the extent of migration when before and after watershed management scenarios were compared in all the watersheds except Mallapuram. This supports peoples' perceptions on migration that significant employment was generated during the period when watershed works were executed. Once the implementation of the watershed was completed, there were no alternative avenues to sustain the employment created. Hence, people have resorted to migration again. Moreover, there was an increase in migration after the watershed. This could be due to the fact that labour participation would have increased consequent to the increased demand for watershed works with in the villages, which was being released into the labour market after completion of the works. This aspect came out in some of the earlier studies on watershed management in Maharashtra (Deshpande and Reddy, 1991). Another explanation could be the release of family labour from support activities like fetching water, fodder and fuelwood. However, migration was expected to come down provided there was growth in agricultural activities, such as increased area under irrigated crops, cropping intensity, etc. It may take some more time for the watershed management to result in increase in area under irrigation, etc. On the other hand, improvements in groundwater availability did not seem to have any impact on migration despite the increase in employment.

Gender

Qualitative research revealed that there were substantial changes in the role of women at the household level due to the advent of SHGs. Watershed management programme has strengthened the SHGs through better employment and wages to women. Thus, watershed management has indirectly contributed to gender development. Work participation rates (main activity) of women were quite high and comparable with male participation rates in all the sample villages. Secondary activity work participation was quite high among women compared to men. In both main and subsidiary activities women participation was mainly in agricultural-related activities while men participated in other activities as well. Besides, women contributed about 80–90 percent towards supportive livelihood activities, such as fetching water, fuelwood and cattle herding. If converted in to money values (opportunity costs) their contribution to the household economy would be substantial.

Involvement of women in the household decision-making process is an important indicator of gender equity. Extent of women involvement in the household decisions was measured at three levels, namely, (a) unilateral decisions by male members,

(b) unilateral decisions by female members, and (c) decisions taken together. While 'A' reflects the lowest level, 'B' reflects the highest level of women's participation and involvement. Women's involvement in various important issues, such as income generation, debt-savings and other household activities was examined. Women's involvement in income-generating activities was total (B) only in a few cases. In two of the villages (Tipraspalle and Mamidimada) men took decisions unilaterally in majority of the cases while in the other two villages decisions were taken together in majority of the households (Table 6.11a and b). That is, at the maximum only 60 percent (S. Rangapuram) of the households involved their women members while taking decisions regarding income-generating activities. At the highest level of participation (B) the percentage of households reporting women's involvement ranged from zero to 10 across the sample villages.

Interestingly, in Tipraspalle, women took unilateral decisions regarding debt and savings in 40 percent of the households, which was due to the activities of the local *mahila samakhya* (women's organisation). In the case of all other decisions, such as purchase of durable goods, children's education, family planning and health, they were decided jointly in majority of the households or unilaterally by male members. Women's participation appeared to be better in the case of decisions, such as health, children's education, family planning, etc. (Table 11b). Women's involvement was particularly better in the case of health where 70 to 100 percent of the sample households involved women in the decision-making process (B+C). In the order of importance, women involvement was the lowest in the case of income-generating activities, followed by financial matters (debt and savings), purchase of durable goods, children's education, family planning and health.

Financial Capital

Improvements in financial capital are a reflection of improvements in the employment pattern, income, etc., due to the changes in

Table 6.11a *Involvement of Women in Decision-Making in the Sample Households (% of households)*

Village/Activity	*Income-generating Activities**			*Major Purchases*			*Debt and savings*		
	A	*B*	*C*	*A*	*B*	*C*	*A*	*B*	*C*
Mallapuram	40	10	50	30	10	60	30	10	60
S. Rangapuram	40	00	60	50	00	50	40	00	60
Tipraspalle	70	00	30	30	00	70	50	40	10
Mamidimada	90	10	10	40	20	40	55	00	45

Note: A = only male decision, B = only female decision, C = together decision.
* Income-generating activities relate to agriculture, livestock, etc.

Table 6.11b *Involvement of Women in Decision-Making in the Sample Households (% of households)*

Village/Activity	*Family Planning*			*Children's Education*			*Health Care*		
	A	*B*	*C*	*A*	*B*	*C*	*A*	*B*	*C*
Mallapuram	17	20	63	20	20	60	00	20	80
S. Rangapuram	47	00	53	60	00	40	00	10	90
Tipraspalle	03	23	74	40	10	50	30	10	60
Mamidimada	00	00	100	10	10	80	00	20	80

Note: A = only male decision, B = only female decision, C = together decision.

cropping patterns, cropping intensities, etc. Larger income from these activities creates the potential for greater savings and consequently an increase in financial capital. These changes are directly linked to access to water for irrigation purposes. Agricultural activities, such as farm labour (own or hired), are also the main activities in these villages. Only a few of them work in construction or *beedi*-making. Given the difficulties in obtaining accurate information on savings (something that people were understandably reluctant to talk about), improvements to financial capital are assessed in terms of sustainable increases in income potentials.

Yields and Returns

Despite the poor rainfall during the preceding three years land productivity has increased considerably in all the watersheds. Yield rates per acre have gone up in irrigated (paddy) as well as unirrigated (especially groundnut) crops, though the increases were not statistically significant (Table 6.12). Paddy yields have gone up by 15 (Tipraspalle) to 44 percent (S. Rangapuram), while groundnut yields have increased by 16 (Tipraspalle) to 81 percent (S. Rangapuram). This clearly indicates that watershed management not only enhanced the availability of groundwater but also improved the *in situ* soil moisture content that helped the increase in yield rates of groundnut. This also indicates that watershed management has contributed in terms of improving the resilience and robustness of the natural system. Yields of jowar have not improved, and have even gone down in one of the villages (Mamidimada). On the other hand, performance of non-beneficiary households was not that impressive except in the case of Mallapuram. And, the increases in yield rates were more prominent among the rich and medium households in most of the cases, reflecting the improved availability of irrigation among these households.

However, changes in land productivity may not result in improved livelihoods at the household level. For, these

Table 6.12 *Changes in Yield Rates*

Village/Wealth Rank	*% Change in the Yield Rates*							
	Beneficiary Households				*Non-beneficiary Households*			
	Paddy	*G.nut*	*Jowar*	*Castor*	*Paddy*	*G.nut*	*Jowar*	*Castor*
Mallapuram	24	19	00	00	39	29	00	00
Very Poor	11	–17	00	00	00	00	00	00
Poor	27	–01	00	00	25	31	00	00
Medium	22	54	00	00	66	25	00	00
Rich	31	47	00	00	—	—	—	—
S. Rangapuram	44	81	00	00	00	–38	00	00
Very Poor	—	—	—	—	00	00	00	00
Poor	00	278	00	00	00	00	00	00
Medium	00	50	00	00	—	—	—	00
Rich	44	50	00	00	00	–38	00	00
Tipraspalle	15	16	0.02	00	0.7	00	17	00
Very Poor	00	00	00	00	00	00	00	00
Poor	27	00	–05	00	–04	00	31	00
Medium	–07	16	08	00	06	00	08	00
Rich	25	00	00	00	—	—	—	—
Mamidimada	19	00	–14	08	36	00	00	95
Very Poor	00	00	00	00	00	00	00	00
Poor	12	00	–01	13	00	00	00	00
Medium	18	00	–50	–40	33	00	00	00
Rich	31	00	–84	100	40	00	00	100

Note: In none of the cases changes in yield rates are statistically significant.

improvements in yield rates need not necessarily get converted into net income if the improvements in yield rates were realised at higher costs. Interestingly, only three watersheds have recorded positivc incremental net returns in the case of paddy and two watersheds in the case of groundnut (Table 6.13). When all the crops were taken together, three of the watersheds have positive incremental returns. Interestingly, S. Rangapuram has recorded negative returns while Mamidimada has marginal positive returns. Net incremental returns were quite reasonable in Mallapuram (Rs. 1,105 per acre) and Tipraspalle (Rs. 534 per acre). Gains in access to irrigation to the poor were not converted into net income gains. The differences between beneficiary and non-beneficiary households were quite conspicuous in this regard. However, the changes were not statistically significant in any of the cases.

Aggregate incremental net returns of the non-beneficiary households were negative in all the villages except Mallapuram, though again they are not significant in any of the cases. Even, in Mallapuram the net incremental returns to non-beneficiary households were marginal. This indicates that watershed management had a positive impact on net returns, which is an indicator of economic viability. Under the given conditions (agro climatic and institutional) watershed management is economically viable in Mallapuram and Tipraspalle. Its viability in some cases reflects its potential resilience against drought conditions. That is, when implemented properly, watershed management can protect agriculture from adverse climatic situations at least in the medium term. In this, it is meeting one of its main objectives.

Employment

The sample villages have experienced substantial increase in the employment due to the programme. Total employment gains ranged between 11 (Mamidimada) and 29 (Mallapuram) percent among the beneficiary households, while the increase among the

Table 6.13 *Cropwise Incremental Net Returns (per acre)*

Village/Wealth Rank	*Incremental Net Returns (Rs/acre)*									
	Beneficiary Households					*Non-beneficiary Households*				
	Paddy	*G.nut*	*Jowar*	*Castor*	*All*	*Paddy*	*G.nut*	*Jowar*	*Castor*	*All*
Mallapuram	724	1372	00	00	1105	483	–89	00	00	197
Very Poor	8225	1521	00	00	4873	00	00	00	00	00
Poor	–271	960	00	00	64	1612	1065	00	00	1339
Medium	787	1435	00	00	2591	3285	–330	00	00	1478
Rich	2376	1883	00	00	920	—	—	—	—	—
S. Rangapuram	3932	2257	00	00	–376	00	–618	00	00	–618
Very Poor	—	—	—	—	—	00	00	00	00	00
Poor	00	4015	00	00	277	00	00	00	00	00
Medium	00	879	00	00	–1687	—	—	—	—	—
Rich	3932	2314	00	00	–768	00	–618	00	00	–618
Tipraspalle	2109	–529	–1058	967	534	620	00	222	00	–1049
Very Poor	00	00	463	00	–931	00	00	00	00	00
Poor	1207	00	–2581	1125	1119	–1641	00	31	00	–4048
Medium	2382	–1261	–588	765	293	1378	00	313	00	–383
Rich	1900	00	–717	00	327	—	—	—	—	—
Mamidimada	–945	00	144	1310	166	927	00	–2737	–715	–858
Very Poor	00	00	30	00	30	00	00	00	00	00
Poor	–48	00	–594	825	–344	00	00	00	–418	–418
Medium	–1763	00	–1093	–1520	–1370	–297	00	–2737	–3287	–1763
Rich	2170	00	1242	11775	5063	1230	00	00	00	864

Note: In none of the cases the incremental returns are statistically significant.

non-beneficiary households ranged from 5 (Mamidimada) to 52 (Mallapuram) percent (Table 6.14). Growth in employment was higher among beneficiary farmers in two villages (Mamidimada and S. Rangapuram) whereas non-beneficiary farmers have recorded higher growth in Mallapuram and Tipraspalle. The increase in employment was statistically significant in the case of beneficiary households. The increase in employment was higher during the summer season compared to kharif (July–November) and rabi (November–March) seasons, as the watershed works were often carried out during summer. Besides, activities related to horticultural crops, vegetables, along with non-farm activities, have increased substantially during summer months. There was no clear trend regarding the employment impact across wealth ranks though the benefits seem to be relatively more in the case of medium and rich households, as they have more cultivable area.

Household Income

Household income from all sources, like agriculture, livestock, wage employment, etc., has improved significantly in all the villages (Table 6.15). This was mainly due to the increase in employment and wage rates, whilst the improvements due to crop production and livestock were rather limited. The increase in household income ranged from 54 percent in Tipraspalle to 101 percent in Mallapuram. The contribution of activities other than crop production was also reflected in the distribution of household income. The estimated Gini ratios indicated a substantial decline in inequalities across all situations, including non-beneficiaries (Table 6.15). In general inequalities are lower in the case of total income, which was due to greater dependence on activities other than crop production in most of the sample villages. That was poor households (landless in general) seem to have benefited more in proportional terms from watershed when compared to medium and rich households. While the rich benefited more from agriculture, the poor benefited more from employment outside

Table 6.14 *Changes in Farm Employment across Seasons (Total employment) (in %)*

Village/Wealth Rank	*Beneficiary Households*				*Non-beneficiary Households*			
	Kharif	*Rabi*	*Summer*	*Total*	*Kharif*	*Rabi*	*Summer*	*Total*
Mallapuram	23	24	53	29*	56	48	48	52
Very Poor	14	00	00	10	122	51	87	23
Poor	28	21	52	28	21	33	16	35
Medium	29	31	57	33	55	22	00	35
Rich	18	19	63	25	—	—	—	—
S. Rangapuram	23	20	30	25*	11	14	90	23
Very Poor	—	—	—	—	13	15	200	28
Poor	19	26	28	23	00	00	00	00
Medium	25	43	48	25	—	—	—	—
Rich	25	34	29	28	00	08	50	10
Tipraspalle	16	20	31	19*	25	28	43	28
Very Poor	00	00	00	00	36	36	50	33
Poor	12	21	16	16	20	27	89	29
Medium	18	20	36	21	26	26	00	23
Rich	26	08	50	24	—	—	—	—
Mamidimada	11	08	18	11*	09	03	05	05
Very Poor	00	08	13	04	00	00	00	00
Poor	12	10	11	11	00	05	00	02
Medium	15	10	21	14	07	00	00	03
Rich	00	00	00	00	29	07	25	20

Note: * indicate that the increases in employment are statistically significant at 1 percent level.

Table 6.15 *Changes in Income Inequalities in the Sample Villages (Gini ratios)*

Village	*Beneficiary Households*				*Non-Beneficiary Households*			
	Agricultural Income		*Total Income*		*Agricultural Income*		*Total Income*	
	Before	*After*	*Before*	*After*	*Before*	*After*	*Before*	*After*
Mallapuram	0.49	0.02	0.33	0.29 (101*)	0.80	0.67	0.46	0.16
S.Rangapuram	0.59	0.34	0.34	0.08 (77*)	0.89	0.89	0.89	0.52
Tipraspalle	0.77	0.64	0.50	0.03 (54*)	0.67	0.58	0.67	0.32
Mamidimada	0.81	0.70	0.46	0.01 (63*)	0.67	0.63	0.67	0.24
Overall	0.84	0.64	0.64	0.30	0.86	0.70	0.70	0.33

Note: Figures in parentheses are % change in total income. * indicates that the difference is statistically significant at 1 per cent level. Gini ratios may be taken as indicators only due to the problem of small sample. The overall picture is more realistic.

their own farms. Among the beneficiary households, Mallapuram has the lowest level of inequalities in agricultural income in both before and after situations. However, in the case of total income, the decline was more prominent in Mamidimada, Tipraspalle and S. Rangapuram.

Aggregate Impact on Capitals

For assessing the aggregate impact on livelihoods some of the important indicators are converted into monetary terms and the improvements are presented in radar diagrams (Figures 6.1–6.4). These indicators include benefits from improvements in the availability of fodder, fuelwood and groundwater (natural capital), improvements in household assets (physical capital), total household income (financial capital), changes in the expenditure on health and education (human capital), and changes in income from migratory labour (social capital). Indicators are measured in actual monitory terms and presented as after and before scenarios.[7] Note that increase in migratory labour is treated as negative impact and hence any improvement in social capital ought to be understood as negative impact. However, the changes in some of the variables do not stand statistical rigour. Paired 't' tests were carried out on all the important indicators. As per the tests improvements in area under irrigation (natural capital) are significant in three of the sample villages, while the improvements in net incremental returns (financial capital) are not significant (Table 6.16). On the other hand, improvements in total household income and employment are statistically significant in all the villages. In the case of natural capital, fodder availability improved significantly in Mallapuram only, while fuelwood and water (drinking and irrigation) have not recorded any significant improvement. Both the human capital indicators (education and health) have improved significantly in most of the cases. And social capital (days of migration) has not changed significantly.

Fig 6.1 Impact of WSD in Mallapuram

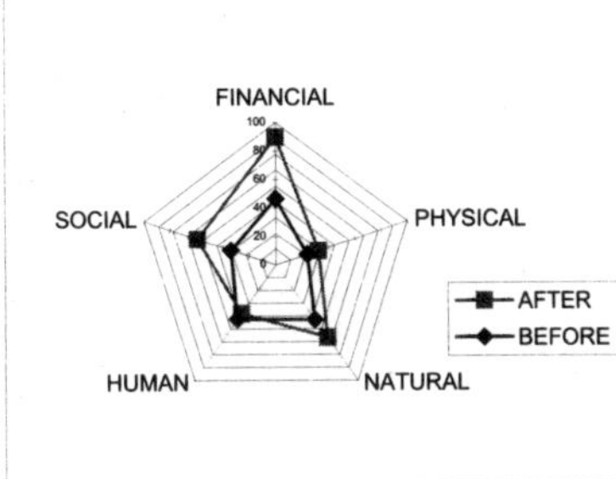

Fig 6.2 Impact of WSD in S. Rangapuram

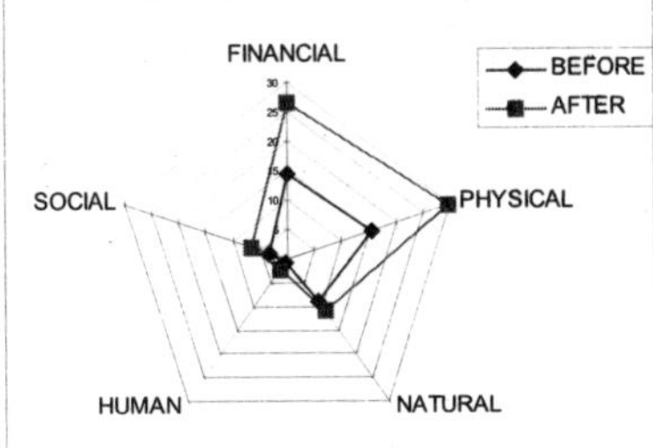

Fig 6.3 Impact of WSD in Tipraspalle

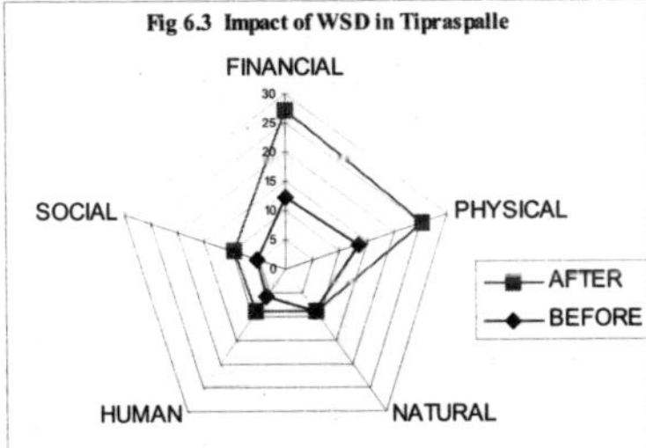

Fig 6.4 Impact of WSD in Mamidimada

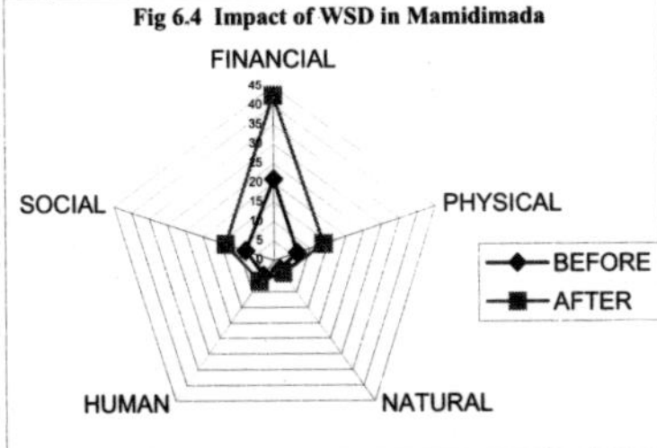

Table 6.16 *Statistical Significance of the Capitals (all indicators in Rs)*

Capital	*Mallapuram*	*S.Rangapuram*	*Tipraspalle*	*Mamidimada*
ΔFinancial	45610*	15702*	19382*	56155*
ΔPhysical	8599	14307**	11650*	13756**
ΔNatural	1539**	1974**	444	3976*
ΔHuman	–510	1536**	3464	6634*
ΔSocial	–2557*	–3506*	–4464*	–13611*
Total	52681	30013	30476	67070

Note: * and ** indicate that the differences are significant at 1 and 5 per cent levels respectively.

Can Watershed Management Sustain Rural Livelihoods?

Can watershed management sustain rural livelihoods? This is a crucial question given the magnitude of the programme in terms of resources (about US$ 1,000 million) and coverage (10 million hectares). As indicated in the framework, watershed management would sustain rural livelihoods if it meets the strong sustainability criteria of enhancing all the five capitals. Our analysis clearly brought out that despite being the model watersheds, in none of the sample watersheds, the programme has a significant impact on all the capitals. Besides, livelihood sustenance is linked to the resilience/sensitivity of the livelihood assets to changes in climatic conditions rather than assets *per se*. For, some assets are more resilient/less sensitive than others. Therefore, enhanced livelihood security should be assessed on the basis of the resilience of various livelihood assets and the improvements thereof. Resilience levels are ranked as high, medium and low and indicated against the impact indicators (Table 6.17). Here resilience is ranked in the context of the impact (positive). For instance, improvements in land assets (even in value terms) provide high livelihood resilience to the household, as it enhances the credit worthiness of the household. On the contrary, increases in migratory labour have low resilience, as it is dependent on external factors. Often investments in other assets like water harvesting equipment are highly sensitive to geological factors and may turn out to be risky.[8] Improvements in ecological indicators, such as groundwater, fodder and fuelwood, are more resilient than direct livelihood indicators like other assets, employment, income, etc. But, in the case of groundwater, the increase in the number of wells is unsustainable in the absence of replenishing mechanisms and hence the increase in number of wells is termed as a low resilience indicator. Whereas, improvement in water table level is a high resilient indicator. Similarly, social indicators, such as education, health, gender equity and economic equity are more resilient.

Table 6.17 *Impact of Watershed on Livelihood Security*

Impact on Assets	*Measure*	*Resilience*	*Impact in Sample villages*			
			Mallapuram	*S.Rangapuram*	*Tipraspalle*	*Mamidimada*
Physical	Land	H	M	H	M	H
	Livestock	M	M	M	L	L
	Others	M	M	H	M	M
Financial	Employment	M	H	H	M	M
	Income–Agriculture	M	H	L	M	M
	–Total	M	H	M	M	M
	Stability	H	H	H	L	L
Natural	Water–Drinking	H	M	M	M	M
	Irrigation					
	–no. of wells	L	L	M	H	M
	–depth of water table	H	M	M	M	M
	Fodder H	H	L	L	M	
	Fuelwood	H	M	L	L	M
Human	Education	L	L	M	H	M
	Health H	H	L	M	M	
Social	Migration	H	L	H	L	M
	Gender	H	M	M	M	H
	Equity	H	H	H	H	H

Note: L = low, M = medium and H = high.

From the point of resilience Mallapuram watershed is ranking high in the case of high resilient and low in the case of low resilient indicators. It has better ranking in the case of ecological indicators and ranks high in all the social indicators (including migration). However, in the case of education, it is showing low ('L'). The performance of Tipraspalle and Mamidimada is not impressive from the sustainable livelihoods point, while S. Rangapuram falls in between. From the SRL angle none of the watersheds meets the strong sustainability criteria, though Mallapuram watershed comes close. This indicates that participatory watershed management in its present form is a necessary condition but not a sufficient condition to sustain rural livelihoods. But, watershed management holds the potential for enhanced livelihood security even in the given geo-climatic conditions where watershed cannot bring direct irrigation benefits on a large scale. Moreover, distribution of these benefits is not egalitarian given the distorted agrarian structure and factor markets. Even, the spill over or externality benefits like employment are extremely limited in the absence of significant improvement in irrigation benefits. At the same time, watershed management is necessary in these fragile regions in order to strengthen the ecological base such as soil quality, water resources (including tanks), grazing lands, wastelands, etc. In this context, watershed management should not be viewed as a programme for income and employment generation for all sections of the population.

In order to realise the full potential of watershed technology, pro-poor programmes that complement the benefits of watershed management need to be introduced. These programmes include horticultural and dairy development that would benefit from the improved resource conditions like *in situ* moisture, grazing lands, water bodies, etc. Households, in fact, seem to prefer these activities in the context of an improved resource base. Though some of these activities are being introduced recently, their success is dependent on infrastructure (transport, storage, markets, etc.) and credit (institutional finance) support systems apart from a conducive policy environment that is propitious for institutional (collective systems, self-help groups, etc.) evolution and development. In the absence of an integrated view on resources-livelihoods-institutions-infrastructure, these programmes may not fulfil the objective of sustainable rural livelihoods. Even, the success of non-farm activities like petty business, services, etc. (often seen as an alternative to rural development) critically hinges upon the overall improvements in the rural livelihoods (effective demand). As such, it can be concluded that watersheds development, where implemented effectively, will have a range of impacts upon the recipient villages, but these impacts are not as effective as they could be in terms of equity (with the better off benefiting more) or sustainable livelihoods development. The full potential of watershed programmes will only be realised where they are linked to other activities needed to support livelihood development (such as access to markets) and enhance equity (especially in terms of access to water resources). More recent approaches to expand the classic watersheds model and incorporate other aspects of development (sometimes called 'watershed-plus' or the proposed neeranchal guidelines) are certainly a move in the right direction.

But these initiatives emphasise more on new structures of implementation than strengthening the implementation process. They are yet to grapple with the equity issues, especially in groundwater. For, most of the proposed livelihood initiatives are linked to water resources. In the absence of water poor cannot avail these initiatives effectively. In fact, in some of arid and semi-arid regions, water reforms assume greater importance when compared to land reforms. In this context, unless groundwater brought under the community management regime with principles equity in sharing the water, any efforts to address the livelihoods and poverty may not materialise. The collective action institutional arrangements for watershed management should go beyond watershed structures and address the most pertinent issues like groundwater management. For, equitable and sustainable management of groundwater is at the core of effective and sustainable watershed management.

Notes

1. Externalities are defined as the impact on the utility one person due to the activities (usually production) activities of other person. These externalities could be positive and negative. Watershed management is an example of positive externalities, as the treatment of land in area (belonging to a person or community) could result in improved resource (say water) availability in the neighbouring area. On the other hand, groundwater exploitation in a watershed could lead to negative externalities, i.e., exploitation (over) groundwater by one farmer (for agriculture production) may result in drying of wells in the neighbouring plots (loss of production).
2. Now the importance of integrating livelihood aspects in to watershed management is well recognised and the proposed watershed guidelines (*Neeranchal*) have adopted this approach. But, in the absence of systematic anaysis of impacts, livelihood impacts of watershed development tend to be overemphasised.
3. See Campbell et al. (2000) for an earlier attempt in this regard.
4. There are no changes in the access variables (distance) such as distance during the reference period.
5. Depth of the wells was assessed based on the information provided by the sample households on the depth at which groundwater is available before and after the watershed.
6. Distress or survival migration denotes extreme economic and often social hardships faced by labourers in rural India and migration becomes an outlet as part of their strategy for survival (GoI, 1991).
7. For clarity in presentation figures are converted into Rs. in '000' and Rs. in '00' (only in figure one for natural, human and social capitals).
8. Well failures are identified as one of the main reasons for farmers' suicides in recent years.

7

Participation and Impact: GO-NGO Syndrome

Success of watershed development was often attributed to active people's participation and the involvement of non-governmental organisations (NGOs). Several studies observed that the performance of an NGO-implemented watershed is much better than those implemented by the government. NGOs seem to ensure active people's participation (Vaidyanathan, 1991 and 1999; Farrington et al., 1999). What is nature of impact of the participatory guidelines on people's participation? Can the guidelines help fill the gap between NGO-GO dichotomy as far as participation and performance is concerned? What is the outcome of the policy changes emanating out of this concern at the ground level? More importantly, is the widely argued NGO advantage true or design? These questions are pertinent, as the new guidelines emphasise people's participation as well as the role of NGOs in watershed management. The success of the programme depends on how seriously participation is understood and incorporated in the implementation of the programme. Is there discernable improvement in the process of participation due to this and the performance of the programme? In fact, better participation across the board means improvement in the performance of government implemented watersheds as well. The hypothesis that needs to be tested is whether there is an overall improvement in the performance of the programme, including the government-implemented watersheds or does it still depend on the quality of NGOs, and how far the new policy guidelines have helped in improving the implementation process. Finally, how widespread is the NGO advantage and how far one can generalise the role of NGOs in higher performance of watersheds?

While the new guidelines emphasise involvement of all sections of the community,[1] the distribution of benefits from the watershed to all sections of the community need not be *suo motto*. Watershed development on its own does not guarantee the distribution of benefit flows across the community. Watershed development is essentially a land-based technology and hence most of the benefits naturally accrue to those who hold large share of land. Impact of current watershed development activities, as observed in some of the recent studies, in terms of groundwater recharge, cropping pattern changes, etc., seems to be impressive as compared to the earlier programmes (Rao, 2000). As observed in some of the best-implemented watersheds (Chapter 6), the impact is clear in terms of improvements in livelihoods despite three continuous below normal rainfall years. The externalities are conspicuous in the case of new watersheds over the older ones. In general, the impact is visible in terms of improved natural resource base, namely, availability of *in situ* moisture and water for longer periods in the vicinity of check dams, etc., but the impact is rather weak in terms of livelihood improvements and poverty alleviation (Bekele et al., 2008).

Recent field studies have clearly established that economic impact is visible in the places wherever project implementing agency (PIA) was committed to the work (Reddy et al., 2001 and Reddy, 2000). Further, there are differences even among the good PIAs as far as economic impact is concerned. These differences could be explained in terms of the method adopted by each PIA in implementing the watershed as distinct from the differences in the local endowments (Chapter 6). The limitation of these assessments is that it covers only a limited number of best-implemented (NGO) watersheds and hence, cannot be generalised. Needless to add, that the canvas ought to be wider for generalisations in the policy context. Further, NGOs implement hardly 10–20 percent of the watersheds leaving the rest to the government for implementation. Hence, the implementation process is not representative in character notwithstanding the differences in approaches.

This chapter attempts to examine the process and assess the impact of watershed development programme under the 1994 guidelines in the context of GO-NGO implementation. An important issue in this regard is the variations in the process of implementation of the programme. Here, the linkages between watershed activities, crop production, and resource structure also matter. The nature of impact of watershed on the productivity and employment of different sections of the community, distribution of benefits from the watershed development to various sections of the community, sustainability of the benefits will be largely toned by these factors.

Watershed Management and Contours of Comparison

During the last decade, Andhra Pradesh is on the forefront in regard to implementation of watershed development programme. AP has taken up the watershed management programmes and implemented strictly adhering to the new watershed guidelines since 1995–96.[2] As per the guidelines implementation of the watershed has to be completed in four years covering 500 hectares of area with an outlay of Rs. 20 lakh per watershed

(Rs. 4,000 per hectare).[3] Desert-prone districts like Anantapur receives Rs. 22.5 lakh per watershed (Rs. 4,500 per hectare) due to its unfavourable agro-climatic conditions. The average area under watershed is limited to about 500 hectares in line with the guidelines. Twenty-two districts have been covered under this programme till 2001–02. Though there are variations across districts, the fund utilisation ratio is about 70 percent, which varies from 34 percent in West Godavari district to 102 percent in Ranga Reddy district. In 2001–02, the number of watersheds initiated in the state stood at 7,809 and covered about 47 percent of the unirrigated area.

In order to assess the performance of watershed development programme implemented by different agencies eight watersheds were selected in the districts of Prakasam, Anantapur and Medak representing three agro-ecological and geographical regions, viz., Coastal, Rayalaseema and Telangana. A matching sample of another eight villages was selected to represent the non-watershed scenario. All these villages were selected after visits to several watersheds/villages in the respective districts and consultations with the project directors of DPAP, DRDA and NGOs. Criteria for selection of watersheds broadly were: (a) the selected watershed should have the treatments completed; and (b) it should be one among the better-implemented and managed watersheds. The reason behind these criteria is that the impact can be assessed only in technically completed and reasonably well-implemented watersheds. Watersheds are so selected as to include watershed implemented by both government organisations and non-government organisations. In all except one case, funding was from the government. Accordingly, three watersheds from each district, two NGO-implemented and one GO-implemented, were selected. There were no GO-implemented watersheds in Medak district and hence we selected only two NGO-implemented watersheds. Details of the location of the selected watersheds are presented in the Table 7.1. The data refers to the years 2001 and 2002.

Table 7.1 *Location of the Sample Watersheds*

District/Name of the Watershed Village	*Mandal*	*Implementing Agency (PIA)*	*Year of Starting*	*Year of Completing*
PRAKASAM				
(a) Tadivaripalli	Tarlupadu	DPAP-GO-Markapur	1994	2000
(b) P. Bommalapuram	Dornala	SNIRD- NGO-Ongole	1995–96	2000
(c) Lingapuram	Cumbhum	PRRD-GO-Cumbum	1996	2000
ANANTAPUR				
(a) Kannepalli (A)	Brahma Samudram	MDT-GO-Kalyandurg	1998	2001
(b) Mamdoor	Brahma Samudram	RDT-NGO-Kalyandurg	1995	2000
(c) Seeboi	Kalyanadurg	RDT-NGO-Kalyandurg	1996	2000
MEDAK				
(a) Sekhapur	Zaheerabad	KVK-NGO-Zaheerabad*	1996	2000
(b) Vanampalli	Jharasangam	KVK-NGO-Zaheerabad	1997	2000

Note: * This is NGO-run Krishi Vigyan Kendra (KVK) and hence falls under the NGO category.
Source: Field Study.

Both qualitative and quantitative informations were collected from the selected watershed areas. Discussions with MDT members, PIAs, Project Directors at the district level were helpful to get an overview of the situation. A sample of 50 households was drawn from the beneficiaries of each watershed and a control group of 25 households was selected from villages falling outside the treated watershed. Here, we looked into a few important aspects for comparing the performance under the two regimes of implementation. First, we compared the changes in the crop economy and cropping pattern. The aim was to look into the returns from agriculture in two different situations. Secondly, employment generation in the changed crop economy also attracted the attention as this supports the economy. Thirdly, the important effect of watershed treatment is on water availability, both as replenishing the source of groundwater as well as feasibility of new water bodies in the region. Besides, the watershed treatment also makes available irrigation water for more number of days than earlier. Lastly, we also looked into the allied implementation parameters both in terms of participation and effectiveness of implementation.

We have carefully selected a control group, which is similar to the participating group in all respects except thc programme. The control group provides the counter factual of the participating group, but this is not uncomplicated, as it is difficult to find such a matching group at least in terms of observable indicators. Alternatively, one can compare 'before' and 'after' situations of the same households that participated in the programme. This approach calls for baseline data, which again is not available in all situations. Second best solution in this regard is 'reflexive comparison' where 'before' and 'after' the treatment scenarios are compared for the participating households. Otherwise, this method gives biased assessment of the impact (Ravllion, 2001). Memory lapse is directly linked to the time lapsed after initiating the programme. These biases could be further minimised by using the 'double difference' method where 'before' and 'after' situations are examined for both control and participating groups.

Impacts: Economic and Ecological

Watershed treatments have technical, economic and environmental implications. Economic impacts are measured in terms of changes in area under irrigation, cropping pattern, net returns, employment, and other economic variables. Whereas, environmental impacts are assessed in terms of changes in fodder, fuelwood, livestock, drinking water and many other non-measurables. It was observed that proportion of area under irrigation has gone up by more than 10 percent among sample households, which ranged between 11.1 percent (NGO watershed of Anantapur) and 47.5 percent (NGO watershed of Prakasam). While poor gained more in three cases (one GO and two NGO-implemented watersheds), non-poor gained in two cases (one GO and one NGO-implemented watershed) (Table 7.2). While the GO-implemented watershed performed better in Anantapur, it was the NGO-implemented watershed that has done better in Prakasam. Impact of watershed development on irrigation was substantial as could be seen from the comparison between beneficiary and non beneficiary groups (Tables 7.2 and 7.3). Almost all the non-beneficiary households reported either no change or decline in area under irrigation. The overall impact of watershed on irrigation was positive despite the poor rainfall during the preceding three years of our field research.

Despite the increase in area under irrigation, there were no substantial shifts in cropping pattern in terms of new crops, though there were changes in the area allocated to high value crops like cotton, sugarcane, horticulture, etc. Paddy was the single largest crop in the sample villages of Prakasam district. Area under paddy has increased substantially in a number of cases, the increase ranged from 2 to 208 percent across the sample watersheds (Table 7.4). Similarly, all other irrigated

Table 7.2 *Impact on Area Irrigated: Beneficiary*

Village/PIA/ Category	*Prakasam*				*Anantapur*				*Medak*	
	GO		NGO		GO		NGO		NGO	
	B	*A*	*B*	*A*	*B*	*A*	*B*	*A*	*B*	*A*
Area under irrigation (acres)										
Poor	24.4	29.5	19.8	33.5	4.0	23.0	3.1	3.7	10.9	12.3
Non-poor	21.3	27.7	34.5	46.6	45.3	46.8	38.4	47.5	18.8	21.1
All	45.7	57.2	54.3	80.1	49.3	69.8	41.5	51.2	29.7	33.4
% change										
Poor	20.5		69.2		475.0		19.4		12.8	
Non-poor	30.0		35.2		3.3		23.7		12.2	
All	25.2		47.5		41.6		23.3		11.1	
% Area irrigated										
Poor	13.4	12.9	17.6	22.0	8.1	33.1	1.8	1.8	9.1	9.2
Non-poor	11.6	12.1	30.7	28.0	91.9	67.3	23.1	23.2	15.8	15.8

Note: B – Before; A – After. The second set of rows refers to percent change between the two situations – before and after the treatments.

Source: Field Survey.

Table 7.3 *Area under Irrigation: Non-beneficiary*

District/Village	*Before (Acres)*		*After (Acres)*		*% Change*	
	Poor	*Non-poor*	*Poor*	*Non-poor*	*Poor*	*Non-poor*
Prakasam						
China Cumbum	1.4	1.2	1.1	1.0	–30	–20
Buddapally	1.7	19.3	1.6	19.0	–10	–1.6
Jammy Dornala	1.4	6.3	1.4	6.0	0	–4.8
Anantapur						
Rayalappa Doddi	2.6	7.7	2.6	7.5	0	–2.6
Timmigani Pally	2.9	3.7	2.9	3.7	0	0
S. Kondapur	1.1	3.0	1.1	3.1	0	–3.33
Medak						
Jadi Malkapur	0.1	0.9	0.1	0.8	0	–1.11
Siddapur	0.1	6.2	0.1	6.2	0	0

Source: Field Study.

crops have gained almost similarly with the overall increase in area under irrigation. On the other hand, shifts in cropping pattern were marginal in the case of non-watershed villages. Majority of the irrigated crops recorded gains in yield rates. Gains were higher in NGO-implemented watersheds for most of the crops. Yield improvements were mainly due to better availability of groundwater, especially near the check-dams and better *in situ* moisture availability. In majority of the cases, non-poor households have performed better due to their comparatively better access to groundwater. However, the gains in yields were marginal in the case of unirrigated crops. When compared to non-beneficiary households, beneficiary households have recorded larger improvement in yields, especially in the case of irrigated crops. This indicates a qualitative improvement in the availability of irrigation due to the watershed development programme.

Increased crop productivity has largely brought in higher net returns to the farmers in majority of the crops and watersheds. Interestingly, all the watersheds have recorded positive incremental net returns for most of the crops. Overall, incremental net returns have gone up for irrigated crops, which ranged from Rs. 79 to Rs. 919 per acre (Table 7.5). Poor households gained more in Prakasam and Medak districts, while non-poor households gained more in Anantapur. It was observed that while, GO-implemented watersheds performed well in Prakasam district, NGO-implemented watersheds performed well in Anantapur district. Net incremental returns are quite reasonable in unirrigated plots of watershed area as well. Even in the case of unirrigated crops, non-poor gained more than the poor in majority of the cases. Net incremental incomes of non-beneficiary households have shown negative trend in all the villages. This indicates that watershed development has had a positive impact on net returns and that watershed development has been economically viable in most cases.

Table 7.4 *Changes in Cropping Pattern of Watershed Area (% change in the share of area under different crops)*

Village/PIA/ Category	*Prakasam*		*Anantapur*		*Medak*
	GO	NGO	GO	NGO	NGO
Irrigated Paddy					
Poor	75.0	208.3	113.6	3.3	4.75
Non-poor	108.3	87.5	11.5	25.19	2.3
Cotton					
Poor	78.6	131.0	—	—	—
Non-poor	65.0	–51.0			
Sweet Lime					
Poor	67.2	—	—	—	—
Non-poor	86.7				
Chillies					
Poor	—	198.9	—	—	—
Non-poor		–14.0			
Sugarcane					
Poor	—	—	—	—	36.6
Non-poor					7.1
Groundnut					
Poor	—	—	–16.7	20.0	—
Non-poor			–55.2	40.3	
Total					
Poor	21.5	67.9	225.0	4.0	95.4
Non-poor	38.7	40.5	4.9	10.1	26.6

Source: Field Study.

Household Income

Household income has improved in all categories of households—ranging from 10 percent to 46 percent (Table 7.6). Income gains were more for the poor households in majority

Table 7.5 *Incremental Net Returns from Irrigated Crops in Watershed Area*

(Rs per acre)

Village/PIA/ Category	*Prakasam*		*Anantapur*		*Medak*
	GO	NGO	GO	NGO	NGO
Paddy					
Poor	655	881	383	494	204
Non-poor	–37	500	778	910	425
Cotton					
Poor	0	995	—	—	—
Non-poor	163	513			
Chillies					
Poor	1402	0	—	—	—
Non-poor	2225	350			
Sugarcane					
Poor	—	—	—	—	–93
Non-poor					128
Groundnut					
Poor	—	—	0	0	—
Non-poor			–175	225	
Total					
Poor	919	833	79	360	178
Non-poor	513	453	146	581	154

Note: The differences are not statistically tested.
Source: Field Study.

of the cases, especially among the GO-implemented watersheds. While growth in poor households income was grater than the non-poor households in both the GO-implemented watersheds, income gains were better for the poor only in one of the three NGO-implemented watersheds. As far as source-wise incomes were concerned the differences between poor and non-poor categories are not consistent across watersheds. Income from livestock recorded substantial improvement in all the categories,

Table 7.6 *Total Household Income by Sources (% share): Beneficiaries*

Village/PIA/Category	*Prakasam*				*Anantapur*				*Medak*	
	GO		NGO		GO		NGO		NGO	
	B	*A*	*B*	*A*	*B*	*A*	*B*	*A*	*B*	*A*
Agriculture										
Poor	21	20	55	54	61	48	53	55	26	28
Non-poor	64	54	63	50	77	78	78	80	56	54
Livestock										
Poor	05	05	10	11	01	01	03	03	06	05
Non-poor	07	11	06	05	01	01	02	02	07	08
Labour										
Poor	21	20	28	20	49	50	32	31	52	53
Non-poor	06	09	01	01	13	12	08	07	32	33
Others										
Poor	05	05	03	03	0	0	12	11	15	14
Non-poor	03	06	22	21	10	09	12	10	05	05
Horticulture										
Poor	49	50	04	12	—	—	—	—	—	—
Non-poor	20	20	09	12	—	—	—	—	—	—
Total (Rs./hh)										
Poor	35,196	40,651	24,205	29,640	14,092	17,372	18,876	23,015	32,230	38,835
		(15)		(22)		(23)		(22)		(20)
Non-poor	1,67,675	1,85,225	1,71,400	2,50,999	2,74,900	3,13,100	3,80,950	4,24,750	91,125	1,16,005
	(10)		(46)		(14)		(11)		(27)	

Note: B – Before; A – After.
Source: Field Study.

and non-poor households seem to have gained more than poor households as far as improvement in livestock holdings is concerned. This indicates that the non-poor reaps more benefits from allied agricultural activities. This supports one of the recent findings in Anantapur district where the distribution of assets, including livestock, is biased in favour of rich (Reddy et al., 2003). Income from horticulture has increased manifold in the NGO-implemented watersheds in Prakasam district. The annual income of non-beneficiary households is substantially lower than that of beneficiary households and the differences got steeper in the case of poor category of farmers.

Employment Effect

Sample villages have witnessed substantial increase in employment due to the watershed development activities (Table 7.7). Increase in employment was higher among beneficiary households in most of the sample watersheds. NGO-implemented watersheds have performed better than GO-implemented watersheds in terms of increase in employment. However, in the case of Medak (NGO) watersheds, the growth in employment was less than that of the other two districts. It may be noted that in the case of Prakasam district the difference between beneficiary and non-beneficiary households was marginal as far as the changes in employment among the poor households are concerned. In all the villages, increase in employment was higher during the kharif and rabi seasons (Table 7.7). In summer season also, there was considerable improvement in employment indicating the favourable impact of watershed development on summer activities too. Poor farmers seem to have benefited more in the watersheds of GO in Prakasam, NGO watersheds in Anantapur and Medak districts, than the non-poor during the summer season. In other words, activities related to horticulture crops, along with non-farm activities, increased substantially during summer months in Prakasam district.

Table 7.7 *Employment Generated per Household*

Village	*Before (Days)*				*After (Days)*				*% Change*			
	K	*R*	*S*	*T*	*K*	*R*	*S*	*T*	*K*	*R*	*S*	*T*
Prakasam-GO												
Poor	38.5	30.5	14.5	83.5	45.3	36.8	18.8	100.8	17.8	20.4	30.4	20.9
Non-poor	28.8	22.3	11.3	62.3	33.5	26.5	13.5	73.5	12.5	14.3	15.0	13.6
NGO												
Poor	36.0	26.0	14	76.0	43	30.5	18.5	92.0	19.5	17.3	34.1	21.2
Non-poor	40.0	27.5	23	80.5	55	45.5	30.5	131.0	37.5	66.7	43.8	62.7
Anantapur-GO												
Poor	54.0	42.0	30.5	127.0	54	42	30.5	127	0	0	0	0
Non-poor	57.5	48.0	37.0	143.0	57.5	48.5	37.5	144	1.1	1.5	0.75	0.75
NGO												
Poor	31.8	23.5	8.8	62.5	33.8	24	24.3	82	5.0	8.3	94.3	22.8
Non-poor	51.3	36	11.3	98.5	54.3	39.3	26	119.5	6.0	9.4	88.7	21.1
Medak-NGO												
Poor	64	46.5	31.5	142	70.3	50.5	35.3	156	8.8	9.8	26.5	9.9
Non-poor	75.8	40	24	140	79.8	41	24	145	6.8	2.7	0	3.6

Note: K = Kharif season; R = Rabi season; S = Summer season; T = Total for the year.
Source: Field Study.

Seasonal Migration

Migration is one of the time-tested adjustment mechanisms to cope with the seasonal employment stress and to get better income opportunities. On an average, each person has spent 5–10 days in a year away from home in the sample villages. The average distance travelled was 30–40 kilometres in general but in Vanampalli village, people go up to 200 kilometres (Table 7.8). Among the beneficiary households, the total number of days migrated in a year per household ranged from 1 day (Seeboi) to 35 days (Vanampalli). Consequent upon the watershed treatments, there has been a decline in the extent of migration as compared to the situation before watershed. However, migration has shown an upward trend in Medak district.

Employment opportunities were generated during the execution of the watershed works. But, once the technical work on the watershed gets completed, there would be only a few alternative avenues to sustain the employment created. Often, the extent of migration would be the same when scenarios as of 'before' and 'after' watershed treatment were to be compared. In fact, migration has gone up in some cases (Reddy et al., 2004) as in the case of Medak district. On the other hand, migration tends to decline when there is substantial improvement in agriculture activities like large area being put under horticultural crops, improved cropping intensity, etc., due to the advent of watershed management. Interestingly, while migration has more or less halted in the case of non-poor, poor still continue to migrate. NGO-implemented watersheds in the two districts, where comparisons could be made, performed well in curtailing migration. Adoption of location-specific activities, such as appropriate management of CPRs, livestock and other livelihood activities, has reduced the propensity to migrate.

Table 7.8 *Pattern of Migration Among the Watershed Villages (no. of days/year)*

Category	*Prakasam*				*Anantapur*				*Medak*	
	GO		NGO		GO		NGO		NGO	
	B	A	B	A	B	A	B	A	B	A
No. of Persons										
Poor	5.8	3	8	5.5	4	5.5	4	3	7.8	9
Non-poor	0	0	0.5	0	1.5	1	0.5	0	0.3	0
No. of Days										
Poor	62.5	45	118	80	128	85	124	100	205	238
Non-poor	0	0	7	0	48	40	13.3	0	15	0
Distance (km)										
Poor	14.6	16	11.5	7.8	8.8	8.8	5.9	5.3	101.3	136.3
Non-poor	0	0	5	0	3.8	6.3	3.8	0	11.3	0

Note: B – Before; A – After.
Source: Field Study.

Ecological Impacts

Understanding ecological impact is tricky. Ecological variables are not firm and static parameters and hence could at best be indicative than firm. Sustainable usage of natural resources is essential to realise sustainable agricultural growth and development to meet the food needs of a growing population. In this context, the concept of watershed and ecological concerns has become quite relevant. The main components of watershed treatments such as contour-bunds, check-dams and vegetative barriers, are targeted at increasing soil moisture content, groundwater recharge and reducing soil run-off and facilitating vegetative growth. The important environmental benefits identified are improvement in groundwater recharge, augmenting drinking water supplies and increase in biomass (fodder and fuelwood) production.

Groundwater

The impact of watershed on groundwater was assessed in terms of changes in number of wells[4] and also in the depth of the water table. Most of the villages in Medak district continued to depend on open wells after the watershed treatment. The sample villages of Prakasam and Anantapur districts have recorded an increase in number of bore wells in all the watersheds, the rate of increase ranged between 3.6 percent in Mamdoor of Anantapur district and 45 percent in Tadivaripalli of Prakasam district. Percentage change in the depth of groundwater table has ranged between –2.2 percent and 992 percent with significant variation between villages (Table 7.9). Groundwater tables improved ('–' sign) in three cases and remained stable ('0' sign) in three cases and the GO-NGO differences are evident mainly in Prakasam district where groundwater levels have improved in the NGO-implemented watersheds. Notably, in most of the cases, it is the poor farmers who own majority of the wells. But knowing fully well that the aquifer parameters change according to the recharge

Table 7.9 *Changes in Groundwater Situation in the Watersheds Villages*

Village/PIA/ Category	*Prakasam*				*Anantapur*				*Medak*	
	GO		NGO		GO		NGO		NGO	
	B	*A*	*B*	*A*	*B*	*A*	*B*	*A*	*B*	*A*
No. of Wells										
Open Wells										
Poor	0	0	0	0	0	0	0	0	6	6
		(0)		(0)		(0)		(0)		(0)
Non-poor	0	0	0	0	1	1	1	1	2	2
		(0)		(0)		(0)		(0)		(0)
Borewells	9	13	10	12	5	6	1	1	1	1
Poor		(44)		(20)		(20)		(0)		(0)
Non-poor	3	4	7	7	11	11	7	7	1	1
		(33)		(0)		(0)		(0)		(0)
Depth (ft)										
Borewells										
Poor	29	139	90	88	59	59	22	22	29	138
		(379)		(–02)		(0)		(0)		(376)
Non-poor	12	131	68	59	72	72	96	90	120	133
		(992)		(–13)		(0)		(–06)		(11)

Note: Figures in parentheses indicate percentage change.
Source: Field Study.

zones, the effect on groundwater has to be viewed cautiously, even the GO-NGO differences.

A clear and positive impact is seen with regard to drinking water consumption across all the watersheds in terms of quantity and time spent (Table 7.10). In terms of quantity used, the GO-watersheds showed better performance, while in the NGO-implemented watersheds households now save more time. These differences reflect qualitative and quantitative improvements, i.e., in some of the watersheds drinking water is available at a closer location than earlier, in other cases more and assured water is available but at a distance. On the whole, the picture indicates substantial improvement in the drinking water situation. The decline in time spent was as high as –42.5 to –41.1 percent in Sekhapur (Medak) and P. Bommalapuram (Prakasam) and as low as –14.1 percent in Lingapuram (Prakasam).

Fodder and Fuelwood

Fodder availability has improved in all the sample watersheds. The GO-implemented watersheds in Prakasam recorded better performance while it was the NGO-implemented watersheds that performed well elsewhere. The main sources of fodder in these sample villages were CPRs and own fields. Dependency on CPRs for fodder varied across the sample watersheds. The increase in the dependency on CPRs was the highest in the GO-watershed of Anantapur and lowest in the NGO-watershed of Medak (Table 7.11). However, open grazing, in CPR as well as own fields, has increased substantially in all the sample watersheds while stall-feeding has declined. This is indicative of the increase in the biomass in the sample villages, which is at variance with the earlier observation of the shift in livestock composition in favour of small ruminants (Chapter 6). Poorer households are benefiting more by this shift. This supports our field observation that the marginal and small farmers benefited more through the development of watershed treatments

Table 7.10 *Availability of Drinking Water in Watershed Villages*

Village/PIA/Category	*Prakasam*				*Anantapur*				*Medak*	
	GO		NGO		GO		NGO		NGO	
	B	*A*	*B*	*A*	*B*	*A*	*B*	*A*	*B*	*A*
Quantity (lt./day/hh)										
Poor	10.1	11.8	10.7	11.3	9.4	11.1	10.2	11.6	13.5	15
Non-poor	6.6	8.3	11.8	12.4	11	12.3	13.3	14.2	12.6	14
% Change										
Poor	18.7		5.8		17.4		10.8		12.5	
Non-poor	19.3		5.6		12.3		6.6		12.3	
Time Spent (hrs/day/hh)										
Poor	0.6	0.3	0.75	0.4	1.2	1.2	0.5	0.3	1.1	0.8
Non-poor	0.5	0.4	0.48	0.3	0.8	0.5	0.4	0.3	0.7	0.4
Change %										
Poor	–21.9		–42.5		0		–14.5		–32.5	
Non-poor	–14.1		–31.7		–25.0		–22.2		–41.1	

Source: Field Study.

Table 7.11 *Fodder Availability in the Watershed Villages (% Change)*

Village/PIA/Category	*Prakasam*		*Anantapur*		*Medak*
	GO	NGO	GO	NGO	NGO
Stall Feeding					
Number of Days					
Poor	–3.0	2.2	0	0	–6.2
Non-poor	–1.4	0.25	0	0	–0.4
Quantity (kgs/day)					
Poor	7.6	16.4	0	0	3.1
Non-poor	3.4	7.2	0.5	5.5	0
CPR Grazing					
Number of Days					
Poor	13.8	10.4	29.2	21.5	4.4
Non-poor	7.7	2.3	34.9	14.5	1.3
Quantity (kgs/day)					
Poor	11.2	37.2	–6.7	17.6	3.2
Non-poor	13.3	–4.8	2.4	27.7	3.3
Own Field Grazing					
Number of Days					
Poor	16.2	13.6	8.9	10.3	0.7
Non-poor	16.8	4.0	15.3	2.1	0
Quantity (kgs/day)					
Poor	23.5	34.3	5.9	14.8	1.2
Non-poor	20.9	–9.0	0.8	11.2	0

Source: Field Study.

in the CPRs. That is heartening as far as equity aspects are concerned.

The fuelwood needs of sample households were met by collections from CPRs and purchases from the market.

Table 7.12 *Changes in the Availability of Fuelwood in Watershed Villages*

Village/PIA/Category	*Prakasam*				*Anantapur*				*Medak*	
	GO		NGO		GO		NGO		NGO	
	B	*A*	*B*	*A*	*B*	*A*	*B*	*A*	*B*	*A*
Quantity (cl./day/hh)										
Poor	0.014	0.016	0.017	0.018	0.019	0.018	0.012	0.012	0.015	0.017
Non-poor	0.012	0.013	0.016	0.018	0.027	0.027	0.012	0.017	0.018	0.021
% Change										
Poor	15.6		9.7		0.16		0.15		0.13	
Non-poor	6.7		8.2		0.19		0.19		0.17	
Time Spent (hrs./day)										
Poor	0.19	0.19	0.19	0.21	0.27	0.27	0.16	0.15	0.31	0.28
Non-poor	0.19	0.15	0.25	0.20	0.23	0.20	0.19	0.19	0.30	0.25
% Change										
Poor	0		14.5		0		–2.9		–9.9	
Non-poor	–12.5		–20.8		–12.5		0		–12.8	

Source: Field Study.

Changes in the fuelwood availability were assessed in terms of households' dependence on different sources as well as the time spent by the households in collecting the fuelwood. It was clear that the fuelwood situation has improved, though marginally in all the sample watersheds (Table 7.12). The improvements can be noticed in terms of quantity used and time spent in fetching. The gains seem to be higher in the case of Prakasam district. Evidently, poor households gained more in terms of quantity and non-poor gained more in terms of time saved. This could be due to the dependence of poor on the external sources (CPRs) that are far off. This aspect came out clearly when we looked at source-wise use of fuelwood (Table 7.13). Dependence on CPRs was more for the poor households in majority of the cases, which shows that availability of CPRs directly benefits the households, particularly the poor, in terms of both money and time savings. When 'before' and 'after' scenarios were compared, the dependency on CPRs has declined in all the watersheds for both poor as well as non-poor farmers. This is mostly offset by the purchase of fuelwood by all the households. On the other hand, marginal improvement is observed in own sources of fuelwood. But that influences the house expenditure pattern as well as impacts time taken for fuelwood collection.

The performance of eight sample watersheds varied in their impact on economic and ecological factors. This may be attributed to agro-climatic conditions, and the institutional arrangements of watershed implementation. Watershed implementation process differs across implementing agencies though they follow almost identical guidelines. Though the performance of the NGO-implemented watersheds was better in general, this hypothesis does not hold good in all the cases. Performance of the PIA and the watershed is critically linked to the existing social and human capital at the village level. This indicates that good PIA is necessary but not a sufficient condition for the better performance of the programme. For, some of the PIAs—GO or NGO—could not implement the guidelines due to political interference (Lingapuram of Prakasam,

Table 7.13 *Sourcewise Availability of Fuelwood (% change)*

Village/PIA/Category	Prakasam				Anantapur				Medak	
	GO		NGO		GO		NGO		NGO	
	B	A	B	A	B	A	B	A	B	A
CPR										
Poor	69.5	64.3	92.0	88	80.0	79	49	45.5	80.5	79
Non-poor	49.3	43.50	76.0	72.5	67.0	66	61.3	54	71.3	68.5
Own										
Poor	12.8	16.0	5.5	8.5	11.0	11.0	9.5	10.0	10.5	9.0
Non-poor	9.5	10.3	7.5	10.0	13.5	13.5	13.3	15.3	11.8	11.8
Purchase										
Poor	17.8	19.8	2.5	3.5	9.5	11.0	16.5	19.5	9.0	12.3
Non-poor	16.3	21.3	16.5	17.5	19.5	20.5	25.5	30.8	17.0	19.8

Source: Field Study.

Kannepally of Anantapur-GO watersheds) or lack of cooperation from the local communities (Vanampalli of Medak-NGO watershed). On the other hand, watersheds like Seeboi, Mamdoor of Anantapur district (both NGO watersheds), Tadivaripally (GO watershed) of Prakasam district and Sekhapur (NGO watershed) of Medak district, have better performance indicators. These aspects of implementation are taken up in the next section.

Community Participation and Implementation Process

The concept of participation is interdisciplinary but it originates in the discipline of Social Psychology. From a social psychological perspective, participation forms an analysis of the group behaviour in a small group or large group (Cartwright and Zander, 1968). Here, one also needs to know the psychological theories of group behaviour. The questions relating to group behaviour have also bothered social scientists from the perspective of development initiatives but the fact that it involves basic social psychological parameters is always overlooked. For social scientists, it is the question of success or failure of a group initiative, which is at stake and thus the determinants of success or failures are confused with the factors influencing group behaviour. But, for a social psychologist, analytically explaining group behaviour has always posed greater challenge and group behaviour takes various forms. Psychological theorists indicate that people join together generally due to common needs, shared goals and imminent common threats.

People's cooperation is achieved by providing some incentives and the best incentive is through financial support. Participation of the community in the watershed management project is ensured by roping in the NGOs. NGOs that have familiarity with the people, and are aware about the local social dynamics, play important role in motivating people to participate in the watershed management projects. Moreover, credibility of the NGO and competent staff also impinges on the community participation in the watershed projects. The formation of watershed committees at micro-watershed level, providing representation not only to farmers but also to the members of self-help groups (SHGs), landless labourers and women members, helps in wider participation of the people in the project. The financial support for various land-based and non-land-based activities ensures active participation of the local communities. Technical support plays an important role in watershed management. Presence of technical persons or group (WDT) infuses confidence among the participants. In most of the watershed management programmes, the technical group had the responsibility to organise the people to undertake project activities. It has also the capacity to attract the people around them and convince it about the benefits accruing from the project and thus enlist their participation.

The definition of the group as well as its sustainability is conditioned by these factors. The group behaviour is dictated by the weights assigned to these factors. Therefore, depending on these relative weights, one watershed (Ralegaon Shindi) became successful watershed while the other (Mokhada) did not give similar results (Deshpande and Nikumbh, 1993). Moreover, the long-term sustainability of the group depends on the composition of the group. Any group participating in a research-based programme will have four components or sub-groups namely, the dominating, adhering, simmering and splintering. The dominating sub-group consists of the stakeholders who are equipped with social-economic capital to dominate the group decisions. Therefore, if the sub-group is strong in the group dynamics, the group sustains for a long but distribution and innovation are always in question. The adhering sub-group contains the stakeholders who generally follow other members and rarely raise objection. The domination of this sub-group also results in sustainability of the group, but at times innovation is feasible here.

The third sub-group described here is the simmering constituents of the group. The stakeholders coming under this component are those, who are not quite happy with some of the decisions, but may not express it without some support. They need back-up and the larger presence of this component in the group makes it fragile. The last sub-group is that of the splintering members. These stakeholders are unhappy over the decisions or some other activities. Often it becomes difficult to internalise them and thus the domination of this component causes the break-up of the group with slightest provocation.

Participation in the project is directly associated with the level of stakes involved. Higher the stake, higher the probability of sustenance of the project. If the aggregate stakes are negligible, then the level of sustenance will also be low. As the stakes increase probability of sustenance also increases and reaches a peak at some level of stakes and then turns asymptotic thereafter. Within the group, those having larger stakes may participate in the watershed project more actively when compared with the people in the group anticipating peripheral benefits from the project.

Level of Community Participation

Community participation implies the participation of all the beneficiaries, direct and indirect, in the watershed activities, and it is one of the pointers to assess whether watershed management is sustainable in the long run. The extent of community participation in the watershed programme is assessed on the basis of households' responses about their participation and attendance at the watershed committee (WC)/watershed association (WA) meetings besides participation in training and exposure visits. The level of community participation is expected to be high in watersheds implemented by NGOs. NGOs functioned as a facilitator and capacity builder in many cases (especially Anantapur district), helping to bridge the gap within the local communities as also between communities and the government agencies. NGOs offer different types of training, which include legal rights to the use of CPR and management techniques. NGOs have also played a crucial role in promoting gender equity in watershed management issues. Out of eight sample watersheds, the level of community participation[5] is assessed as 'good' in four watersheds, poor in three, and average in one (Table 7.14). Interestingly, the level of community participation has been found to be independent of the status of the implementing agency (NGO/GO). In Prakasam district, while the participation in the NGO-implemented watershed is average, it is good in one GO-implemented watershed and poor in the other. In Medak district, of the two watersheds implemented by the same NGO, one has better participation (good) while the other does not (poor). In Anantapur district, both the watersheds implemented by the same NGO have recorded good participation in contrast to the poor participation in the GO-implemented watershed. This gives a mixed picture of the linkages between the PIA and the participation on one hand

Table 7.14 *Distribution of Sample Watersheds by Level of Community Participation*

Village/Disrtrict	*Poor*	*Average*	*Good*	*PIA*
Prakasam				
Tadivaripalli			1	RDPR (GO)
P.Bommalapuram		1		SNIRD (NGO)
Lingapuram	1			RDPR (GO)
Anantapur				
Seeboi			1	RDT(NGO)
Mamdoor			1	RDT(NGO)
Kannepalli(A)	1			MDT(GO)
Medak				
Vanampalli	1			KVK (NGO)
Sekhapur			1	KVK (NGO)

Source: Field Study.

and NGOs and participation on the other. That is, participation is not automatic in the NGO-implemented watersheds. The linkage between participation and performance is vindicated further in our preceding analysis.

Process of Implementation

The process of watershed implementation and management is critical to its sustainability in the long run. It depends on how strictly the guidelines are followed, adopted to local (community) needs and the level of involvement of local people in the whole process. This paves the way for the sustenance of the treatments. The modus operandi and the time taken depend on the approach of the PIA towards the watershed management. Besides, attitudes of the local community in terms of social capital (cooperative nature, leadership, etc.) determine the time required for the social mobilisation and organisation. While NGOs seem to have better leverage in social mobilisation due to their continued proximity, there could be differences among them corresponding to their experience with and commitment to the watershed activities. NGOs with long experience in the locality would have more credibility and rapport with the local communities over that or a new NGO. Similarly, such NGOs with involvement in rural development activities are likely to continue their field presence beyond the completion of the watershed programme. More importantly, recognition of the importance of the total involvement of the local communities in the implementation and ensuring their cooperation are critical issues for the success and sustainability of the programme. These factors would facilitate better sustainability of the programme when compared to the PIAs with little experience and commitment to people's participation.

The GO-implemented watersheds represented the two extreme cases of social mobilisation. In Prakasam, the GO PIA had to conduct eight Gram Sabha meetings to arrive at a

Table 7.15 *Process of Watershed Implementation*

District/ PIA	*No. of GS (prior) meetings*	*Process of selecting WA/WC*	*Time taken in formation of WA*	*Time taken for initiating WS works*	*Number of meetings (after)*		
					GS	*WA/WC*	*WDT*
Prakasam							
GO	8	High political interference	4 months	1 year	8	Monthly (48)	Monthly (48)
NGO	2	Through GS meetings	2 months	1 year	6	10	16
Anantapur							
GO	1	Through GS meetings	4 months	3 months	15	18	4
NGO	4	Through elders initiative	4 months	2 months	4	Monthly Twice (96)	Monthly (48)
Medak							
NGO	5	Through discussions with people	5 months	17 months	4	4	Weekly (208)

Note: GS = Gram Sabha; WA = Watershed Association; WC = Watershed Committee; WDT = Watershed Development Team.

consensus as a result of political interference (Table 7.15). On the other hand, the GO PIA in Anantapur could do so in just one meeting. In the case of NGO-managed watershed, the number of Gram Sabha meetings ranged between two (Prakasam) and five (Medak). Though the time taken for this process did not differ much between the PIAs, the process of forming the WA/WC differed. In two cases the selection was made in the Gram Sabha meetings, in the other two cases the process was initiated through dialogue with the village elders and informal discussions with the people. In one case, the nomination of WA/WC was purely apolitical. The PIAs in Anantapur, GO as well as NGO (RDT), took about 2–3 months to initiate the watershed works, whereas in the other districts the process took more than one year.

It was noted that the focus in the process of implementation differed across the selected watersheds. One typology was to emphasise on the watershed development teams whereas the others depended solely on the technical treatment. Often, it is argued that watershed treatment is more technology-oriented forgetting the predominant social capital aspect of it. This was visible in the models of implementation followed by the two groups of PIAs.

It is quite clear that PIA is the pivotal element in the process of watershed management. Therefore, it is necessary to identify the right type of PIA to implement the watershed programme in order to achieve the project objectives. From the PIA's point of view, the task of bringing the entire village on to a single platform, making them think and act in unison and also aware of the programme, seems to be much more complex than what it is perceived to be at the policy level. Factionalism, political rivalry and non-cooperation are the common evils in the village. Among these, party politics is the most harmful, which virtually divides the village into different groups that fight for their petty interests and deprive the common people of benefits from the common assets. This always intersects the implementation process of any state-run participatory programme, as participation is largely dictated by these factors.

Recognising the seriousness of the divisions at the village level, PIAs adopt different approaches to bring about cohesiveness or consensus among the communities. The most commonly followed strategy, by the GO as well as NGO PIAs, is combination of incentives and disincentives. It was pointed out that in most of the cases there was unanimity in the selection of the office bearers to the watershed association. The initial community meetings are usually marred by groupism and often end in a tussle for the positions. After two such meetings WDT issues a warning that unless there is some consensus in selecting the leader (s), the programme would be shifted to the neighbouring villages. The amount of money being huge (about Rs 14 lakh), this trick often worked and hence being widely used. The main reason is that the WDTs do not get enough time to interact with local communities to explain and convince them to work towards the common good. The second approach is to hammer out a deal between the opposing groups through apportionment of key positions, i.e., President, Chairman and Secretary, among the aspiring political parties and ensure 'just' representation to all the groups. This is more common in GO PIAs. Group rivalry (conflicts) or disputes were common in almost all the villages, though not as harmful as party politics. Some of the NGO PIAs followed a process-oriented approach, viz., to begin with, the PIA tries to resolve the conflicts within the groups, and if it should fail at the group level, then, it takes the matter to WC. Finally, when it fails at the WC level too, the matter is put before the Grama Sabha, where the conflicts are usually resolved through some sporadical arrangements (either distribution of posts or through 'carrot and stick strategy'). The NGO PIA in Anantapur follows its own devised approach.

Rural Development Trust (RDT) is a leading NGO in Andhra Pradesh with more than 30 years of standing in Anantapur district. RDT implements several activities, focusing on the poor, specifically on the weaker sections among them. It also involved awareness building and cohesive group formation. RDT has been involved in environmental development and drought mitigation activities for the past 11 years. These activities constitute the foundation for formation of WCs and for undertaking additional activities. At present, RDT is working in more than 50 micro-watersheds in addition to which, the government, under new guidelines, provided funding for another 22 watersheds for execution. Irrespective of the source of funding RDT follows the following guidelines:[6]

1. Emphasis on selecting villages with the potential for collective action. That political rivalry and groupism are discouraged. Watershed is sanctioned to a village only when the demand comes from the village community and the communities should prove their resolve by creating a common good through collective action during a period of one year.[7]
2. Watersheds to cover an entire village rather than being restricted to 500 hectares. This ensures widespread benefits and participation.
3. Two members from each household (from at least 90 percent of the total households) should become members of the watershed association by paying a membership fee of Rs. 11 each.
4. Cooperation from the president and other members of the Gram Panchayat is mandatory.
5. Collecting the farmers' share prior to the implementation of the project ensures user contributions. In some instances, user contribution could be as high as 30 percent.
6. The organisational structure of watershed management is somewhat different from that of the official pattern: there is, for example, no watershed secretary, who is usually a paid employee.
7. The watershed committee to be supported by a watershed advisory committee consisting of village elders and influential people.
8. RDT employs broad-based, barefoot technical and non-technical specialists on a (more or less) permanent basis.

9. RDT emphasises a gender-sensitive approach. A separate woman staff member (a watershed women organiser) is employed for every 10–12 watershed villages. She should live in the village and regularly interact with women about their concerns, roles and responsibilities.
10. It uses a two-pronged approach to watershed management and poverty alleviation. It follows: (a) land-based watershed development targeting the whole village population and the entire natural resource base, private as well as common, and (b) poverty-based socio-economic development targeting only the poorest, i.e., SCs and STs. The approach is designed in such a way that the poorest communities get the benefits of watershed development and poverty alleviation inputs. As a result, equity and sustainability are also strengthened.

The merits of RDT's philosophy are evident in the process of watershed implementation (Table 7.15). Social mobilisation is mainly done through negotiations rather than resorting to any compromise solutions. This is possible due to their selection criteria. No efforts were made towards social mobilisation by the GO PIAs. Further, the NGO PIA in Prakasam district did not receive any cooperation from the community due to factions. The NGOs both in Anantapur and Medak districts had initiated training and watershed-related works in the villages prior to the implementation. The concept of user contribution and stakeholder's involvement in the programme was hardly adhered to in the process. In almost all the cases, the user contribution, kind or cash, was marginal or nil. Users' participation was usually limited to supervising the works in their own field and in some cases contributions were accounted by deduction from the wages of the labourers. In other words, labourers were paid lower than the stipulated wage rate and the difference between the stipulated rate and actual pay is adjusted against the farmers' contribution. RDT is the only PIA that collected the contributions in real terms, and all others were found adjusting wages against contributions.

NGOs and Watershed Implementation

It is often argued that NGOs perform better as far as watershed implementation is concerned (Kerr et al., 2002; Goud, 2005). The bias in favour of NGO PIAs is mainly due to the reason that they are often better equipped for social mobilisation as well as articulation with the visiting researchers. More than that NGOs operate on a smaller scale, have better quality of manpower and therefore identify appropriate human resources and allocate funds. Further, it is well known that the performance record of NGOs keeps it afloat to get their funds from various sources. The NGOs that have outside funding seem to have a better track record and performance than those implementing the government programmes. Therefore, unit costs often tend to be higher in the former case.

It was observed that 4–5 WDT members manage 9–12 watersheds, irrespective of the fact whether they are implemented by GO or NGO. In the case of RDT they have a dedicated staff of 120 people to manage 100 watersheds. This shows that RDT deploys three times more human resources per watershed than that of other PIAs. Besides, RDT would have used more human resources (certainly of better quality) during the pre-selection phase. On the other hand, many government PIAs have only part-time workers. However, the success of RDT, which also implements watersheds with outside funding, points to a more efficient use of resources. In fact, RDT's per acre expenditure (average of all their watersheds) is less than that of other PIAs. Nevertheless, it is necessary to compare the actual (per unit) costs of GO funded with externally funded watersheds in order to prove the better performance of NGO PIAs. However, we could not really compare this aspect, as government funded all the sample watersheds.

Given the process followed, it appears that the scale of the programme could be a bottleneck. That is, either the size of WDT should be larger or the number of watersheds allocated to each PIA should be reduced to one-third of the present. Since all the PIAs implement government-funded watersheds, it is difficult to estimate the cost differences. In addition to efficiency in fund use, the success of the watershed programme depends on commitment and honesty of the PIA. The evidence presented here, while vindicating the hypothesis of the need for NGO involvement in watershed management cautions against any sweeping generalisations in this regard. A committed PIA, GO or NGO, is necessary but not sufficient to ensure the success of watershed management. It is well accepted that unless the PIA puts in enough efforts in terms of human resources and time to iron out the intra-community differences or disputes within the village, the implementation of the watershed could rarely be effective.

Conclusions

Despite the emphasis in the guidelines on participatory process and building up social capital, only cursory attention is given to this aspect. Often participation is defined to suit the convenience of the implementing agencies, i.e., some define it as voluntary contribution of labour, cash or involvement in post-implementation maintenance. A few NGO-led projects have ensured comprehensive participation in terms of community involvement right through designing, executing, contribution in terms of cash or/and kind and or take over of the maintenance, etc. Only in the case of comprehensive involvement of local community, is the impact sustainable and that cannot be to the credit of the PIA alone (Kerr et al., 2000). Strengthening the social capital base and ensuring community participation is a difficult job, demanding lot of time and sustained efforts from the implementing agencies. Only the best projects are found to have devoted substantial time towards social organisation when compared to less than 2–3 months in general. Not surprisingly, the better performing projects were found to be those where PIA had devoted a year or more to organise people before committing funds for the watershed treatment (Kerr et al., 2000). More importantly, scanning the villages for potential, especially social, to receive and absorb the technology is a prerequisite for watershed technology to sustain.

Apparently, there is a conflict between extensive versus intensive approach to watershed development. While the nature of watershed development technology requires intensive approach, the state is more interested in scaling up of the programme due to political interests. Intensive approach is followed by the established NGOs (PIAs) which devote more time towards social development. In Andhra Pradesh, participatory approach is being implemented from above at macro level. Unfortunately, the grandeur of the scheme belies the effectiveness of the programme. More importance is given to spread than intensity in order to cover more people due to the pressure from local politicians or to attract more central funds. As a result, the long-run sustainability of the programme is often held at stake. The problems here are more practical. It is clear from our case studies that more number of PIAs are required to implement the programme on a large scale and given the critical link between the quality of PIA and the impact of the programme, it is necessary to identify good PIAs, which are sadly in short supply. In order to cover more area and watersheds DRDA was opting either for lesser-known NGOs as PIAs or entrusting the work to various departmental officials. This approach was not only resulting in proliferation of dubious NGOs but also affecting the quality of work, as most of the officials work as part-time PIAs.

In order to address the issue of scaling up watershed programme in a sustainable manner and to meet the constitutional obligation of decentralisation through PRI involvement, the watershed guidelines were revised during April 2003 and christened as *Haryali Guidelines*.[8] As per these guidelines village PRIs have replaced the watershed committees (WCs) as PIAs. Money is transferred directly to PRIs from the DRDA or the DWMA (District Water Management Agency) in Andhra Pradesh. Village

PRIs implement the watersheds with the help of line departments. The Gram Panchayats have to execute the works and keep the necessary records apart from carrying out the day-to-day watershed activities. NGOs are given the last priority as PIAs only in the absence of PRIs or line departments. Another major departure is the reduction in the allocation towards capacity building and community mobilisation.

Though the 2003 guidelines appear to address some of the serious concerns expressed earlier, these were strangely formulated without any consultative process, feedback or understanding the ground realities. First of all, it distorted the broad-based user participation by abolishing the WC and user group framework. Second, in the absence of proper human capital at village level, PRIs get overburdened with traditional responsibility of implementing the watershed development. While capacity building was the major concern, the channels of capacity building, i.e., role of NGOs and fund availability for capacity buildings have been drastically reduced. In fact, it was argued that the PRIs should be capacity-enabled prior to giving them the responsibility of implementing the watersheds (Reddy et al., 2002). In the process the implementation of watershed development might still continue effectively under the control of line departments with the excuse that of PRIs do not have required capacity. The argument was always on how to bring the WC under the pur view of PRIs. The guidelines failed to take into account some of the new initiatives followed by NGOs and the state in the recent years in this regard. For instance, in Karnataka, PRIs implement the watershed development with the help of sub-committees, while in Andhra Pradesh it was an NGO (RDT) that introduced the village development council (VDC) to oversee the smooth implementation of watershed development (Sivanna and Reddy, 2005). In any case, the objective of getting wider participation still needs to be reckoned with. Unless the dynamics of and factors influencing collective action and people's participation are clearly understood, attaining sustainable watershed management and rural livelihoods remain a distant dream. While some of the theoretical issues in this regard are discussed in Chapter 4 the following chapter discusses some of the practical issues pertaining to collective action in watershed management.

Notes

1. Participation may not be total in all situations due to divergent livelihood activities such as migration, trans-humans, etc.
2. Prior to this, the National Watershed Development Project for Rainfed Areas (NWDPRA) has been introduced in 1990–91. Till 1996–97, under this programme, 94 watersheds covering 1.76 lakh hectares were treated with an expenditure of Rs. 5,116 lakh.
3. These rates are now revised to Rs. 30 lakh per watershed (Rs. 6,000 per hectare).
4. Increase in number of wells not necessarily reflects the improvement in groundwater situation, as it is part of the secular trend in groundwater exploitation in these regions.
5. Participation is defined as good in terms of number of meetings, actual functioning of the WC in terms of conflicts, works done and people's perception about the process of watershed implementation.
6. These guidelines are somewhat similar to the guidelines of Accion Freterna (AF) discussed in Chapter 4. AF and RDT are sister concerns. Given the importance, we present these guidelines again at the cost of repitition.
7. These conditionalities are over and above the geo-physical guidelines (extent of degraded lands, CPRs, availability of drinking water, etc.) laid in the guidelines.
8. The guidelines were modified earlier during 2001 but only marginally in terms increasing the duration from 4 to 5 years and allocation from Rs. 4,000 to Rs. 6,000 per acre.

8

Collective Action and Watershed Management

The 1994 watershed guidelines have provided a definitive space for collective action through its emphasis on participatory watershed management. There is a clear recognition that collective action is a prerequisite for sustainable watershed management. How to achieve participation remained a moot point despite some directions provided in the guidelines in this regard. Till the advent of 1994 guidelines collective action strategies/issues in watershed management remained cursory in policy, though participation has become a buzzword. This is clearly reflected in the low adoption rates till the mid-1990s and limited success even after the new guidelines. The rhetoric on "people's participation and watershed management" continues and NGOs occupy a *prima donna* place in achieving people's participation. As observed in the previous chapter, though NGOs in general are good implemententing agencies (PIAs), there is no guarantee that impact is uniform across NGO-implemented watersheds. On the other hand, it is also not true that impact is poor in all the watersheds implemented by governmental organisations (GOs). For, there are variations in the process of implementation within NGO and GO PIAs. However, three general variations can be observed based on the implementing agency: GO, NGO or the combination of GO and NGO (Table 8.1).

In the context of watershed development, as is the case with other commons, the focus was mainly on the participation or collective action perspective. The discussion was always on why collective action failed to take off in majority of the cases while it is effective in others. Most of the fact-finding was carried out on the basis of implementation process and identifying the PIAs that have done/not done a proper job. But the ball stopped at the implementation level, as fewer watersheds sustained after the implementation phase, irrespective of who implemented it. The reason could be that property rights issues are either avoided or taken for granted. That is, the approach is to honour the existing rights. In the process equity issues are sidelined. The linkages between property rights and collective action on one hand, and equity and collective action on the other, are less understood. This is true at the policy as well as implementation levels.

Collective Action in Watershed Management

In this section, we examine the context, actors and the action arena (process of collective action) and their linkages in the context of watershed management in semi-arid regions. We developed framework based on the existing literature along with our practical experience with participation and collective action in watershed management as well as other resources. In what follows we discuss the framework in detail (Fig. 8.1).

Context

The context of watershed management is the initial conditions in the semi-arid regions. These can be grouped under internal,

Table 8.1 *Variations in Implementation of Watershed Programme by Type of Implementing Agency*

State-Run Programmes (GO)	*Projects Implemented by Non-Governmental Organisation (NGO)*	*Projects with Coordination of GO and NGO*
• Implemented by technocrats therefore technically sound • Top-down approach in planning and implementation • Structures and activities do not have location specificities • Number of line departments are involved in the implementation and this process provokes low coordination among them • High density of administrative staff • High overhead charges and therefore chance for more pilferages • Forced participation of the community	• Technically focussed towards NGO's specialisation • Lack of sufficient and trained technical people that impinges on the span of technical aspects • Non-holistic approach as activities taken up are influenced by past experience or expertise of the NGO • Participative approach in planning and implementation of the project • Less overhead charges and low pilferages • Participation of community is conditioned by the voluntarism of the NGO	• Hybrid approach involves best of both state agencies and NGOs • Technically sound and conditioned by the dominance of the partners • Mix of bottom up and top down • Low overhead cost • Approach is holistic in nature • Participation is ensured and people friendly

Sources: Deshpande and Nikumbh (1993), Deshpande and Narayanamoorthy (1998) and Deshpande, Bhende and Erappa (2003).

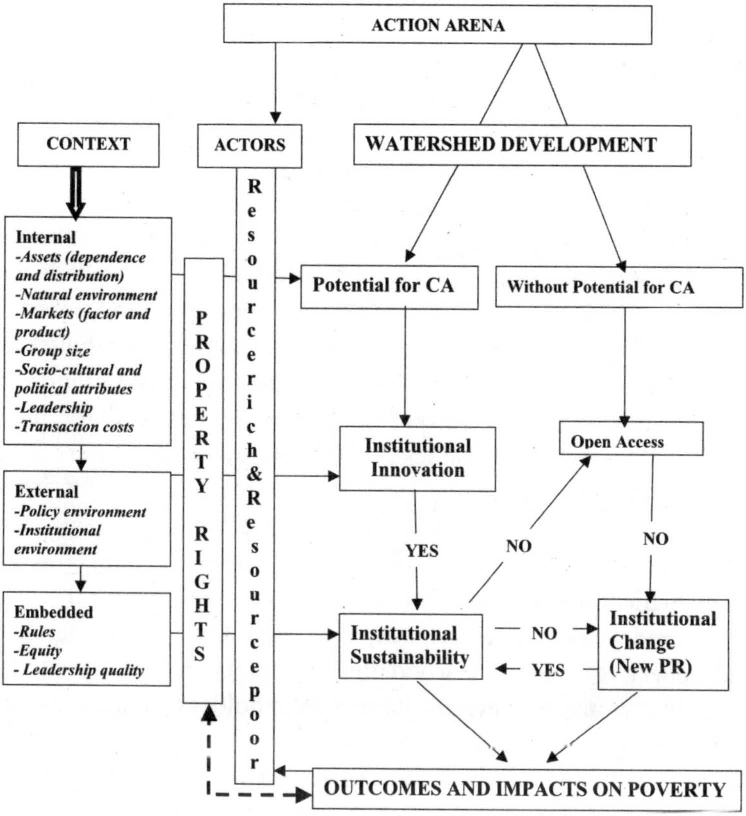

Figure 8.1 Analytical Framework for Sustainable Watershed Management

external and embedded. Internal conditions pertain to asset endowments of the local community, while external conditions are those that influence the internal conditions from outside the community and the embedded conditions are those that the community possesses traditionally and are difficult to alter in the short run. Embedded conditions are relevant in the context of existing institutional arrangements, especially informal.

Internal Conditions

Internal conditions include asset endowments, in terms of five capitals, asset distribution and dependence. The main asset endowments in the context of watershed include land, water, livestock, forests, etc. Apart from their quality, how these assets are distributed among households of the community is important from the point of poverty. Dependence on the assets is relative, as some households may depend more and some less. Dependence on assets is linked to quality of assets, property rights, external sources like non-farm income (including income from labour). A typical case would be that most of the households possess land but do not have access to water, resulting in low productivity, high risk, vulnerability and shocks. Similarly, livestock owners may not have access to grazing lands or forests or even water. This makes them less dependent on their assets. Economic dependence on the assets determines a community's interest in managing it. The higher the dependence of the community on its natural assets like land, water, grazing lands, etc., the higher the probability of collective action. Clearly defined property rights with equity would not only broaden the base of stakeholders but also sustain the efforts in the long run (see Chapter 4).

Factor and product markets reflect the level of economic development, which influences the opportunity costs of time of the stakeholders. The higher the opportunity cost, the lower will be the households' willingness to contribute towards resource management. More importantly, households' dependence will be lower when opportunity cost is higher, i.e., returns from alternative employment will also be more. Essentially, the availability of market for labour may thus influence reliance on natural assets. Markets help in determining the allocation of time between different avenues, i.e., households can compare the returns from time invested in land improvements and labour markets. It was observed that in the regions where non-farm employment is available, households tend to invest more in soil conservation activities (Shiferaw et al., 2004). In irrigated conditions households choose to buy fodder and fuelwood from the market rather than harvest their farm trees due to high opportunity costs of labour (Reddy et al., 1997).

In the context of watershed management, size of the group would be, at least, as big as the landowning households covered under the watershed. Such community tends to be quite big (ranging between 300–500 households) in most of the villages. As argued earlier, in order to make watershed management pro-poor, this group needs to be broad based, including the landless as well as the landed households outside the watershed. For, watershed has positive and negative externalities that would affect these households. Neither the negative externalities are compensated nor the positive externalities are charged (World Bank, 2006). In order to internalise these externalities participation in the programme needs to be broad based. This would not only increase group size making collective action difficult but also makes the group heterogeneous. The size of a group is considered to be crucial for collective action. It is often argued that the smaller the size of the group, better will be the potential for collective outcomes (Olson, 1965). This is found to be true even in the context of formal institutional organisations like agricultural production cooperatives (Kirsch et al., 1984). Smaller size facilitates better coordination and communication resulting in lower transaction cost in organising community action. Though there is no optimum size of the group that facilitates better collective action situations, the group should not be so big as to increase the transaction costs. At the same time, it should not be so small that it would result in higher provision costs (per capita costs to provide the public good). Obviously, the potential for collective action would be higher when the total (transaction + provision) cost is on the lower side. For, higher per capita costs may make mobilisation and organisation difficult and thus lead to higher transaction costs.

Apart from the size, the socio-cultural milieu of the group determines the heterogeneity of the group. Role of heterogeneity in collective action is highly contested (Heckathorn, 1993; Varughese and Ostrom, 2001; Poteete and Ostrom, 2004). According to Olson (1965: 45), the potential for collective action will be easier in a community with highly unequal degrees of interests. This may be true in the context of 'privileged groups' where some of the members can bear the entire costs of providing public goods due to their self-interest (higher benefits in relation to costs). But, in situations where a dominant group has a little or no interest in public good while the peripheral group has greater interest, the public good may not be provided. If it happens that the dominant group also happens to be in the majority, the potential for collective action is extremely dim. On the other hand, a majority group might have larger interest but lack the ability to provide the collective good though there exists the potential. In most situations, it is observed that the poor have higher stakes and hence deeper interest when compared with the non-poor.[1] The potential for collective action is greater when the entire community has interests tied to the common resources. This is possible only when there is equity rather than inequity in the degree of economic interests of the community. Such homogeneity in economic conditions across the households in the community is observed as one of the important determinants in the success of community-based lift irrigation schemes (Panipanchayat or water council) in Maharashtra, India (Deshpande and Reddy, 1991). Various other studies have also shown that equity in economic and social structure of the community facilitates collective action (Tang, 1992; and a number of other studies as quoted in Bardhan, 1995). This calls for clearly defined and equity-oriented property rights in the benefit flows.

Socio-cultural aspects do have a major influence on individual perceptions. For instance, perceptions regarding common grazing lands differ between farming and animal herding communities. In India, where occupation is identified by caste, different caste groups have differential interests in natural resources. In villages, where a majority of the households belong to one particular community, the potential for collective action will be greater. Social networks are also stronger among homogeneous communities. Together, they make the social capital, which determines the potential for collective action. It is observed that effectiveness of the implementing agency (even in the case of same NGO) varies depending on the social cohesiveness and leadership among the communities. In the absence of such social cohesion, the implementing agency had to put extra effort in order to make the social conditions conducive for collective action (Reddy et al., 2005).

The importance of leadership and authority comes out clearly from the studies that have dealt with institutions in detail, i.e., studying the origins, process and rules (Jodha, 1985; Guha, 1985, 1989; Wade, 1987; Chopra et al., 1990; Deshpande and Reddy, 1991). Institutional innovations are easier and sustained for longer periods in feudal societies where leadership is strong. The continuation of feudal norms in some communities explains the success of institutional arrangements even today (Wade, 1988). In a study of communal irrigation in the Philippines, Kikuchi, Dozina and Hayami (1978: 225) noted, "unless there had been good leaders in the community who perceived the high rate of return and managed to organise the programme with the consent of community members, such a project would have not materialised". The role of leadership is increasingly becoming important as the politico-economic transformation in most of the societies is giving rise to individualistic and self-centred behaviour. Besides, the political factions at the community or village level are making it difficult for community action for the common good. In the context of political and social factions there is nothing like common good. This underscores the importance of leaders who can see beyond these short-run benefits and who are strong enough to convince the groups to sideline their political rivalries for achieving the common good. In a study of Rajasthan villagers wanted some outside support, either from an NGO or the state, to solve their problems relating to water, as there is no cohesion within the communities. Everybody was interested in cooperating but nobody was interested in taking the lead to initiate. This is mainly due to political divisions in the communities. Similarly, it is observed in the context of watershed development that in some instances the performance of watersheds is good in the presence of good leaders at the village level (Reddy et al., 2005).

Transaction costs are present in formulating and changing property rights regimes as well as collective action strategies. Transaction costs of negotiation and organisation are to be borne and shared within the community. There would be information costs pertaining to determining the quantity and quality of the resources, which arise when equity concerns are incorporated in to property rights (Libecap, 2002). These costs tend to be lower in homogenous communities who share the same resource for similar productive purposes. Nevertheless, the process of negotiation could be long drawn due to information asymmetries. Often transaction costs associated with equity and measurement disputes delay or block the moves towards effective property rights regimes (Libecap, 2002). This explains the existence of ineffective or inefficient (in terms of poverty alleviation) property rights arrangements. Despite high transactions costs and long drawn process, it is necessary to move in the direction of pro-poor property rights regimes. State should bear the transaction costs, as the social benefits outweigh individual benefits in this case.

External Conditions

External conditions include (i) policy environment, and (ii) institutional environment. Policy environment is vital for institutional innovation as well as its sustenance. Policies can lead to institutional innovations or the disintegration of existing ones. For instance, colonial policies of viewing natural resources (water, forests, etc.) as sources of profit led to the decline of age-old community management systems in South India (Reddy, 1990).

Similarly, even in independent India centralised policies of not involving local people have not only led to breakdown of local institutions but also resulted in the degradation of resources (Reddy, 1996). Binswanger's study (1991) also highlights the impact of policies on deforestation in the context of the Amazon in Brazil. Unless policy and political aspects are duly internalised, it is difficult to explain many cases of misuse of the resources, especially those turning into open access from common property. On the other hand, policy support to involvement of local people in watershed development and forest management has resulted in the innovation of successful institutions like 'watershed committees' and 'forest protection committees' in India. These policies have provided incentives to the communities through providing usufruct rights of varying degrees on various benefit flows. The success of Taiwan's irrigation systems is mainly due to the state policies of co-production and management (Lam, 1996). Basically, policies destroy or provide/strengthen the existing property rights—formal or informal—regimes.

In the context of globalisation, it is argued that most of the policies are biased against the poor. As a result, poor are excluded from sharing the benefits of liberalisation process in India. This is mainly because poor are not equipped to participate and benefit from the markets. Poor produce less from their degraded natural resources and a substantial share of it is used for self-consumption leaving little to sell in the market. Unless poor join together in collective efforts, they cannot benefit from improved product prices. Similarly, they are in a disadvantageous position to improve their land quality as the technologies like watershed development are of long gestation nature. This insecurity in returns to investment and lack of property rights in other complementary inputs like water work as a disincentive to join the collective efforts. Consequently, they turn myopic and adopt low yielding livelihood strategies (Di Gregorio, 2004).

While most of the policies are pro-poor in nature, their effectiveness in addressing poverty depends on the institutional environment fostering the policies. Institutional environment is comprised of legal and governance structures. Unless policies are enforced through institutions, they may not have much impact on poverty. That is, property rights need to have legal standing and institutions to enforce them. Pro-poor policies backed by legally honoured property rights and enforcing institutional structures together make good governance. Of late, decentralisation of governance is often argued to be more effective and efficient framework for delivering pro-poor programmes.

Embedded Conditions

Embedded conditions pertain to the informal institutional arrangements existing in the village communities. These institutional organisations and their functioning might have evolved historically in order to address specific problems faced by the community. These are embedded in the community because they are evolved from within the system with no or little support from outside. Embedded institutions are found to be more robust and efficient when compared to the formal and imposed institutional arrangements (Reddy and Reddy, 2002). Important conditions that make the informal institutions vibrant and sustainable include: (a) rules and regulations including operational rules, collective-choice rules and constitutional-choice rules as described by Ostrom (1990), (b) equity, and (c) quality of leadership.

Allocation of rights and distribution of costs and benefits (equity) are the most important among the rules and regulations. The attitudes of free riders are more prevalent under institutional arrangements, where costs and benefits are distributed unequally across households. This is the case in most of the common grazing lands. Everybody apparently has equal right for the cattle to graze in the commons without any compensation. Equity problems arise because there will not be equity in the distribution of cattle holdings across the households. Therefore, the households owning a large number of cattle derive maximum benefits from grazing on commons without having to contribute anything extra. As a result, those who are on the other extreme (deriving least benefits) tend to assert their user rights inappropriately, such as encroaching. That is, when people view an established system as inequitable according to established social standards, they have incentives to undermine it (Hanna, 1996). This happens mainly due to two reasons: (a) inequity in the distribution of benefits as explained above, and (b) absence of any stakes, as the households do not contribute to the maintenance of the CPR. The principle of contribution (on equity basis) seems to be important in some successful collective action situations (Deshpande and Reddy, 1991; Agrawal, 1994). In other words, when use rights are not *gratis,* chances are better for institutional sustainability.

Unless sanctioning is used against rule breakers, there is no other way to maintain rule compliance, which is termed as quasi-voluntary compliance. This is "*quasi*-voluntary because the non-compliant is subject to coercion—if they are caught" (Levi, 1988 as quoted in Ostrom, 1990). Who, insider or outsider, can carry out monitoring and enforcement effectively is an important aspect that needs to be addressed. Ostrom (1990) has observed that monitoring and sanctioning are undertaken by the participants themselves rather than by any external authorities in long enduring institutions. However, in the context of changing socio-political conditions, insiders (appropriators) are reluctant to carry out monitoring and sanctioning activities. Internal monitoring would be fearless and effective under a strong and effective leadership. In the absence of such conditions, one should not underscore the importance of external authorities in taking up monitoring and sanctioning. In fact, appropriators seem to prefer external forces to doing it themselves (Reddy, 1996). A mix of internal and external forces may also prove a better alternative, as is the case with *Pani Panchayat*. In this case, appropriators undertake monitoring, while sanctioning is enforced by the water council consisting of appropriators with the help of the trust (NGO), an external organisation (Deshpande and Reddy, 1991). Quality here is not limited to leaders' skills and assets, but includes their commitment (to the cause) and character (upholding the societal values) in discharging duties. These qualities are emulated by others in the community and uphold the tradition of following rules and norms in the long run. In the absence of such leaders, self-interests (leaders) can override the societal or common interests and result in degeneration of institutions.

Action Arena

From the point of poverty alleviation the community consists of two main actors, viz., resource-rich and resource-poor. Poverty alleviation requires pro-poor changes in policy and property rights. In the process of reallocating the resources resource-rich ought to forego some of their benefits for the overall improvement in the socio-economic conditions. Therefore, consensus between the rich and the poor is required to arrive at an acceptable trade off. While bringing different actors together is central to collective action and poverty alleviation, we discuss here the conditions that would facilitate collective action.

In the watershed-related literature participatory management is defined as a process, which operates at various levels right from planning through execution and finally ensuring sustainability for future. This however excludes the necessary and sufficient conditions as well as different forms and layers of participation. Pimbert and Pretty (1997) identified a few forms of participation, which range from passive to self-generated. These forms are however not exhaustive and can change in priorities and intensity according to situation (Deshpande and Nikumbh, 1993). Sharma (1997) viewed the process of participation from traditional efforts, culture and mores of people. His observation was from the specific standpoint of an upper Himalayan watershed. In a similar setting, Ostiani and Warren (1995) documented the learning from the field experience of the

Inter-regional Project for Participatory Upland Conservation and Development. They classified participation on the basis of activity, such as planning, contribution, monitoring and evolution, etc. A good example of this process can be seen in Sukhomajari watershed study (Chopra et al., 1990). Cohen and Uphoff (1980) identified the basic four layers beginning with decision-making and going through implementation, distribution of the accrued benefits and finally, evaluating for correction of the shortfalls in the process of implementation. A common feature observed from the above classification of forms is that these authors have specifically concentrated upon the functional aspect and the utility of these aspects is limited to testing of the extent of participation and the depth of involvement (Deshpande and Reddy, 1991).

Broadly, in the real world, one could distinguish three types of collective choice situations (Fig. 8.1). They are: (a) potential situations for collective action or institutional innovation, (b) conditions for initiating collective action or institutional innovation and change, and (c) conditions for sustaining collective action or institutional sustainability. All the communities faced with resource management problems might not have the potential for institution building, i.e., potential situations are subsets of the larger set. In the absence of this potential[2], resources tend to degrade. Similarly, all the potential situations need not necessarily lead to institutional innovation, i.e., a subset of potential situations, and all the institutional innovations are not necessarily sustainable in the long run, i.e., a subset of institutional innovation. While the last subset represents the success stories of institutional innovation, the first subset represents the cases of failure. Besides, institutions that fail to sustain may either change or often remain as failures. This distinction is important as different factors tend to operate at different levels and the degree of their importance also differs across situations. That is, different factors operate and exert differential impact on these situations though they overlap at times.

As is clear from the literature (see for a review Reddy, 1998), some of the assumptions, especially behavioural, made in various theories, are not very realistic and do not reflect the rural communities we are dealing with. This calls for the articulation of assumptions necessary to understand rural societies. These assumptions include:

1. Individuals are *boundedly rational*, i.e., individuals act rationally within the limits of information available to them. In the conditions of low awareness and information lags obtaining in rural communities in developing countries, a *full justification* or a priori expectations would be erroneous. Moreover, calculating costs and benefits pertaining to natural resources which continuously change needs a higher order or computational ability that is beyond the capability of ordinary people (without training) leave alone rural people.
2. Individuals are often *intentionally irrational (economic)*. Individual's actions, sometimes, may not reflect even bounded rationality. This is mainly due to socio-political factors, which are increasingly becoming central to rural societies. Here group rationality overtakes individual rationality and masks the latter. The implicit rationale is political gain for the group as a whole, though a particular individual may or may not get any tangible benefits in the immediate future. What is rational for the group may be irrational for an individual, and individual may simply follows the group, even if she/he is aware of the irrationality of (economically) choice. This may be attributed to expected socio-political benefits in the future.
3. All the people in a community are *not opportunistic* as defined by Williamson: "self-interest seeking with guile" (Williamson, 1985: 47). They trust one another though we do not rule out the possibility of opportunistic behaviour, whatever the size of such a group. It is observed that trust, truthfulness and acting with justice are essential lubricants of societies (Dasgupta, 1996; Sethi and Somanathan, 1996).

4. Individuals are aware of the behavioural pattern of others, as they know each other for a long time and would have faced a variety of situations together (*involved in repeated games*). And, they *communicate freely* even in a faction-ridden community and hence are neither prisoners nor victims of isolation.
5. In general, a majority of individuals are *trend followers, rather than trendsetters*. That is, individuals are willing and ready to cooperate but not ready to take initiative or lead in creating institutions.

These assumptions largely reflect the basic characteristics of rural communities. One has to find ways to bring them together. According to Mr. Rajendra Singh (the Magsaysay award winner for his seminal work on organising rural communities to develop water harvesting structures in Rajasthan), there are five types of groups among rural communities. These are: (a) base (influential due to their background, credibility, character, etc., boundedly rational); (b) negative (oppose everything and anything, intendedly irrational); (c) opportunists (always take the side of majority); (d) target group (vulnerable and no voice); and (e) motivated (eager to do something or trend followers). Mr. Singh synthesizes that the task in the collective action strategy is to bring the base and motivators together. Once these two are together involving the target group becomes easy. Together, these three groups become the majority in the villages and hence attracts the fourth group, i.e., opportunists. The negative group then gets marginalised leaving them the option of joining or quitting.[3] The village development council concept in the watersheds, promoted by the rural development trust is somewhat close to this approach (Sivanna and Reddy, 2005). The three collective choice situations identified above arise due to the variations in the composition of these groups in the community, i.e., communities with greater proportion of negative and opportunist groups, etc. The conditions discussed (external, internal and embedded) in the context influence or determine the three types of collective choice situations (Fig. 8.1).

Implications for Poverty Alleviation

Watershed implementation becomes effective with the help active and sustainable participation/collective action. Watershed development, if properly implemented, leads to resource improvements, land productivity, employment generation, etc. However, the density of impact depends mainly on the resource context. As mentioned earlier, water is the major constraining factor in agricultural improvements in the semi-arid regions. Water resources, surface as well as ground, are limited. Rainfall is 250–700 mm per year and falls in the monsoon period of three months (July–September). Today, rainfall patterns have become totally unpredictable. The result has been crop failure, which is a regular phenomenon in these regions. Some localities have ephemeral streams or rivers. Villagers have, from time immemorial, had access to tanks and open wells, some of which are still in use. There is a link between surface and groundwater resources. By diverting surface water flows into tanks, open wells and the groundwater through specific infiltration areas, rainwater is harvested. Tubewells are the main source of water supply in most of the semi-arid regions.

Uncertain rainfall is the major water-related vulnerability and characterises agriculture and life in these areas. The main source of irrigation is groundwater, which is extracted through open and borewells. Though tanks used to be the main source of irrigation, most of them have degenerated over the years due to poor maintenance and lack of policy support. Groundwater extraction has become the privilege of large farmers due to its capital-intensive and lumpy nature (one-time investment). The advent of deep borewells and submersible (deep) bore pumps has further aggravated the problem. In the absence of any initiatives to strengthen groundwater-replenishing mechanisms, the expansion of bore wells has led to depletion of the groundwater table and the drying up of open wells. Resource-poor farmers are the main victims. Even some common accessible handpumps for drinking water have gone dry as private pumps extract groundwater for irrigation. As a result, the local institutions that were managing these systems have become dysfunctional, though in some villages their traces remain. In the process, water has been transformed from a community resource into one in the private domain. Thus majority of people have been denied their right to the common pool of resource.

Villagers are aware of the links between ground and surface water bodies, but due to the magnitude of the investment and the collective effort required, communities have shied away from reviving surface water bodies. Instead, they expect the state to take up such activities. They seem to be comfortable with the private exploitation of groundwater though they are aware of the fact that its overexploitation results in the degradation of the resource and in widening inequalities. These stresses have not yet reached the stage of an outright conflict, though, partly because the level of awareness of the people about their rights in resources and entitlements is low. Still, the impact of declining water tables and the resultant well failures, coupled with uncertain climatic conditions, adverse input-output prices and poor quality of inputs (especially seeds), has brought the agriculture sector to a flash point in these regions. Reports of farmer suicides and widespread migration, even among large farmers, are common.

The introduction of watershed development in such adverse conditions, as seen in the previous chapters, is expected to improve the standard of living of the local communities in various ways. These improvements can range from moderate to nominal (Chapters 6 and 7). Watershed development is a land-based development approach comprising various components aimed at land, water and conservation of vegetation. Every inch of land is a micro-watershed, which is in turn a sub-set of a macro-watershed. When a micro-or macro-watershed is treated physically, the quality of land will improve because the erosion of soil by wind and water will be checked. Activities like contour bunding, pebble bunding, trenching, *nala* bunding, *gulli* plugging and plantation are some techniques implemented to check erosion, enhance *in situ* moisture levels and improve vegetative cover. As a result of the improved quality of soil and heightened availability of moisture, land productivity also increases. In addition, the rainwater harvested per unit of land increases, as does groundwater recharge. When all micro-watersheds are treated, the overall availability of water improves due to the augmentation of groundwater recharge and to the increased capacity of reservoirs less vulnerable to siltation. With the help of check-dams, small-scale local reservoirs, which provide multiple benefits, including groundwater recharge, can be built. However, upstream-downstream externalities appear to cause conflicts between communities (World Bank, 2006; Ray and Bijarniya, 2006; Reddy, 2004).

At the local level, improving water availability depends on local rainfall pattern, soil type, slope and geology—all of which vary from village to village. Given the socio-economic context of the region, the key beneficiaries from the programme are the landed households, which form the majority. Large farmers are generally better off, who can invest in borewells. But large farmers are also getting into debt due to widespread well failures in recent years. Marginal and small farmers diversify by working part time as labourers or by getting into non-agricultural income-generating activities. Labourers cope with setbacks by temporarily migrating out of the area to places of work; in the worst cases, they sell themselves as bonded labourers. Even large farmers adjust by reducing social expenditures such as that on education, religious festivals and marriages. Of late, due to the well failures caused by severe drought, even medium and large farmers are migrating. For households that have always lived of their land honourably, the process of pauperisation creates social and psychological trauma.

The impacts of watershed development can be termed short and long run as well as direct and indirect. As a land-based programme, watershed development mainly helps landed households. All soil conservation activities are beneficial to the landed in the medium to long run. In addition, the landless and landed poor also benefit from increased employment and wages in the short run. All watershed works are implement on a specified standard unit-rate basis by local labourers. As there are no middlemen, earnings result in daily wages 2–5 times the normal rate. Because of the volume of work, wage-earning households, as well as small and marginal farmer households with extra labour capacity, benefit considerably from interventions.

Watershed development has also provided the poor with some benefits in the long run in addition to the earnings from wage labour during the implementation stage. The increase in wage employment at the village has resulted in the decline in outmigration. But, studies have shown that the reduced migration is limited to the implementation period. In fact, migration was observed to have gone during the post-implementation period, due to the increased participation rates in response to demand and wage rates. Similarly, the impact of higher wages is normally short-term, i.e., lasting only during the period of implementation However, in some cases, there is clear improvement in livelihoods and standard of living conditions due to the increased area under irrigation and diversified cropping pattern made possible by the assured availability of groundwater.

Landed households benefit in the medium and long run, as the yields tend to improve by 20 percent (Chapters 7 and 8). Changes in cropping patterns are noticed even in the rainfed agriculture, though on a smaller scale, than in irrigated areas, where the cropping pattern has shifted from paddy and *ragi* cultivation to the cultivation of sunflower, horticultural crops like papaya, flowers and vegetables. Because of the uncertainty in the amount and distribution of rainfall, these benefits are not, however, stable. Unless these vulnerabilities are addressed, the benefits from watershed development remain unpredictable even for the landed. In contrast, farmers with access to groundwater reap stable benefits from watershed activities, which have improved and stabilised groundwater yields. Access to groundwater is, however, for the most part limited to large and medium farmers (Table 8.2). Marginal farmers do not usually have access to groundwater. In sum, while in the short run agricultural labourers' (landed as well as landless) benefit from the programme, farmers, especially those with access to groundwater, accrue the medium and long-term benefits.

Table 8.2 *Distribution of Well Owners by Farm Size*

Farm Size (acres)	*% of households having open wells*	*% of households having borewells*
0–3	00	00
3.1–5	04	11
5.1–10	08	09
Above 10	88	80

Source: Reddy (2004).

While it is clear that land distribution is biased in favour of large farmers in all the regions, water resources are more unevenly distributed than land in the semi-arid tracks (Table 8.3). In a comparative study of irrigated and rainfed villages within the semi-arid region, distribution of irrigated land and irrigation equipment found to be less equitably distributed in the rainfed villages. Distribution of irrigated area is more even in the case of irrigated village, which is due to the canal irrigation. This is true even in the case of irrigation equipment. Better income levels in this village may be the reason for equitous distribution (Reddy et al., 2004). Similarly, the ownership of dairy animals is also skewed in favour of large farmers in all the villages, as they own more that 60 percent of the milch animals. Most of the large and medium farmers own milch cattle. Same is the case with small ruminants, except in the irrigated village where a quarter of the small ruminants are owned by landless households. However, distribution of small ruminants is less skewed when compared

Table 8.3 *Distribution of Land and Water in Semi-arid Regions (Gini-coefficients)*

District/Village	*Land Resources (owned)*	*Water Resources (% area irrigated)*
Anantapur		
(i) Mallapuram	0.47	0.64
(ii) Vaddupalli	0.67	0.93
(iii) Bandarlapalli	0.52	0.94
(iv) Virupapuram	0.77	0.99
Adilabad		
(i) Vadal	0.35	0.92
(ii) Laxmipur	0.36	0.76
(iii) Ashapalli	0.46	0.56
(iv) Hattijhari	0.31	0.97
Rangareddy		
(i) Kothapalli	0.46	0.78
(ii) Naganpalli	0.58	0.93
(iii) Meerkhanpet	0.44	0.57
(iv) Mandipal	0.42	0.90

Source: ICRISAT (2006).

milch animals. On the whole, animal husbandry, big or small, is the domain of large farmers.

It is often argued that livestock is more equally distributed than land assets. In fact, this appears to be true at the aggregate level (Rao and Birthal, 2002). On the other hand, it may be hypothesised that access to irrigation or water resources is more skewed than land in fragile resource regions where groundwater is the main source of irrigation. The variations in the distribution of different types of assets can be seen clearly in terms of Gini-ratios (Table 8.4). Defying our expectations, livestock is distributed more skewedly when compared to land and water resources. This

Table 8.4 *Distribution of Important Assets (Gini-ratios)*

Gini-ratio of	*Mallapuram*	*Hanimireddy Palle*	*Obulapuram*	*Neelareddy Palle (irrigated)*
1. Land	0.62	0.65	0.52	0.60
2. Water				
–Area irrigated	0.81	0.86	0.82	0.68
–Irrigation equipment	0.92	0.92	0.83	0.88
3. Livestock				
–Total animals	0.95	0.94	0.89	0.95
–Milch animals	0.96	0.93	0.88	0.93
–Small ruminants	0.95	0.96	0.91	0.95

Source: Reddy et al., 2004.

happens to hold good even when we separate the milch animal and small ruminants. For, poor households are found to own small ruminants. But, in three of the sample villages, milch animals are more equitably distributed than small ruminants through the difference is marginal. Access to irrigation is more equitable in the irrigated village when compared to less irrigated villages. This indicates that canal irrigation is more equitous when compared to well irrigation due to the high capital-intensive nature of the latter. This argument is well supported by the less equitous distribution of irrigation equipment when compared to area under irrigation in all the villages. This brings out clearly the concentration of all the important assets in the hands of few rich farmers. Of all the assets, access to water is the most critical factor that determines livelihood strategies and well-being of the household.

There is a clear bias against the landless and the landed poor as far as receiving sustained benefits are concerned. The main reason for this is the absence of clearly defined property rights in water resources. Though water is a common pool resources (CPR), mostly the large farmers access the water depriving the marginal and small farmers. Landless along with marginal and small farmers form the core group of poor. One way of addressing the needs of the poor is by strengthening CPRs with legitimate provision of equitable usufruct rights to them. There is, however, concern over how to maintain CPRs as in many places there are no effective institutional arrangements in place for maintenance.

Making the Watershed Benefits Pro-poor

The Andhra Pradesh government's stress on poverty eradication calls for an all-out effort to ensure a more equitable distribution of watershed development benefits. At present, the major benefits of watershed development go to the richer households as 70 percent of the expenditure goes to interventions that benefit them. At the same time, only 7.5 percent of the input is used to support the livelihoods of poor and landless families (GoI, 2001). The watershed-plus approach of the APRLP is a step in this direction, but more innovation and experimentation is needed. Here, we discuss some the pro-poor initiatives that need attention at the local level. A major way to target long-term watershed benefits to landless and other poor households is to strengthen the CPRs, making them accessible to the poor through collective action strategies.

An example is the arrangements concerning palm trees in the CPRs of Guddella village in Anantapur district. Palm leaves are used in basket and mat making activities, while toddy (local liquor) is extracted from mature palm trees. Two economically and socially poor communities depend on these activities for their livelihoods (Reddy et al., 2003). Guddella village has 1,000 palm trees under the 30 hectares of temple lands (CPR). Before the watershed committee was started, these palm trees were treated as open access. Even neighbouring villagers would cut their branches for various purposes. The households from within the village often used to face shortage of leaves and were forced to travel far to procure palm leaves. The watershed committee and the Village Development Committee (VDC) have now taken charge of these trees. Two guards are employed by the VDC at Rs 600 per month to protect the trees year round. Yearly, the households depending on the palm trees pay some money to the VDC to get use rights. The amount is decided on a consensus basis, rather than on an actual cost basis. This arrangement has ensured that the village poor have better access to the resource and led to a more productive use of their time. There are similarly instances of giving exclusive fishing rights in tanks and behind check-dams to the local fishing community. Furthermore, in some villages, SC people are given the exclusive use rights of roadside plantations.

Another important activity, which has potential for improving rural livelihoods, is dairy activity. Dairy development, along with horticulture development programme, is expected to complement and hence the benefit flows from watershed development, especially to the poor communities. Both these activities are dependent on water and other CPRs like wastelands or common grazing lands. While these two programmes are being launched in a big way, their impact on poor communities is rather ambiguous. This is mainly due to the reason that the prevailing policy environment is not conducive for such benefit flows towards poor. Dairy development is actively pursued in some of the villages. Nationalised banks provide loans to the households up to 90 percent of the cost. The banks finance on unit basis (two buffaloes). The total loan amount ranges between Rs. 20,000 to Rs. 28,000 per unit. Some of the conditions for getting the loan include: (a) a deposit of Rs. 2,000 per animal as guarantee, (b) ownership of land, irrigated is preferred, and (c) a guarantor. Besides, most of the loans are given to hybrid (murra) buffaloes. The borrower is expected to repay the loan with 50 percent of the earnings from milk on a monthly basis.

These conditions exclude the poor from participating in the programme. While landownership is necessary to maintain the high feed intensive murra buffaloes, their suitability to local environment is questionable. For, our discussions with the beneficiaries revealed that murra breed is a failure due to the water and fodder stress in the region. On the other hand, the local varieties may be more profitable. Provision of loans to local varieties will not only be low cost but also accessible to poor. For, even the landless households can maintain local varieties, as their fodder requirement is much lower. Now, the efforts, especially by a local NGO (Rural Development Trust), are on to convince the bankers to finance the local varieties and also improve the local breeds through cross insemination. Only then landless poor households can benefit from the programme. Renovating water bodies, horticulture and dairy activities are eagerly pursued by the district administration in the study region. While dairy development has lot of potential, it needs to be tuned to the local constraints. At present, the programme is not favourable to the poor households. Dairy could be an effective pro-poor programme under the watershed development if the policy support is tuned to the needs of the poor.

One more activity under the watershed programme, which has greater potential for poverty alleviation, is the formation of self-help groups (SHGs). Forming and strengthening institutions at the village level is an innovative feature of the watershed development guidelines. Small (10–15 members) groups are organised to generate money through savings. During watershed development wage rates go up 3–5 times and employment opportunities also increase. During that time it is relatively easy for even the poor to start savings. The savings are circulated amongst the group members who use it for investment or consumption, paying a pre-decided interest rate (usually 24 percent per annum).

Once these self-help groups are established, a revolving fund of Rs 50,000 per watershed is available to support them through matching grants. The watershed in Mallapuram (Anantapur district), implemented under NGO-GO partnership, demonstrates the potential of such programmes in poverty alleviation. Under the watershed programme, in Mallapuram, there were eight SHGs. These were organised around occupations and there were two tailoring groups (women), two groups of cane workers (women), two groups of masons (men), one group of carpenters (men) and one group of cobblers (men). Membership ranges between 5–10. Most of the groups are very active and have generated substantial savings. They not only lent money for their own vocational activities, but also towards new activities, such as petty business, etc. One of the women groups has about Rs. 1,50,000 in savings, and they have lent out money for purchase of two auto-rickshaws. The main reason for the success of these groups is that they concentrated on individual-based lending rather than community based activities. While collective activities can be very profitable, most of the times they are dogged by the classic collective action dilemmas. The real strength of SHGs lies in identifying activities that match local resources, skills and needs, and are economically profitable.

As it is clear from our discussion that institutional innovation and sustenance is the key for the success of the watershed development and also making it a pro-poor activity. Participatory watershed management emphasises evolution of institutions and strengthening the existing ones. While number of institutional arrangements, such as watershed associations, user groups, self-help groups, etc., are evolved in order to utilise the benefits of the programme, their sustenance in the long run is questionable. For, these institutional arrangements are imposed from outside rather than socially embedded. Socially embedded or informal institutions are more sustainable than formal institutional arrangements, because they evolve out of a genuine requirement. Evolution of such institutions is a time-consuming and costly (transaction costs) affair and hence their impact is rather limited. On the other hand, the impact of formal institutions could be widespread and effective at the macro level. Though it is too much to expect the evolution or replication of socially embedded institutions in every village, formal institutions should draw lessons from such institutions in order to sustain in the long run. Often, the success of socially embedded institutions is critically linked with their financial sustainability and socio-economic equity in the distribution of costs and benefits. There is need for integrating market principles with the institutional approaches.

Marrimakulapalle (Anantapur district) is an example of such institutional sustainability and provides some useful insights for institutional strengthening and sustenance. While the formal watershed committee was established only during 1998, Marrimakulapalle had 20 years of experience in maintaining traditional institutions. About 20 years back, the village elders, with the help of a local NGO (RDT/AF), initiated three institutions, namely, Anjaneya Swamy Committee (ASC), Peerla Swamy Committee (PSC) and Vidya Committee (VC). All the committees have proportional representation from all the caste groups in the village.

The ASC has eleven members and looks after the law and order issues in the village. In the village meetings the committee discusses all minor and major offences. Those declared guilty are fined depending upon the seriousness of the offence. Even members of the committee itself are not spared from the procedure. It also has eleven members and works as a community bank. The PSC generates money from various common resources, such as income from temple lands, sale of dung in the streets, fines from punishments by ASC, etc. It has constructed quarters for school teachers and rents them out to teachers. Money thus generated is distributed among community heads, proportionately to their population. This is given as loans to the needy within the community at a 24 percent per annum interest rate, and the loan is collected with interest on a particular day in the year for redistribution. The PSC has accumulated savings to the tune of Rs 3,00,000. The VC has 30 members representing all the caste groups and collects funds from the members on a voluntary basis. Donated money is used for extension of the school building, employing assistant-teachers, etc. Since the construction of quarters most of the teachers stay in the village.

The needs of the landless are taken care of in a unique fashion. The village council has acquired 10 hectares of land with the help of RDT/AF, on which a bore well is drilled for irrigation. This land is auctioned to groups of landless households on yearly, rotational basis. Usually, a group of 4–5 households take the land for cultivation purposes. In this manner, the equity issues are resolved to some extent as far as land is concerned. However, inequity in water distribution is yet to be resolved. Some of the economic and equity principles of these informal institutions could be useful for strengthening the formal institutions.

Conclusions

The policy reaction to the growing recognition of the importance of participatory institutions in natural resource management at best can be described as ad-hoc and misguided. As a result, the term 'participatory process' has found its place in all development project documents with little or no concern for its implementation. Participatory process is being advocated in all developmental projects as if it were a technology rather than treating it as a philosophy. While it is difficult for an implementing bureaucracy to understand this philosophy, the effort to understand some of the successful and enduring institutional arrangements are clearly missing at the policy level. On the contrary, the policy environment is rather more hostile than conducive to the innovation and sustainability of existing institutions. Unless the existing policy perspective changes towards facilitating institutional innovation, let alone institutional promotion, successful and enduring institutional arrangements at the local level continue to be exceptions and unlikely to spread even to neighbouring areas.

The present framework, though not focused on how these policy changes could be brought about, stresses the importance of policy and political environments for institutional innovation and sustainability. This framework distinguishes CPR situations with differential institutional capabilities and thus facilitates better targeting of policies. Assessment of institutional capabilities has to be made an important input for policy formulation. Political economy aspects, along with cost-benefit aspects, are of prime importance for institutional innovation and change. While costs and benefits determine the potential for institutional innovation, the actual creation of institutional arrangements is critically linked with political economy aspects. Creation of policy environment for institutional arrangements is more important and sustainable than direct imposition of institutions. Policy changes (or environment) need to be matched with the contemporary political environment. There is thus a great need to recognise the role of external forces, like NGOs, as catalytic factors promoting institutional arrangements through providing leadership and promoting leadership from within the community. The policy environment should be conducive to facilitate their role. The grassroots level success and effectiveness of development policy largely depends on the synergy between the government and NGOs.

The challenge is to understand and analyse the origins and process of institutional innovation. Understanding the process rather than limiting oneself to situational analysis, assists in designing broader macro-policies for promoting institutional arrangements. It also provides clues as to whether it is feasible at all to design macro-policies for successful institutional arrangements. At the moment devising such policies appears to be very much feasible. Policies need to be more targeted and to limit the role of the state in implementing the policies. The state should be assigned a more important and critical role in assessing institutional capabilities, identifying and promoting external agencies (NGOs), wherever necessary, and monitoring their activities. This role can only be performed by the state in order to achieve the intended policy objectives. This aspect deserves utmost attention as recent years have experienced mushrooming of local NGOs, not all of which are genuine. Though this is not to the liking of the implementing bureaucracy, which is used to rent seeking, we are confident that the attitudes will change once the hard decisions are taken.

Notes

1. This is only to suggest that the poor depend more on natural assets and commons for their livelihoods. Their critical dependence, however, makes them vulnerable to changes in resource conditions.
2. Identifying the potential situations has become important, of late. As per Haryali Guidelines (GoI, 2003), one of the criteria for selection of watershed is community's willingness to contribute for the development and for operation and maintenance. This is seen as potential for watershed development. Some NGOs go a

step further in asking for evidence of collective efforts in terms of creating some common assets as an indication of potential (Reddy et al., 2005)

3. Based on the discussion with Mr. Rajendra Singh on 6th February 2005 at Tarun Bharat Sangh, Alwar, Rajasthan.

9

Political Economy of Watershed Management

The process of watershed development can be better understood in the political economy framework. For, the attitude, philosophy and ideology of the policy makers are crucial in determining the development path. Here, we focus our attention on two important issues, which have political undertones. These include: (a) adhering to the basic philosophy (guidelines) of participatory approach, and (b) involvement of Panchayati Raj Institutions (PRIs) in the implementation of watersheds. Though both the issues are concerned with decentralisation, the institutions involved differ in terms of their constitutional mandate. While PRIs are constitutionally mandated and democratically elected institutions, participatory institutions are formally created for the purpose of specific programme delivery.

Decentralisation of governance is often argued to be more effective and efficient framework for delivering pro-poor programmes. The perceived benefits of decentralisation range from stimulation of economic growth, alleviation of rural poverty, strengthening the civil society and reducing the responsibilities of the centre (Manor, 1999). For, political accountability is often greater at the local level (Seabright, 1996). It was observed that project costs are four times higher in centralised systems when compared to decentralised systems. Besides, asset maintenance is much better in the decentralised systems (Bardhan, 1996). Decentralisation with its potential benefits, coupled with the declining legitimacy of centralised systems, has attracted support from a diverse range of ideological schools. However, it is cautioned that decentralisation is not effective or efficient in all situations. Under conditions of greater inequality it may result in political and elite captures and nexus formation between interest groups (Bardhan, 2002). While decentralised systems are found to be superior in terms of intra-regional targeting efficiency, their delivery systems target better in low poverty regions and worse in high poverty regions (Bardhan and Mookherjee, 2000).

Decentralised governance relies on the local institutional structures for delivery of pro-poor programmes. In India, decentralisation is often understood as devolution of powers to the locally (district and village) elected constitutional bodies, i.e., the Panchayti Raj institutions.[1] While these democratic institutions had an effective role in the early decades of independence, they experienced erosion of powers during the later years.[2] This is mainly due to the absence of constitutional mandate for these institutions and leaving their fate to the whims and fancy of the state governments. Over the years state governments curtailed their powers in order to centralise the governance structures. The 73rd constitutional amendment in 1993 was an attempt to resurrect these institutions. While the amendment helped in strengthening and systematising these institutions in terms of conducting regular elections, constituting the state finance commissions, etc., the option of devolution of powers, crucial for their vibrancy, is still in the hands of the state governments. Despite the fact that the amendment requires devolution of functions (29 in total), functionaries and funds, as per the 11th schedule, most of the state governments have not done so.[3]

On the other hand, some states like Andhra Pradesh have adopted different institutional arrangements in the name of participatory institutions as decentralised delivery systems. These institutions effectively by passed the democratic institutions and are also known as parallel institutions or community-based organisations (CBOs) or user committees. Financially, these institutions are much stronger when compared to the PRIs. The rationale for promoting these institutions include: (a) user groups understand the day-to-day problems better than the elected and political representatives, (b) PRIs failed to deliver the benefits over the last five decades,[4] and (c) PRIs are known for elite capture and political patronage. However, divergent views are held on the role of these institutions regarding their effectiveness and their linkages with the PRIs (GoI, 1998; Sastry, 2000; Manor, 2001; Sitaram, 2002). Manor (2000 and 2001) argues that these institutions have not only weakened the PRIs but are also potentially damaging the development. He calls for the integration of the user committees with the elected committees. The arguments favouring the convergence between PRIs and CBOs include: (a) improves the accountability, (b) addresses the inadequacy of powers and funds of the PRIs, (c) improves the sustainability of the programmes, as PRIs are permanent constitutional bodies.

It is often argued that these CBOs insulate development from politics. Manor (2001) counters: "This notion is myth—and a dangerous myth at that. Politics—that is, the interplay of interests and forces in pursuit of power, resources, status, etc.—is pervasive." Elite capture was found to be a serious problem even the case of community-driven development in West Africa (Platteau, 2004). How far these participatory institutions function above political and class interests (elite capture) is a moot point? This chapter attempts to understand the extent and nature of elite capture in the newly created participatory institutions in the context of watershed development in Andhra Pradesh. The prevailing pattern of forming the parallel institutions or CBOs in the state and the compelling political-economy reasons made this a significant avenue of inquiry.

Approach and Setting

This chapter is based on the experience from the process of watershed implementation in the government-implemented watersheds, which account for 80 percent of the watersheds in the state. Besides political dimensions, which are at the core of our study, are often addressed or overcome in the NGO-implemented watersheds through consensus building.[5] A sample of three villages was selected for an in-depth study after visiting a number of villages. The sample selection is purposive using multiple criteria. All the sample villages are located in Anantapur district, which is one of the most severe drought-prone regions of the state with high concentration of watersheds. Sample villages should have the watershed programme going on for the past 2–3 years and not with a completed watershed. This would provide us insights into the political dynamics in the process of implementation. Besides, we have visited a sample of six villages in various mandals across the district (government PIAs) for

Table 9.1 *Important Features of the Sample Villages*

Village Name	*Mandal*	*Political Status*	
		Before (1994–99)	*Present (2001–2005)*
TV Puram	Rayadurg	General category, BC-boya, Congress.	SC-reserved, TDP
DK Puram	Rayadurg	BC (reserved-women), TDP	BC, Congress
JR Palli	Rayadurg	SC-reserved, TDP	BC, Congress

the purpose of cross-checking our findings in the three sample villages where we have conducted the intensive study.

Further, the selection of the main sample villages was anchored on the shift in power during the last elections to local (panchayati raj) bodies in August 2001. All the sample villages have experienced the shift in power from one party[6] to another, i.e., from Telugu Desam to Congress in two villages and from Congress to Telugu Desam in one. The details of the sample villages are presented in Table 9.1. The study was based on qualitative as well as quantitative information elicited from various levels (processes) of watershed implementation. These include the PIAs, watershed associations, watershed committees, user groups, households, etc. The focus, however, was more on qualitative research, viz., group discussions, focus group interviews, time trends, individual interviews, etc. These interactions were not one time and the process was continued for one year on a regular basis, i.e., every quarter from February 2002 till March 2003. The idea was to capture the changes in the political process and its impact on the watershed development programme. Quantitative information is elicited pertaining to the coverage of the watershed programme, financial and physical allocations, components of watershed, distributional aspects, etc. All the sample villages differ from one another as far as their socio-economic profiles are concerned (Table 9.2).

Despite being the drought-prone region, the primary livelihood activity in the sample villages is agriculture. Landless account for about 10 percent of total households in two of the villages, while they account for 22 percent in one. Landless households along with small and marginal farmers work as agricultural labour to eke out their earnings. Migration to other places as labourers is another important livelihood activity. Some households also practise sheep or goat rearing, as part of their vocational activity. Though a number of other activities, such as construction, forest works, agro-processing

Table 9.2 *Socio-economic Profile of the Sample Villages*

Village	*No. of HH*	*Population*	*Social Composition (percentage of HH)*			*Economic Composition (percentage of HH)*				
			SC/ST	*BC*	*OC*	*Landless*	*Marginal & small*	*Medium*	*Large*	*% area irrigated*
TV Puram	600	2800	20	76	04	08	16	68	08	02
DK Puram	500	2300	20	78	02	10	30	30	30	07
JR Palli	320	1717	30	47	23	22	52	08	18	08

Note: SC/ST = Scheduled Castes/Scheduled Tribes; BC = Backward Castes; OC = Other castes or forward castes who do not get special reservation status by the constitutional authority; HH = Households.

works, etc., exist, their contribution is marginal in the overall village economy. Of late, watershed works have become the main source of employment in these villages. Crop production is mainly rainfed with little scope for irrigation facilities. The only source of irrigation in these villages is well irrigation that accounts for less than 10 percent of the total cropped area. Of late open wells are getting dried up due to overexploitation of water and farmers are shifting to bore wells, which are more expensive. Of the three villages, TV Puram is the most backward with only 2 percent of its net sown area under irrigation, while the other two villages have about 7–8 percent irrigation. Groundnut is the single most important crop in these villages. Paddy is grown under wells. Other dry crops, such as ragi, bajra, etc., and irrigated dry crops, such as cotton, chillies, etc., are also grown.

Political Profile

All the villages are politically divided between the Telugu Desam Party (TDP) and the Congress Party. In general, according to the people, political conflicts arise during the election time and subside immediately after the elections. However, these are not very uncommon. For instance, in JR Palli, control over the Gram Panchayat has shifted from TDP to Congress in the recent elections. The mandal president (Congress) was from this village.[7] It appears that there was regular interaction between the Gram Panchayat and watershed committee, which is headed by TDP chairman. The Congress-controlled Gram Panchayat was interested in overseeing and monitoring the watershed works so that no undue favours are done to the TDP supporters. This works as a kind of checks and balances. But this kind of activism was not seen in other two villages though there are political undercurrents that surface less frequently. The partywise composition before and after the last local body elections indicated latent conflicts between the groups

Table 9.3 *Composition of PRIs in the Sample Villages during the Last Two Elections*

Village	*No. of wards*	*% of women*		*% belonging to*						*% belonging to*			
				SC/ST		*BC*		*OC*		*TDP*		*Cong*	
		A	*B*	*A*	*B*	*A*	*B*	*A*	*B*	*A*	*B*	*A*	*B*
TV Puram	11	09	00	18	27*	72*	73	—	—	45	73*	55*	27
DK Puram	10	40*	30	10	10	80*	90*	10	—	50*	30	50	70*
JR Palli	11	36	18	55*	27	36	55*	09	18	55*	18	45	82*

Note: A = previous elections (1994–99); B = recent elections (2001–2006).

* Indicate the category of the sarpanch or president of the PR body.

(Table 9.3). There was total reversal in the power equations in all the villages. In all the villages there was a balance between the two political groups during 1994–1999 period but turned into single party domination (accounting for more than 70 percent of the ward members) in the 2001 elections.

Given their numerical strength BCs (backward castes) dominate the composition of the PRIs. Unless the post of the president was reserved for SCs/STs, BCs hold the coveted position. Interestingly, forward caste groups, which are often the economically strong and historically/politically dominant groups, did not seem to wield any political power in these villages. In fact, there seems to be some kind of marginalisation of this group during the last elections, as they held fewer positions (ward members). On the other hand, vulnerable sections like SCs/STs and women got a chance through reservation. This was a positive fallout of the reservation policy.

TDP dominated the watershed associations (WAs) and watershed committees (WCs) in two of the villages and held half of the membership in the other. Note that these bodies were constituted one or two years prior to the elections to the PRIs. Hence, the political affiliations of the members did not reflect that of the PRIs. Interestingly, the TDP has dominated both WA and WC even prior to the panchayat elections in TV Puram. TV Puram was an example of how the contractor-bureaucracy nexus could dominate the WC. Since the contractor belongs to the TDP, he had become the chairman of the WC and got his supporters as members and WA president. In the other two villages there was a compromise between the parties and hence they shared the WA and WC positions. However, in these villages, this compromise did not last long. In JR Palli one party failed to honour a pre-poll alliance for the 1999 PRI elections. In the other village (DK Puram) the compromise broke down due to the failure of the PR president to implement a fair division of spoils between members of the two parties.

Politics, Contractors and Watershed Management

Contractors and Politics

The three sample villages portray three different scenarios regarding the political dynamics of implementation. Clearly, the contractor-official-politician nexus seems to be unlikely to deliver the programme-intended benefits, especially those that should be directed at the poor. This happens because of the sharing of rents. The three scenarios include situations in which:

1. contractors have little or no presence (DK Puram);
2. contractor is the dominant figure (TV Puram); and
3. contractor and political elements are active (JR Palli).

Though the financial and administrative controls were in the PIAs hands, their discretion to make biased spending decisions was diluted when there were strong benevolent leaders with political influence at the village level. In the absence of such leaders, the effectiveness of the programme depends on the benevolence and honesty of WC chairman and members. Though strong political leaders were present in JR Palli, they were self-seeking contractors and effective only to the extent of ensuring proper distribution of benefits between the political groups, but not necessarily to the poor and vulnerable people.

Added to this there was 'social nexus' in JR Palli. That was one family, due to its economic and political strength, leading the Congress group. Often, the poor and vulnerable get the spill over benefits, as the endeavour was often to please the politically active groups. Some apolitical households and landless poor in JR Palli stated that watersheds, despite the conflicts, might bring some improvements to their lands and also some employment benefits. That is, there is rationality in politicisation, in that leaders of political factions, in order to consolidate their hold over a group of political supporters, must deliver at least some benefits. Politicisation, however, because it involves appeals to higher levels of political influence, tends to delay the process of implementation.

In TV Puram everything was left to the contractor who was also the WC chairman. This reduces the potential for overt partisan conflict of the sort that could delay implementation. The WC chairman followed the technical guidelines suggested by the PIA and Watershed Development Team (WDT). His interest was in carrying out the works and making profits. One problem was that the quality of works suffered.

In the case of DK Puram works were carried out as per the technical guidelines and often under the supervision of the WC. Even when outside contractors were used (very rare) the quality of works was ensured with the supervision. The WDT was not dominated or controlled by the chairman and hence more participatory (with other WC members and fellow farmers).

In all the three cases, however, the role of the WA was limited to the initial meetings and electing the WC members, chairman and WA president. Often WA president was not aware of the happenings in the watershed, except in the case of JR Palli where he was also village president. There was no preparatory work prior to constituting the bodies in the sample watersheds, as there should have been according to the programme guidelines. Villagers were informed about the Gram Sabha two days prior to the meetings. The general impression obtained through our qualitative research was that officials name the members of the committees, including the president and chairperson. People neither visualise nor understand the connection between PR and watershed bodies. They consider them as separate entities.

Relations between PRIs and Participatory Institutions

In the villages that are politically active, however, a lot of groundwork was necessary for formulating the mutually agreeable WA and WC. Interviews in the sample villages and elsewhere revealed that the prevailing situation across the villages with regard to the relationship between PRIs (democratic bodies) and WAs/WCs (participatory institutions) can be broadly grouped under (a) conflict ridden, (b) competitive checking, (c) political nexus, and (d) passive observation.

Conflict Ridden

Our qualitative research indicated that conflict-ridden villages are almost always torn between two party-affiliated political groups or factions. Development programmes rarely enter into these villages. Even if they enter, they will be forced to withdraw due to persistent conflict. For instance, murders have taken place in some villages in Rayalaseema region in order to gain control of the watershed committees. Initial compromises made by the officials often failed to hold firm; factions are deep-rooted and often stem from within a kin or a lineage group. For instance, in the SR Puram village, two neighbours who were powerful in the village led the two factions. One group became dominant with the 1999 assembly elections where its party (TDP) MLA won. Watershed programme was initiated in the village as a result of the local TDP group leader's contacts with the new MLA. All the positions in WA and WC were given to the associates of the TDP leader, unanimously approved by a hastily called Gram Sabha under the watchful eye of the PIA officials. Within hours of the proceedings, the opposition (Congress) group gathered at the same spot and started shouting slogans and abuses. This resulted in the killing of three people from the Congress group. The case is currently pending in the court.

Similar incident, though not bloody, has brought the programme to a standstill in another village. In a multi-caste and conflict-ridden village (R K Kunta) watershed project was introduced by the district administration by forming the WA and nominating the members and the chairman of the WC. No group protested about the distribution of positions initially, thinking that chairman will not have any financial and administrative role in implementing the watershed programme, as this had been the village's experience with an earlier World Bank-aided watershed development programme. But, as soon as people began to realise that the WC chairman has the financial control over Rs. 2 million, the conflicts started. The opposing groups insisted that unless the appointment of WC chairman was reopened, no watershed works would take place in the village. This turned out to be prophetic. Though we had gathered evidence of the existence of this syndrome in a number of villages, none of our sample villages fall in this category. The research design intentionally avoided these villages, as the objective was to examine the impact of election-induced shifts in party control on project implementation, focusing on cases in which inter-institutional and inter-group relations were relatively harmonious prior to the elections.[8]

Competitive Checking

'Competitive checking' villages are those where political groups work in a competitive situation (competitive politics). The competition was for gaining maximum credit for their developmental activities. In such situations panchayats seek involvement in the day-to-day activities of the watershed committees, especially when leadership of the panchayats and the watershed bodies belong to different parties. The purpose was to check whether benefits are favouring the party followers of the WC chairman. Our broad finding, based on the information from across the range of cases beyond those that form the core sample of this study, was that this takes place more often in the villages where a shift had taken place in the recent elections. Our sample village JR Palli is a good example of such a situation. Congress replaced TDP as the majority group in the village panchayat in the 2001 elections. This replacement appears to be widespread in this region. There were also cases where the tension between two local factions—one in charge of PRI and the other in charge of WC—helped to create some checks and balances which reduced biases/benefit-hogging.

Political Nexus

In this category there exists a nexus between PRIs and watershed management institutions (WA and WC), irrespective of the control over positions by different groups. There were many variations on this theme, but it takes two main forms. It was observed in the case of JR Palli that the Congress group leader's younger brother was nominated to the post of WA president when there was a compromise between the groups in sharing the WA and WC positions. This facilitated the division of spoils (contracts) between the groups even prior to the PR elections. The watershed (contract) works were shared in 50:50 ratios between the two groups. This type of arrangement tends to occur more frequently in 'reserved' (for social groups or women)PR constituencies. Allocation of posts between groups depends on their relative (bargaining) power and information. As we have seen, in many cases, people opted for lower positions, as they do not have perfect information or knowledge.

Another form of nexus or compromise was the sharing of PR and parallel institutions between two groups. A case in point was that of R K Kunta village, which had the experience of watershed development under the World Bank programme. This village was severely divided along caste lines, though both the main castes belong to the backward caste (BC) category. A member from one of the dominant castes was interested in contesting for the post of president in the PRI elections. The village elders convinced him to withdraw from the context by luring him with a promise of some other prominent position in future. The candidate from the Congress group was elected unanimously to the village panchayat. When the village was selected for watershed programme, keeping in view the promise during the election period, the village elders have proposed, for the post of WC chairman, the name of the TDP member, who had foregone the election contest earlier. The election was unanimous in the Gram Sabha.

Another slightly different case was found in K Padu village. This village was led by an economically dominant but a numerically minor (eight out of 200 households) caste group. This group was divided equally between the Congress and the TDP, and consensuses were usually reached to ensure distribution of spoils and the decision-making authority between these groups. When the watershed programme was introduced in the village, the TDP group opted for the WC chairman post. The chairman then nominated all his party people in proportion to their caste strengths as members of the committee. The chairman was a full-time contractor and stays in the district headquarters of Anantapur. His prime interest was making money. The Congress group silently supported and accepted the unanimous selection of the TDP men as WC chairman and members. This was because both party groups had reached an agreement that the Congress group person would be unanimously elected as the village president in the forthcoming elections (in 2001). Since there were no contractor interests in the Congress group, there was no conflict of economic interests. As promised, the Congress man was unanimously elected as panchayat president despite the fact that the village panchayat was in the hands of TDP. In effect, the creation of a parallel body through the watershed programme made it possible to accommodate leaders of both the main party-affiliated factions in the village.

Because of the clear understanding between the groups, which could be charitably characterised as collective action, or disparagingly described as collusion, there was no accountability on either part. In fact, informants revealed that Gram Sabha was held only once, i.e., at the time of formation of WC/WA, and never again after that. PIA officials have simply instructed the WC chairman to regularly obtain signatures from committee members and ordinary villagers in order to create the illusion, on paper, that meetings were conducted regularly every month. Whenever the officials visit the village, they recorded it as a meeting held. No advance intimation is given to the people regarding official visits. It is also reported that these officials come to village merely to supervise the works, as they themselves are the contractors.

The chairman of the WC was illiterate, and has no awareness regarding the watershed guidelines or works in progress. He agreed to whatever the PIA and his associates told him. Some of the villagers have informed that the WC chairman shared money with other prominent members in the village to assure their support in future, particularly in case of any questions or enquiries regarding the watershed works. Chairman himself confessed, though indirectly, that the officials demanded 25 percent commission for sanctioning the bills, which he used to deliver at their residence, while another 10–15 percent commission was used for some other expenses. He further informed that of late he refused to pay the 25 percent to the officials and hence the work progress has slowed down. Such arrangements were often termed as informal convergence between PRIs and parallel institutions.

Sharing of spoils and compromise between groups was possible when there exists equally strong groups. In the absence of a strong opposition the powerful group takes over the situation, especially when their party is in power at higher levels of the political system. In one village, when officials initially introduced the watershed programme in the Gram Sabha, there was a clash between TDP and Congress groups. Given the situation the officials resorted to show of strength (through raising hands). The TDP ended up winning the contest for WC chairman. Later, group as well as caste balance was maintained in WC membership, and the WA presidentship was given to the Congress group. It was reported that the watershed works were going on smoothly without any conflicts between the groups. The main reason appeared to be that the 2001 PRI elections confirmed the electoral strength of the TDP, undercutting any nascent grumbling among the Congress group that their group had more popular support, and therefore should have been awarded the post of the WC chairman.

The preceding discussion indicates that there is blurring of the lines between inter-group conflicts based on economic divisions and those based on political differences. This is due to a significant trend: the tendency either for politicians to turn into contractors or for contractors to turn into politicians. This, in turn, is mainly the result of the financial incentives in the programmes like watershed development and water user associations. Not only the financial flows to these programmes are much higher than the funds available to PRIs, but also the institutional arrangements have facilitated the access to funds to the village people. While this is a good indicator of decentralisation, its misuse appears to be more widespread in the absence of transparency and accountability. As a result, even the powerful and dominant groups at the village level, as observed in one of the villages, prefer the WC chairman position to the position of president in the elected village panchayat. This narrowing of gulf between money and politics at the village level is a reflection of trend at higher levels of the political system. In effect, the means by which watershed programmes have been permitted to operate has assisted this percolation of money politics down to the base of political pyramid.

The ability to secure the conditions under which money can be made from watershed programmes has driven the emergence of compromises between party-affiliated groups in a number of case study villages. The positive side is that the nexus, though not inherently desirable, facilitated the smooth running of the programme in some of the villages. That is, while collusion in sharing of rents is not something generally to be desired, it may be a positive thing to the extent that it creates the necessary (though not sufficient) precondition for pro-poor collective action.[9]

Recent developments indicated that there was also a nexus between the dominant political parties at the higher level. This nexus appears to be more widespread and deep-rooted than imagined. Heavy fund flows into the developmental programmes are the main incentive for bridging the political divisions leading to sharing the rents. For instance, corruption charges levelled against the TDP chairman of the Zilla Parishad (reported in the press) were, surprisingly, denied by majority of Congress opposition members of the Zilla Parishad in an open press conference. This attracted the ire of state-level Congress high command.[10] This kind of cross-party nexus was also noticed even in JR Palli when we discussed this issue with the Mandal Panchayat president. He was not all that opposed to the notorious *janmabhoomi* programme[11] though he belongs to the Congress and *janmabhoomi* is widely criticised for benefiting supporters of the ruling TDP. This particular Congressman was getting 50 percent share in the works allotted at the village and also outside as a result of the opportunities his position provided to act as a break on implementation activities, were he not satisfied with the way in which the projects were being carried out. This form of collusion, however, placed him in conflict with his state-level party, one of the main election planks of which is the abandonment of the *janmabhoomi* programme.

Passive Observation

The final, and perhaps the most common scenario is that of passive observation. Two of our sample villages (TV Puram and DK Puram) represented this situation. PRIs accepted the parallel institutions as another initiative or programme by the government. PRIs are not keen to know about the detailed activities of the watershed development projects, though they were aware of the programme in general. At best PRIs were indifferent to the activities of watershed development. This was mainly due to the nomination process followed in the formation of watershed committees and associations. In majority of the cases officials carry out these nominations. These watershed institutions were treated as temporary bodies established to facilitate the implementation of the watershed programme, whereas PRIs were permanent and more prestigious.

One key reason for the situation of passive observation was the non-existence of contractors within a village (or the existence of one dominant contractor). But other reasons were related to the political equations at the village level. One important difference between these two villages on the one hand, and JR Palli on the other, was the presence of forward caste households in substantial numbers in JR Palli. Often, these social elites were interested in capturing power one way or the other.[12]

In the case of DK Puram TDP was a dominant group, but they lost the previous PR elections to Congress, mainly due to internal dissension. The watershed project had been previously established, with the WA president belonging to the TDP and WC chairman belonging to the Congress. This happened during the tenure of TDP at all levels (village, *mandal* and constituency) when officials distributed the posts between the groups and castes. The TDP group miscalculated the powers of WA president and WC chairman and opted for the former. As a result, village panchayat president and WC chairman turned out to be from the same group in the post-election scenario.

Since there were no contractors from either group in the village, there was little conflict over shares in the construction contracts, and watershed works were carried out smoothly. Observations and discussions with the villagers indicated that the works were carried out systematically in a technically appropriate manner. No favouritism was attributed to the WC chairman, even by the opposition (TDP) group. During the initial visits, it was expressed that there was no conflict between the village panchayat and the WC, not only because their leaders belonged to the same group, but also because the village panchayat president was of the opinion the WC was nominated by the district officials to carrying out watershed works for a period of four years.

But, during March 2003, the WC members complained that the village panchayat president was siphoning the watershed funds to his kith and kin with the help of PIA and other officials.

This was facilitated by the recent changes in the watershed guidelines stipulating that funds would be directly provided to the user groups rather than to the PIA and WC. The village panchayat president had formed some fictitious groups and opened bank accounts in the name of his family members or relatives or close associates as heads of the user groups without informing the WC. Officials have supported him in order to gain a share in the spoils, and because the village panchayat president has also political support at mandal and constituency levels. The TDP group within the village was yet to react to the situation. One reason was that they might need the village panchayat president's support in future, even after the completion of the watershed. This case emphasises the point made earlier that economic interests cut across party lines.

TV Puram, on the other hand, is characterised by the dominance of a single contractor. Though there was a power shift from the Congress to the TDP in the 2001 PR elections, the groups were not active and the conflicts, if any, were limited to the election time. The contractor (who belonged to the TDP) had already managed to benefit from the watershed project prior to the elections. The village panchayat was reserved for SCs during the previous tenure. The SC president was not active, adding to the passive political situation in the village. The contractor, using his political connections and financial muscle-power, got himself nominated to the WC chairman's post and acquired all the other positions (including the WA presidency) filled up with people from his group. Taking advantage of passive situation in the village, the officials did not perform any balancing act (which was the normal practice) in nominating the members to WC or the WA.

During the PR elections, the contractor-cum-WC chairman's candidate was elected as village panchayat president. Interesting point here was that contractor did not venture into politics despite the fact that he could easily have won, as he did not have interest in politics. Perhaps, he was getting the double advantage of getting the benefits of power without identifying himself closely with either party that he could not exert influence higher up the political pyramid were the Congress to take power in the state. As things stand, the contractor carries out all the works in the village, whether these involve watershed projects, *Janmabhoomi*, *Jawhar Rojgar*, and so forth. He has cordial relations with the PIA and officials,[13] with whom he is most likely sharing the spoils.

The passive nature can also be viewed in terms of indifference. People are indifferent to the programme due to the non-participatory approach in this generally docile community. This dimension is observed in K Padu village.[14] Watershed committee and association were composed of all the castes. Villagers have attended the meeting only once, i.e., at the time of formation of committees. Though officials, PIA and team leaders often visit their village, no meetings were conducted. There was no participation of farmers in taking up or prioritising the works. It is reported that there is a mismatch between the requirement and the provisions in the guidelines. Officials and WC are reluctant to be flexible in order to fulfil the people's demands, especially the marginalised sections. Machinery was widely used for the watershed works, depriving the villagers of wage employment.

The chairman of the WC lives in Anantapur town. He visits the village only on Sundays to look after the watershed works, to lend and collect money, and to settle matters related to his personal agricultural works. Though there were political groups in the village, they were active only during the election period.[15] The WC chairman and WA president were close relatives. SCs and labour groups were given due importance only during the election time and never after that. The WA president has informed that neither the WC chairman nor the officials were working in association with the farmers. Neither the villagers nor the president knew anything about the physical or financial details related to watershed. He attended a meeting of watershed at the time of formation of WC and WA, after that he was never called for any such meeting. This was mainly due to lack of awareness among the people. Though sufficient money and time were earmarked for this purpose, the PIAs have neither time nor personnel and inclination to carry out the process in a systematic fashion.

To recapitulate, collective action potential at the village level depends on socio-economic-political structure of the community. A combination of these factors, rather than individual factors, helps explain the divergent outcomes found throughout. When political conflict (on party/factional lines, or on the basis of caste or personality clashes) was particularly acute, the result was the absence of collective action on project works. These conflict-ridden situations were relatively rare, however, as PIAs have strong incentives to avoid locations characterised by severe conflict. There was another large category of cases in which 'passive observation' was found. Here awareness was lacking and project norms were easily flouted.

But a large bulk of the cases were characterised by the two middle scenarios—either' competitive checking' or one or another form of 'nexus'. The domination of political groups by key representatives of economic (contractor) interests often resulted in a form of collusive collective action in order to protect the rents to be obtained through smooth functioning of the project. Other forms of collective action, however, were more benign, representing less egregious theft of public resources, and in effect shading towards the 'competitive checking category'. The latter sort of situations, while relatively rare, appeared likely to be found more often in contexts in which competition between contractors coincides with acute electoral contestation. The situations reflecting the collusive form of nexus appeared to be on the rise. This was mainly due to the availability of sizeable funds coupled with the increasing overlap between economic and political power.

Politics of Participatory Institutions

The promotion of parallel institutions was politically motivated. That is, these parallel institutions were not only created (nominated) by the bureaucrats but also dominated by the social elites and rich in the villages, whereas majority of the PRIs are occupied by the socially disadvantaged people due to the reservations. There still exists an invisible wall between the village elite and other communities, more so in the backward regions.

As per the reservation policy seats in PRIs are reserved as per the following quota system: Scheduled Castes: 15 percent; Scheduled Tribes: 7.5 percent; Backward Castes: 33 percent; Women: 33 percent; and the remaining 11.5 percent of the seats are left for other castes (forward castes) males. Within women's category same reservation policy is followed, i.e., 55.5 percent of the 33 percent are reserved for SCs, STs and BCs. This leaves out less than 30 percent of the seats (including women) for the forward (elite) classes.

This situation is a big drawback for these communities who previously held a majority of seats in the PRIs. The 'opportunity vacuum' created by the reservation policy seems to have been

Table 9.4 *Number of Families Involved in the Watershed (Social Status-wise), 1998–99*

Category	*Total Families*		*President*		*Chairman*	
Scheduled Castes	217290	(19.1)	123	(6.3)	128	(6.8)
Scheduled Tribes	126652	(11.1)	209	(10.7)	160	(8.5)
Backward Castes	454817	(39.9)	626	(32.0)	608	(32.2)
Others (Forward Castes)	340411	(29.9)	996	(51.0)	992	(52.5)
Total Families	1139170	(100.)	1954	(100.)	1888	(100.)

Note: Figures in parentheses are respective percentages.
Source: Status Report, 1998, Department of Rural Development, Government of Andhra Pradesh, Hyderabad.

Table 9.5 *Number of Families Involved in the Watershed (Land Class-wise), 1998–99*

Category	*Total Families*	*President*	*Chairman*
Large Farmers	141249 (12.4)	420 (21.5)	474 (25.1)
Small Farmers	402373 (35.3)	682 (34.9)	652 (34.5)
Marginal Farmers	330643 (29.0)	410 (21.0)	390 (20.7)
Landless	264905 (23.3)	442 (22.6)	372 (19.7)
Total Families	1139170 (100.)	1954 (100.)	1888 (100.)

Note: Figures in parentheses are respective percentages.
Source: Status Report, 1998, Department of Rural Development, Government of Andhra Pradesh, Hyderabad.

filled by the parallel bodies like watershed committees or associations. The positions of president (watershed association) and chairman (watershed committee) are disproportionately held by forward castes. On the other hand, all the other communities are underrepresented (Table 9.4). This is true even in the case of economic classes (Table 9.5). This dimension is clearly reflected in our sample villages too (Tables 9.6 and 9.7).

There are arguments in favour as well as against the parallel institutions. The main argument in favour of the parallel institutions is that user groups or CBOs know their problems better when compared to politically oriented PR bodies. As our analysis clearly brought out that there is no evidence to say that these parallel institutions (WC / WA in our case) are apolitical.[16] In fact, they are equally politicised. Nominations are often made on political or group basis. Further, these bodies often form nexus with political functionaries in PRIs or at higher levels of political system. As the data clearly indicates (Tables 8.4 and 8.5), parallel institutions are used to by pass the PRIs in order to strengthen the cadre base of the party in power.[17] Empowering the PRIs with substantial funds could go against the state-level ruling party's interests by providing opportunities for political patronage to the opposition groups.

Table 9.6 *Composition of the Watershed Association*

Village	No.	% members belonging to									
		Women	*SC/ ST*	*BC*	*OC*	*LL*	*MF*	*SF*	*Md.F*	*LF*	*TDP/ Cong.*
TV Puram	9	—	—	100*	—	11	—	22	67*	—	78*/22
DK Puram	9	—	11	78*	11	—	45	11	—	44*	56*/44
JR Palli	8	25	38	50*	12	25	13	—	12	50*	25/75*

Note: * Indicate the category of the president of the watershed association.
LL = Landless; MF = Marginal Farmers; SF = Small Farmers; Md.F = Medium Farmers; LF = Large Farnmers

Table 9.7 *Composition of the Watershed Committee*

Village	No.	% members belonging to									
		Women	*SC/ST*	*BC*	*OC*	*LL*	*MF*	*SF*	*Md.F*	*LF*	*TDP/Cong.*
TV Puram	11	09	18	73*	—	09	—	18	64*	09	82*/18
DK Puram	12	25	17	75	08*	—	17	33	08	08*	50/50*
JR Palli	09	11	11	33	56*	11	11	11	—	67*	56/44*

Note: Same as in Table 9.6. * Indicate the category of the chairman of the watershed committee.

This type of subversion is not new to Indian polity.[18] Maharashtra has long bypassed the PRIs and used the administrative route to implement the massive employment guarantee scheme (EGS) in 1980s precisely for the same reason. On the other hand, West Bengal used the PRIs to strengthen the CPI-M's cadre, despite the fact the local bodies were in the hands of the opposition (Congress Party). Schemes, such as National Rural Employment Programme (NREP), are in theory designed to strengthen the marginalised sections and nullify the elite dominance in the PRIs. It may be noted that the AP government was far more hostile to PRIs than any state government in recent times. It systematically diverted funds from the PRIs to user committees and *janmabhoomi* programme because the ruling party could control them far more effectively than it could control PRIs. Interestingly, the AP model has taken a middle path of short-circuiting constitutionally supported structures in order to strengthen the cadre base through creating parallel institutions. This has helped in creating space for meso and micro level politicians in terms of power as well as rents. The political agenda is being pushed in the name of development.

The scale of the programme supports the argument of widespread strengthening of party cadre. No other state has implemented the programme on this scale, as the nature of the programme requires intensive, rather than extensive, approach. In the absence of any controlling and monitoring systems the watershed programmes have become the support systems for the local contractors. As observed in our case studies, contractors prefer WC chairman position to the PRI president position. In the process this programme might end up creating an army of village contractors.

The main problem is that there was no accountability on the part of PIA and WC to any statutory body at the sub-district level. PIA or the WC was not answerable to PRIs at the village or *mandal* levels; they were answerable to the District Rural development Agency (DRDA)[19] at the district level. At the village level, nobody has the statutory right to question the quality of works, distribution of benefits, etc. This happened in practice only when there is active involvement of political groups within the villages. Even this could be surpassed usually when the local faction leader can bring pressure to bear by means of contracts with influential political leaders higher up the political pyramid. There was no transparency in terms of works and money spent unless the PIA and the WC wish to reveal the relevant documentation. More importantly, in the absence of any linkages between the permanent village panchayat and WC and WA, the follow up to the programme was weak. Since the programme is time-bound (lasting no more that four to five years), the PIA automatically withdraws from the village after completing the implementation and WC was also dissolved.

The WA was expected to take the responsibility (as per the guidelines) of sustaining the programme in terms of maintaining the structures, etc. During the implementation of the programme watershed development fund from user contribution was created. The fund size varied from village to village, depending on the contributions. Even, in the best cases—these funds were sufficient for short periods only. The WA was expected to devise methods systems to maintain the fund in order to sustain the programme in the long run. But, given the limited role during the implementation period, the WA was neither interested nor aware of any responsibilities after the completion of the project. The universal response we got from the villagers to our question on the follow-up action was that they "do not have any idea whatsoever".[20] Therefore, the institutional structure or *modus operandi* did not ensure follow up or sustainability of the programme. In this regard, the 1994-95 watershed guidelines were clear in saying that the responsibility of implementing the programme should be shifted to PRIs once the 73rd constitutional amendment comes into effect.

Our field observations clearly brought out that parallel institutions created for watershed development programme were not apolitical. Besides, evidence indicated that they were not above falling prey to the contractor-politician-official nexus. On the contrary, they have become breeding grounds for the proliferation of contractors—as politicians, local project managers (in their role, in some case, as WC) and often as heads of NGO-managed PIAs. Based on our evidence, and given the nature of the programme, we argue that there is a clear need for integrating watershed development programme with PRIs.[21] Given their constitutional validity, PRIs are more accountable, even granting all of their current shortcomings (elite capture, proxy leaders, official complicity in violation of norms) than the existing parallel bodies. When implemented separately (from PRIs), people often treat the watershed programme as another subsidy programme and restrain from actively questioning the process of implementation. This is more so when line departments are involved in the implementation than when NGOs take on the role of PIA.

The dynamics would be different (though not perfect) if the programme were to be implemented through PRIs. Often opposition groups take active interest in the PRI activities at the village level than in an independent developmental programme. We argue there would be more cases of active than passive participation at the village level if PRIs were in charge of implementation. Moreover, the contractor's role also would be reduced to a large extent due to the active participation of the community, especially in the passive or indifferent types of villages. Though there is a danger that the PR sarpanchas may become contractors, the extent and intensity in rent seeking would be on a lower scale due to the active probing of opposition groups. Moreover, the risk of loosing the next elections might lead to a more moderate level of rent seeking. Bringing development programmes under the PRIs would also ensure some kind of balance in the distribution of benefits, especially to the underprivileged sections, due to the reservations to the PRIs. Our analysis clearly revealed that the elite sections of the rural communities mainly control the parallel watershed institutions in the absence of reservations to these structures.

Haryali Guidelines and PRIs

In order to meet the constitutional obligation of decentralisation through PRI involvement, the watershed guidelines were revised during April 2003 and christened as *Haryali Guidelines*.[22] As per these guidelines village PRIs have replaced the watershed committees (WCs) as project implementing agencies (PIAs). Money is transferred directly to village panchayat from the DRDA or the DWMA (District Water Management Agency) in Andhra Pradesh. Village PRIs implement the watersheds with the help of line departments. The village panchayats have to execute the works, keep the necessary records apart from carrying out the day-to-day watershed activities. NGOs are given the last priority as PIAs in the absence of PRIs or line departments. Another major departure is the reduction in the allocation towards capacity building and community mobilisation from 10 percent to 5 percent.

Though the new guidelines appear to be addressing some of the serious concerns expressed earlier, they were formulated without any consultative process of understanding the ground realities. First of all, it distorted the broad-based user participation by abolishing the WC and user group framework. Second, in the absence of proper capacities, the village PRIs are overburdened with more responsibilities of implementing the watershed management.[23] While capacity building was a major concern, the channels of capacity building, i.e., role of NGOs and fund availability for capacity building are drastically reduced. In fact, it was argued that the PRIs should be capacity-built prior to giving them the responsibility of implementing the watersheds (Reddy et al., 2002). In the process watershed management was taken over by the line departments under the guise of poor PRI capacities. Moreover, the argument was always on how to bring the WC under the purview of PRIs instead of thrusting the PRIs with more responsibilities. The guidelines failed to take into account some of the new initiatives followed by NGOs. For instance, in Karnataka,

PRIs implement the watershed development programmes with the help of sub-committees, while an NGO in Andhra Pradesh (RDT) introduced the village development council (VDC) to oversee the smooth implementation of watershed development programmes (Sivanna and Reddy, 2005). While in the case of Karnataka, the sub-committees are formal institutional entities under the PR system while in AP the VDCs are informal arrangements by an NGO.

Political Economy of Watershed Management

- The analysis of the operation of watershed development programmes in the villages studied indicates clearly that the parallel institutional structures, created specifically to facilitate better delivery by operating in an apolitical manner, have not lived up to their promise. These institutions have not only been political in the broad sense of becoming another site of contestation among organised village factions, they have also become implicated in conflicts between political parties. And intentionally bolstered to enhance the control of the ruling party.
- Rather than simply reflecting existing political divisions, and being captured by powerful interests, the framework of governance through which the watershed programmes are managed, can serve actually to make matters worse. In the majority of the cases, parallel institutions are plagued with political conflicts and dominated by rent-seeking economic interests. Given the magnitude of the resources available in the programme, these institutional arrangements are becoming breeding grounds for village contractors and encouraging the conversion of politicians into contractors and vice versa. Even the officials are working as part-time contractors. All this takes place at the cost of equitable development delivery due to the absence of any transparency and accountability at the village level.

- The relationship between the constitutional and democratic PRIs and the parallel institutions is not formal. But, these are informal relationships. These are determined by the dynamics of power equations at the village level. Conflict situations seem to arise when political interests outweigh economic interests. Nexus or compromise situations arise in the event of economic interests outweigh political interests. Destructive conflict situations are often typically characterised by the combination of social and economic powers, i.e., concentration of economic assets in the hands of socially dominant castes. For, the creation of parallel institutions appears to be a political ploy to bypass or short-circuit the democratic institutions, which are no longer under the control of the socio-economic elite due to the reservation policies.
- A comparative analysis of caste and class composition of the PR and parallel institutions clearly indicates a class bias. While this perfectly reflects the 'political design of development', it clearly thwarts the 'development as an instrument for political gains'. The danger is that these two are seen as mutually exclusive, whereas these should complement each other and go in tandem. For, political gains are increasingly getting associated with development gains, especially in the changing context of poor becoming active in articulating their demands. Serving the class interests alone may not guarantee political gains.
- In order to make the parallel institutions better delivery systems of development, they should be made accountable and transparent at the village level itself. PRIs have the constitutional authority and mandate to oversee the activities of developmental programmes. While it is difficult to provide a blueprint on how to integrate the numerous parallel institutions with PRIs, the present study helps in addressing some of the issues in the context of watershed development.[24] These include:

1. The village level PR body (gram panchayat) should be made the project-implementing agency (PIA) with little change in the existing institutional structure at the village level, i.e., WC would continue and carry out the works. The gram panchayat will receive funds directly from the district-level PR body (Zilla Parishad) and spends through WC. It takes the responsibilities of WA such as monitoring the activities and determine on follow-up actions after the completion of the watershed works, etc. While the village level PRI would be accountable to the *Mandal*-level PRI, the *mandal* level PRI to the district-level PRI.
2. The capacity of the PRIs at all levels should be enhanced in a systematic fashion in order to make them effective PIAs. PRIs and WCs at the village level need training in various aspects of watershed development. While PRIs need administrative and accounting skills, WCs need technical skills. Once these skills are imparted, they would remain at the village level for any future needs.
3. Zilla Parishad should identify selected NGOs, with considerable experience in watershed development and these NGOs should be made nodal agencies at the district level (1 or 2 NGOs in a district) to identify and impart training to other local NGOs and WDTs. These nodal NGOs are accountable to the Zilla Parishad.

Notes

1. The approach of direct democracy is adopted in Madhya Pradesh by making *Gram Sabha* central to planning and implementation (Manor, 2001a).
2. These institutions have gone through three different phases of ascendancy (1956-1966), stagnation (1966-1976) and decadency (1976 till early 1990s). A few states like West Bengal, Karnataka and Andhra Pradesh tried to revive these institutions during the 1980s.

3. The Centre is now contemplating to further amend the Constitution making the devolution mandatory, as the states are not yielding to pressure tactics.
4. It is misconceived notion, as the PRIs were never given a chance in terms of rights and responsibilities. Financial devolution has hardly taken place in most of the states. This amounts to devolution of responsibilities without giving any rights.
5. Government PIAs also try to avoid politics in the project implementation but not effective if not counter productive (Chhotray, 2004).
6. It may be noted that elections to PR body (gram panchayat) at the village level are not contested on party basis. But, each group is affiliated to one party or other in most of the cases.
7. Interestingly, even the MLA of the constituency comprising the three sample villages is from Congress. So up to the constituency level Congress is stronger, though TDP can bring pressure from higher levels, i.e., ZP level or state level.
8. Moreover, conducting intensive research is also a problem in the conflict-ridden villages.
9. Though the extent of benefit flows to poor or non-political groups is doubtful (as observed in JR Palli), it (nexus) certainly facilitates benefit flows, i.e., something is better than nothing.
10. This was reported in a series of articles in *Eenadu*, Anantapur District Addition, May 2002.
11. *Janmabhoomi* is a means devised by the Chief Minister to improve the exposure of government officials and politicians to the problems of rural people through direct exposure in high-profile development 'camps'—rural jamborees in which all manner of development benefits are handed out directly to local people. It has been widely criticised as a populist and rather patronizing means of enhancing the personal popularity of the CM, and of course for deeply undermining local government structures.
12. Even the limited number of socially elite households in these two villages is not economically dominant. Adding economic power to social elite radically changes the power equations.
13. This we observed even during our visits. Whenever we went to the PIA, he was present there, either by chance or voluntarily.
14. The indifferent nature is widespread across the villages.

15. Here also the chairman is all-powerful and a contractor too.
16. It is a myth and naïve to say that CBOs are above politics. Politics is pervasive.
17. This is also viewed as an attempt of the ruling party to incorporate different sections of the society and carving new constituencies for its liberalisation reforms (Reddy, 2002).
18. For an interesting comparative study, see Echeverri-Gent (1992).
19. Now, this is changed to District Water Management Agency (DWMA).
20. This is true even in some of the best NGO-implemented watersheds (Reddy et al., 2004).
21. We are restraining from commenting on the possibilities of integrating PRIs with other parallel institutions, as the parallel institutions are different from one another and need different approaches. This is beyond the scope of the present study.
22. The guidelines were modified earlier during 2001 but only marginally in terms increasing the duration from 4 to 5 years and allocation from Rs. 4,000 to Rs. 6,000 per acre.
23. It is reported in the case of Gujarat, the uptake of central money under the watershed development programme has come down drastically after the Haryali Guidelines, as the PRIs are not in a position to implement (personal communication with Prof. Y.K. Alagh). On the other hand, extreme line departments have become all-powerful in the absence of PRI capacity and NGO involvement in the states like AP.
24. We are only providing the indicative guidelines though more details need to be worked out in a systematic manner.

References

Agrawal, A. (1994), "Rules, Rule Making and Rule Breaking: Examining the Fit between the Rule Systems and Resource Use", in Elinor Ostrom, R. Gardener and J. Walker (eds.), *Rules, Games and Common-Pool Resources*, 267–82, University of Michigan Press, Ann Arbor.

Agrawal, B. (2001), "Participatory Exclusions, Community Forestry and Gender: An Analysis of South Asia and a Conceptual Framework", *World Development*, 29(10): 1623–48.

Baland, J.M and J.P. Platteau (1996), *Halting Degradation of Natural Resources: Is there a Role for Rural Communities?*, Clarendon Press, Oxford.

Bandhyopadhyay, D., B.N. Yugandhar and Amitava Mukharjee (2002), "Convergence of Programmes by Empowering SHGs and PRIs", *Economic and Political Weekly*, Vol. 37, No. 26, 29 June.

Bardhan, Pranab, (2002), "Decentralisation of Governance and Development", *Journal of Economic Perspectives*, Vol. 16, No. 4, Fall: 185–205.

——, (1996), "Decentralized Development", *Indian Economic Review*, 31(2). 139–156.

——, (1995a), "Analytics of the Institution of Informal Cooperation in Rural Development", in De Janvry et al. (eds.).

——, (1995), "Rational Fools and Cooperation in a Poor Hydraulic Economy", in Basu, Pattanaik and K. Suzumura (eds.).

——, (1989a), "Alternative Approaches to the Theory of Institutions in Economic Development", in Pranab Bardhan (ed.), *The Economic Theory of Agrarian Institutions*, Clarendon Press, Oxford.

——, (ed.) (1989), *The Economic Theory of Agrarian Institutions*, Clarendon Press, Oxford.

Bardhan, Pranab and Dilip Mookherjee, (2000), "Decentralizing Anti-Poverty Program Delivery in Developing Countries", University of California, Berkeley.

——, (2000a), "Capture and Governance at Local and National Levels", *American Economic Review* (Papers and Proceedings), 90(2): 135–139.

Basu, Kaushik (ed.) (1994), *Agrarian Questions*, Oxford University Press, New Delhi.

Basu, P. Pattanaik and K. Suzumura (eds.) (1995), *Choice, Welfare and Development: A Festchrift in Honour of Amartya K. Sen*, Clarendon Press, Oxford.

Bates, Robert H. (1989), *Beyond the Miracle of the Market: The Political Economy of Agrarian Development in Kenya*, Cambridge University Press, Cambridge.

——, (1995), "Social Dilemmas and Rational Individuals: An Assessment of the New Institutionalism", in Harriss, Hunter and Lewis (eds.).

Baumann, P. (2000), "Sustainable Livelihoods and Political Capital: Arguments and Evidence from Decentralisation and Natural Resource Management in India", Working Paper 136, Overseas Development Institute, London.

Beaumont, P.M. and R.T. Walker (1996), "Land Degradation and Property Regimes", *Ecological Economics*, Vol. 18.

Bekele, A. Shiferaw, Tewodros A., Kebede, and V. Ratna Reddy (2008), "Community Watershed Management in Semi-arid India: The State of Collective Action and Its Effects on Natural Resources and Rural Livelihoods" in Esther Mwangi, Helen Markelova and Ruth Meinzen-Dick (eds.) Collective Action and Property Rights for Poverty Reduction: Lessons from a Global Research Project. CAPRi; Working Paper, p 85.

Bell, Clive (1990), "Reforming Property Rights in Land and Tenancy", *The World Bank Research Observer*, Vol. 5, No. 2, July.

Berkes, F. and M.T. Farvar (1988), "Introduction and Overview", in F. Berkes (ed.), *Common Property Resources*, Belhaven Press, London.

Berkes, Fikret (ed.) (1989), *Common Property Resources: Ecology and Community-Based Sustainable Development*, Belhaven Press, London.

Binswanger, H. (1991), "Brazilian Policies that Encourage Deforestation in the Amazon", *World Development*, Vol. 19, No. 7, July.

Birner, R. (2004), Actors, Institutional Change and Poverty Reduction (5th Session), E-conference organised by CAPRi on Poverty, Property Rights and Collective Action (CAPRi-talk).

Bromley, D.W. (1982), "Land and Water Problems: An Institutional Perspective", *American Journal of Agricultural Economics*, Vol. 64, No. 5, December.

——, (1989), "Property Relations and Economic Development: The Other Land Reform", *World Development*, Vol. 17, No. 6.

——, (1989a), *Economic Interests and Institutions: The Conceptual Foundations of Public Policy*, Basil Blackwell, New York.

——, (1992a), "The Commons, Common Property and Environmental Policy", *Environmental and Resource Economics*, Vol. 2.

——, (1993), "Reconstituting Economic Systems: Institutions in National Economic Development", *Development Policy Review*, Vol. 11.

——, (2004), Actors, Institutional Change and Poverty Reduction (5th Session), E-conference organised by CAPRi on Poverty, Property Rights and Collective Action (CAPRi-talk).

—— (2004), Conceptions of Poverty and the Contributions of Property Rights and Collective Action to Poverty Reduction, E-conference organised by CAPRi on Poverty, Property Rights and Collective Action (CAPRi-talk).

——, (ed.) (1992), *Making the Commons Work: Theory, Practice and Policy*, ICS Press, Institute for Contemporary Studies, California.

Cain, M. and G. McNicoll (1988), "Population Growth and Agrarian Outcomes", in R. Lee et al. (eds.), *Population, Food and Rural Development*, Clarendon Press, Oxford.

Carney, D. (1999), "Approaches to Sustainable Livelihoods", Overseas Development Institute, London.

——, (ed.) (1998), *Sustainable Rural Livelihoods*, Department of International Development (CDHD), London.

Carney, D., M. Drinkwater, T. Rusinow, K. Neefjes, S. Wanamali and N. Singh (1999), "Livelihood Approaches Compared: A Brief Comparison of the Livelihoods Approaches of DFID, CARE, Oxfam, and UNDP", Department of International Development, DFID, London.

Chambers, R. and G. Conway (1992), "Sustainable Rural Livelihoods: Practical Concepts for the 21st Century", IDS Discussion Paper 276, Institute of Development Studies, University of Sussex.

Chatterjee, P.C. (1993), "Status of Ground Water in Rajasthan: Retrospect and Prospect", Research Report No. RR/93-94/59, Institute of Development Studies, Jaipur.

Chhotray, Vasudha (2004), "The Negation of Politics in Participatory Development Projects, Kurnool, Andhra Pradesh", *Development and Change*, Vol. 35, No. 2, April.

Chopra, K. (2002), "Watershed Management Programmes: An Evaluation of Alternative Institutional and Technological Options", in *Principles and Practices of Integrated Watershed Management in India*, W/M Publishing, New Delhi.

Chopra, K., G.K. Kadekodi and M.N. Murthy (1989), *Participatory Development: People and Common Property Resources*, Sage Publications, New Delhi.

Chopra, Kanchan and Gopal K. Kadekodi (1993), "Watershed Development: A Contrast with NREP/JRY", *Economic and Political Weekly*, June 26.

Ciriacy-Wantrup, S.V. and R.C. Bishop (1975), "Common Property as a Concept in Natural Resources Policy", *Natural Resources Journal*, Vol. 15.

Coase, R.H. (1937), "The Nature of the Firms", *Economica*, Vol. 4, November, reprinted in R.H. Coase (1988), *The Firm, the Market and the Law*, The University of Chicago Press, Chicago and London.

Cohen, J.M. and N.T. Uphoff, (1980), "Participation's Place in Rural Development: Seeking Clarity through Specificity", *World Development*, 8(3), 213–235.

Colfer, C. (2004), Conceptions of Poverty and the Contributions of Property Rights and Collective Action to Poverty Reduction (Overview of Concepts), (1st Session), E-conference organised by CAPRi on Poverty, Property Rights and Collective Action (CAPRi-talk).

D'silva, Emmanuel and Sudha Pai (2003), "Social Capital and Collective Action: Development Outcomes in Forest Protection and Watershed Development", *Economic and Political Weekly*, April 5.

Dasgupta, Partha (1996), "The Economics of the Environment", *Environment and Development Economics*, Vol. 1, Part 4, October.

Davies, S. (1996), *Adaptable Livelihoods*, Macmillan, London.

de Janvry, Alain (1993), "State, Market and Civil Organisations: New Theories, New Practices and their Implications for Rural Development", *World Development*, Vol. 21, No. 4, April.

——, S. Radwan, E. Sadoulet and E. Thorbecke (1995), *State, Market and Civil Organizations: New Theories, New Practices and their Implications for Rural Development*, International Labour Organisation, Geneva.

Deshpande, R.S. (1997), "Impact of Watershed Development Programme: Experiences and Issues", *Arthavijnana*, Vol. 39, No. 3, September, 315–414.

—— and A. Narayanmoorthy (1998), "An Appraisal of Watershed Development Programmes, Across Regions in India", *Arthavijnana*, XII(4), December.

——, M.J. Bhende and S. Erappa (2003), "Output and Impact Monitoring: Study of KAWAD Project", ADRT, ISEC, Bangalore.

—— and S.R. Nikumbh, (1993), "Treatment of Uncultivated Land under Watershed Development Approach: Institutional and Economic Aspects", *Arthavijnana*, Vol. 35, No. 1, March 1–21.

—— and N. Rajasekhar (1995), "Impact of National Watershed Development Project for Rainfed Areas (NWDPRA) in Maharastra", *AERC*, Gokhale Institute of Politics and Economics, Pune.

—— and V. Ratna Reddy (1990), "Social Dynamics and Farmer's Society: A Case Study of Pani-Panchayat", *Indian Journal of Agricultural Economics*, Vol. 45, No. 3, July–September.

——, (1991), "Watershed Development Approach in Fragile Resource Regions: An Analytical Study of Maharashtra", Mimeograph Series No. 33, Gokhale Institute of Politics and Economics, Pune.

——, (1991), "Differential Impact of Watershed Based Technology: Some Analytical Issues", *Indian Journal of Agricultural Economics*, 46(3): 261–269.

Di Gregorio, M. (2004), Conceptions of Poverty and the Contributions of Property Rights and Collective Action to Poverty Reduction (Overview of Concepts), (1st Session), E-conference organised by CAPRi on Poverty, Property Rights and Collective Action (CAPRi-talk).

Dietrich, M. (1994), *Transaction Costs and Beyond: Towards a New Economics of the Firm*, Routledge, London.

Dixon, J.A. (1992), "Analysis and Management of Watersheds", in Partha Dasgupta and Karl-Goran Maler (eds.), *The Environment and Emerging Development Issues*, Vol. 2, Clarendon Press, Oxford.

Echeverri-Gent, John (1992), "Politics of Development and the Development of Politics: An Enquiry into the Political Means of Equitable Development", *Contemporary South Asia*, 1(3), 325–349.

Eggertsson, T. (1990), *Economic Behaviour and Institutions*, Cambridge University Press, Cambridge.

——, (1994), "The Economics of Institutions in Transition Economies", in Salvatore Schiavo-Campo (ed.), *Institutional Change and the Public Sector in Transitional Economies*, World Bank Discussion Papers, 241.

Ellis, Frank (2000), *Livelihoods and Diversity in Developing Countries*, Oxford University Press, London.

Fakir, S. (2004), Conceptions of Poverty and the Contributions of Property Rights and Collective Action to Poverty Reduction (Overview of Concepts), (1st Session), E-conference organised by CAPRi on Poverty, Property Rights and Collective Action (CAPRi-talk).

Fan S. and P. Hazell (2000), "Should Developing Countries Invest More in Less Favoured Areas? An Empirical Analysis of Rural India", *Economic and Political Weekly*, 35(17): 1455–64.

Farrington, J. and C. Lobo (1997), "Scaling up Participatory Watershed Management in India: Lessons from Indo-German Watershed Development Programme", *Natural Resource Perspective* 17, Overseas Development Institute, London.

——, C. Turton and A.J. James (eds.) (1999), *Participatory Watershed Development: Challenges for the Twenty-first Century*, Oxford University Press, New Delhi.

Feeny, David (1979), "Competing Hypothesis of Underdevelopment: A Thai Case Study", *Journal of Economic History*, Vol. 39, No. 1, March.

——, (1993), "The Demand for and Supply of Institutional Arrangements", in V. Ostrom, David Feeny and H. Picht (eds.).

Furubotn, Eirik G. and R. Richter (1991), *The New Institutional Economics: A Collection of Articles from the Journal of Institutional and Theoretical Economics* (ed.), J.C.B. Mohr (Paul Siebeck), Tübingen.

Gans, Oskar (1989), "Economic Analysis of Ecological Disequilibria in Industrialized and Developing Countries", in Gans Oskar (ed.), *Environmental and Institutional Development: Aspects of Economic and Agricultural Policies in Developing Countries*, Verlag Breitenbach Publishers, Saarbrüken.

GoAP (1999), Andhra Pradesh Rural Livelihoods Projects, Commissioner of Rural Development, Hyderabad.

GoAP (2001), Watershed Development Programme, Government of Andhra Pradesh, Hyderabad (http://www.andhrapradesh.com/apwebsite/programs/watershed_dev.html)

GoAP (2002), Process Guidelines for Watershed Development Programme, Commissioner, Rural Development, Hyderabad.

GoI (1992), Report of the Committee on Pricing of Irrigation Water, Planning Commission, New Delhi, September.

GoI (1994), Guidelines for Watershed Development, Ministry of Rural Development, New Delhi, October.

GoI (1998), On Watershed Approach for Managing Degraded Lands in India: Challenges for the 21st Century, Ministry of Rural Development, Delhi.

GoI (2000), "Mid-Term Appraisal of the Ninth Plan (1997–2002)", Chapter 10, Planning Commission, Government of India, New Delhi, October.

GoI (2001), Approach Paper to the Tenth Five-Year Plan (2002–07), Planning Commission, New Delhi, September.

GoI (2003), Watershed Guidelines (Hariyali), Ministry of Rural Development, New Delhi.

GoI (2006), From Haryali to Neeranchal: Report of the Technical Committee on Watershed Programmes in India, Department of Land Resources, Ministry of Rural Development, Government of India, January.

GoI (2007), Common Guidelines for Watershed Development Projects, Department of Land Resources, Ministry of Rural Development, February.

Goud, Vinod (2005), "Institutionalising Participatory Approaches in Integrated Watershed Management Programme of Andhra Pradesh: A Case Study of Chittoor District", Unpublished Ph.D. Thesis, Dr. B.R. Ambedkar Open University, Hyderabad.

Grabowski, Richard (1988), "The Theory of Induced Institutional Innovation: A Critique", *World Development*, Vol. 16, No. 3, March.

Guha, R. (1985), "Scientific Forestry and Social Change in Uttarakhand", *Economic and Political Weekly*, Vol. 20, Special Number, November.

——, (1989), *The Unquiet Woods: Ecological Change and Peasant Resistance in the Himalayas*, Oxford University Press, New Delhi.

Hanna, S. (1996), "Designing Institutions for the Environment", *Environment and Development Economics*, 1(1), February, 122–125.

Hardin, Garrett (1968), "The Tragedy of Commons", *Science*, Vol. 162, December.

Harold, Demsetz (1967), "Toward a Theory of Property Rights", *The American Economic Review*, 57, 2.

Harris, John (2003), *Depoliticising Development: The World Bank and Social Capital*, Left World Books, New Delhi.

——, J. Hunter and C.M. Lewis (eds.) (1995), *The New Institutional Economics and Third World Development*, Routledge, London.

Heckathorn, D.D. (1993), "Collective Action and Group Heterogeneity: Voluntary Provision versus Selective Incentives", *American Sociological Review*, 58(3): 329–350.

Hope, Rob (2006), "Low Base Flows and Livelihoods in India: Evaluation of Social Impacts of Water Shed Development Using a Propensity Score Matching Method: An Application to Dudhi Watershed", Madhya Pradesh, Internal Report VII, Winrock International, India: Centre for Land Use and Water Resources Research (CLUWRA), University of New Castle and IIT, Delhi, August.

Husain, Z. (2004), Conceptions of Poverty and the Contributions of Property Rights and Collective Action to Poverty Reduction (Overview of Concepts), (1st Session), E-conference organised by CAPRi on Poverty, Property Rights and Collective Action (CAPRi-talk).

Jodha, N.S. (1985), "Population Growth and Decline in Common Property Resources in Rajasthan, India", *Population and Development Review*, Vol. 11, No. 2, June.

——, (1986), "Common Property Resources and the Rural Poor", *Economic and Political Weekly*, Vol. 21, No. 27, p. 1169.

——, (1995), "Common Property Resources and the Environmental Context: Role of Bio-physical versus Social Stresses", *Economic and Political Weekly*, Vol. 30, No. 5, p. 3278

Johnson, Craig, Priya Deshingkar and Daniel Start (2005), "Grounding the State: Devolution and Development in India's Panchayats", *Journal of Development Studies*, Vol. 41, No. 6, August.

Joshi, Deep and David Seckler (1981), "Economics and Management of Rain Water Harvesting Project", *Indian Journal of Soil Conservation*, Vol. 9, No. 2.

Joshi, P.K., A.K. Jha, S.P. Wani, L. Joshi and R.L. Shiyani (2005), "Meta-Analysis to Assess Impact of Watershed Programme and People's Participation", Comprehensive Assessment Research Report No. 8, International Crops Research Institute for the Semi-Arid Tropics (ICRISAT), Patancheru, Andhra Pradesh.

Joy, K.J. and Suhas Paranjape (2003), "Watershed Development Review: Issues and Prospects", CISED, ISEC, Bangalore.

Kariuki, A.G. (2004), Conceptions of Poverty and the Contributions of Property Rights and Collective Action to Poverty Reduction (Overview of Concepts), (1st Session), E-conference organised by CAPRi on Poverty, Property Rights and Collective Action (CAPRi-talk).

Kerr, John (2002), "Watershed Development, Environmental Services and Poverty Alleviation in India", *World Development*, Vol. 30, No. 8, August.

Kerr, J., G. Pangare, V.L. Pangare and P.J. George (2000), "An Evaluation of Dry Land Watershed Development Projects in India". EPTD Discussion Paper No. 68, International Food Policy Research Institute, Washington DC,137.

——, and V. Pangare (2002), "Watershed Development Projects in India", IFPRI Research Report No. 127, Washington DC.

Kikuchi, M., G. Dozina Jr. and Y. Hayami (1978), "Economics of Community Work Programmes: A Communal Irrigation Project in the Philippines", *Economic Development and Cultural Change*, Vol. 26, No. 2, January.

Kirsch, O.C. et al. (1984), *Self-Help Institutions in Developing Countries: Cooperation involving Autonomous Primary Groups*, Verlag Breitenbach Publishers, Saarbrucken.

Knox, A. (2004). Actors, Institutional Change and Poverty Reduction; (5th Session), E-conference organised by CAPRi on Poverty, Property Rights and Collective Action (CAPRi-talk).

——, Brent Swallow and Nancy Johnson (2001), Conceptual and Methodological Lessons for Improving Watershed Management and Research, CGiAR Systemwide Programme on Collective Action and Property Rights (CAPRi), Policy Brief No. 3, February.

Knudsen, C. (1993), "Modeling Rationality, Institutions and Processes in Economic Theory", in U. Mäki, B. Gustafsson and C. Knudsen (eds.).

Kötter, Herbert (1988), "Institutions and Organisations in Rural Development", *Quarterly Journal of International Agriculture*, Vol. 27.

Lam, W.F. (1996), "Institutional Design of Public Agencies and Co-production: A Study of Irrigation Associations in Taiwan", *World Development*, Vol. 24, No. 6, June.

Larson, B.A. and D.W. Bromley (1990), "Property Rights, Externalities and Resource Degradation: Locating the Tragedy", *Journal of Development Economics*, Vol. 33, October.

Lele, S.N. and R.K. Patil (1994), *Farmer Participation in Irrigation Management: A Case Study of Maharastra*, Horizon India Books, New Delhi.

Libecap, Gary D. (2002), “A Transactions-Costs Approach to the Analysis of Property Rights”, in Eric Brousswau and Jean-Michel Glachant (eds.), *The Economics of Contracts: Theory and Applications*, Cambridge University Press, Cambridge.

Mäki, U., Bo Gustafsson and Christian Knudsen (eds.) (1993), *Rationality, Institutions and “Economic Methodology”*, Routledge, London.

Manor, James (1999), “The Political Economy Democratic Decentralisation”, The World Bank, Washington DC.

——, (2000), “Democratic Decentralisation in Two Indian States: Past and Present”, Unpublished Mimeo, Livelihood Options Project, Overseas Development Institute (ODI), UK.

——, (2001), “User Committees: A Potentially Damaging Second Wave of Decentralisation”, Mimeo, Institute of Development Studies, University of Sussex.

——, (2001a), “Madhya Pradesh Experiments with Direct Democracy”, *Economic and Political Weekly*, Vol. 36, 3rd March.

Marshall, Gordon (1998), *A Dictionary of Sociology*, Oxford University Press, New York.

Meinzen-Dick, R. (2004), Conceptions of Poverty and the Contributions of Property Rights and Collective Action to Poverty Reduction (Overview of Concepts), (1st Session), E-conference organised by CAPRi on Poverty, Property Rights and Collective Action (CAPRi-talk).

, et al (1994), “Sustainable Water User Associations: Lessons from a Literature Review”, paper presented at World Bank Water Resources Seminar, Lansdowne, Virginia, December.

Morrow, C.E. and R. Watts Hull (1996), “Donor-Initiated Common Pool Resource Institutions: The Case of the Yanesha Forest Cooperative”, *World Development*, Vol. 24, No. 10, October.

Morton, J.F. (1996), “Land Resources in Dafur Region, Sudan: Prisoners’ Dilemma or Coase Outcome?” *Journal of Development Studies*, Vol. 33, No. 1, October.

Mwangi, E.N. (2004), Conceptions of Poverty and the Contributions of Property Rights and Collective Action to Poverty Reduction (Overview of Concepts), (1st Session), E-conference organised by CAPRi on Poverty, Property Rights and Collective Action (CAPRi-talk).

Nabli, Mustapha K. and J.B. Nugent (eds.) (1989), *The New Institutional Economics and Development: Theory and Application to Tunisia*, North-Holland, Amsterdam.

Nadkarni, M.V. with S.A. Pasha and L.S. Prabhakar (1989), *Political Economy of Forest Use and Management*, Sage Publications Ltd., New Delhi.

North, Douglass C. (1990), *Institutions, Institutional Change and Economic Performance*, Cambridge University Press, Cambridge.

——, (1995), "The New Institutional Economics and Third World Development", in Harriss, Hunter and Lewis (eds.).

Oakerson, R.J. (1992), "Analysing the Commons: A Framework", in Bromley (ed.) (1992).

Oliver, Springate- Bigenski et al. (2001), "Watershed Development in Andhra Pradesh: A Policy Review", Working Paper 5, Livelihood Policy Relationships in South Asia, Department of Geography, University of Leeds, UK.

Olson, Mancur Jr. (1965), *The Logic of Collective Action: Public Goods and the Theory of Groups*, Harvard University Press, Cambridge.

Ostiani, L. and Patrizio Warren (1995), "Initial Methodological Lessons Learned in Participatory Watershed Management", in Watershed Management in Tropical and Upper Himalayas, www.fao.org/DOCREP/.

Ostrom, Vincent, D. Feeny and H. Picht (eds.) (1993), *Rethinking Institutional Analysis and Development: Issues, Alternatives and Choices*, ICS Press, Institute for Contemporary Studies, San Francisco, California.

Ostrom, Elinor (1990), *Governing the Commons: The Evolution of Institutions for Collective Action*, Cambridge University Press, New York.

——, (1992), *Crafting Institutions for Self-Governing Irrigation Systems*, ICS Press, San Francisco, California.

——, R. Gardner and J. Walker (1994), *Rules, Games and Common-Pool Resources*, The University of Michigan Press.

Pagare, G. and V. Pagare (1994), "A Village Like Ralegan", *Economic Times*, 6 June (The World Report on the Environment).

Pasha, S.A. (2004), Conceptions of Poverty and the Contributions of Property Rights and Collective Action to Poverty Reduction (Overview of Concepts), (1st Session), E-conference organised by

CAPRi on Poverty, Property Rights and Collective Action (CAPRi-talk).

PDI (2001), "Assessment of Watershed Development in Gujarat, Policy and Development Initiatives", Ahmedabad, October.

Pimbert, M. and J. Pretty (1997), "Diversity and Sustainability in Community-Based Conservation", paper presented at the UNESCO–IIPA Regional Workshop on Community Based Conservation, New Delhi, February.

Pingali, P.L. and M. Rosegrant (2001), "Intensive Food Systems in Asia: Can the Degradation Problems be Resolved?" in D.R. Lee and C.B. Barrett (eds.), *Tradeoffs or Synergies? Agricultural Intensification, Economic Development and the Environment*, CABI Publishing.

Platteau, Jean-Philippe (1992), "Formalization and Privatization of Land Rights in Sub-Saharan Africa: A Critique of Current Orthodoxies and Structural Adjustment Programmes", DEP. No. 34, Development Economics Research Programme, Suntory-Toyota International Centre for Economics and Related Disciplines, London School of Economics, London.

——, (1996), "The Evolutionary Theory of Land Rights as Applied to Sub-Saharan Africa: A Critical Assessment", *Development and Change*, Vol. 27, No. 1, January.

——, (2004), "Monitoring Elite Capture in Community Driven Development", *Development and Change*, Vol. 35, No. 2, April.

Poteete, A. and E. Ostrom, (2004), "Heterogeneity, Group Size and Collective Action: The Role of Institutions in Forest Management", *Development and Change*, 35(3), 435–61.

Putnam, Robert (1993), *Making Democracy Work: Civic Traditions in Modern Italy*, Princeton University Press, Princeton, NJ.

Rao, C.H.H. (2000), "Watershed Development in India: Recent Experience and Emerging Issues", *Economic and Political Weekly*, Vol. 35, No. 45, November 4, 3943–47.

Rao, Parthasarathy and P.S. Birthal (2002), "Strategic Assessments and Development Pathways for Agriculture in Semi-arid Tropics", Policy Brief No. 1, Crop, Livestock Systems in India: Research and Policy Issues, ICRISAT, Patancheru.

Ravallion, Martin (2001), "The Mystery of the Vanishing Benefits: An Introduction to Impact Evaluation", *The World Bank Review*, 15(1): 115–40.

Ray, Sunil and M. Bijarniya (2006), "Upstream verses Down Stream: Groundwater Management and Rain Water Harvesting", *Economic and Political Weekly*, Vol. 41, No. 23, June 10.

Reddy, G. Krishna (2002), "New Populism and Liberalisation: Regime Shift under Chandrababu Naidu in AP", *Economic and Political Weekly*, Vol. 37, 2nd March.

Reddy, V. Ratna (1990), "Irrigation in Colonial India: A Study of Madras Presidency during 1860–1900", *Economic and Political Weekly*, Vol. 25, Nos. 18 and 19, May 5–12.

——, (1995), "Environment and Sustainable Agricultural Development: Conflicts and Contradictions", *Economic and Political Weekly*, Vol. 30, No. 12, March 25 (Review of Agriculture).

——, (1995a), "Quenching the Thirst: Means and Costs in Fragile Environments", Working Paper, Institute of Development Studies, Jaipur.

——, (1996), "A Study of Willingness and Ability to Pay for Water", Project Report, Institute of Development Studies, Jaipur.

——, (1998), "Managing the Commons in Transitory Economies: Towards a Theory of Collective Action", paper presented at the International Conference of the European Society of Ecological Economics, Geneva, March 4-7.

——, (1999), "User Valuation of Renewable Natural Resources: User Perspective", *Economic and Political Weekly*, Vol. 34, No. 23, June 5.

——, (2000), "Watershed Development for Sustainable Agricultural: Need for an Institutional Approach", *Economic and Political Weekly*, 35(38): 3435–44.

——, (2001), "Reviving the Traditional Systems for Sustainable Rural Livelihoods: A Study of Tank Renovation Programme in Rayalaseema", Project Report, Centre for Economic and Social Studies, Hyderabad.

——, (2002), "Water Security and Management: Lessons from South Africa", *Economic and Political Weekly*, Vol. 37(28): 2827–81.

——, (2004), "Managing Water Resources in India: A Synoptic Review", *Journal of Social and Economic Development*, Vol. 6, No. 2, July–December.

——, (2006), "Water Pricing Policy: Economics and Politics", unpublished paper, Centre for Economic and Social Studies, Hyderabad.

—— and B.C. Barah (1991), "Ground Water Markets in Rayalaseema: A Note", ODI/IIMI Irrigation Management Network Paper, No. 5, Overseas Development Institute, London, October.

—— and P. Prudhvikar Reddy (2002), "Water Institutions: Is Formalisation the Answer?, A Study of Water User Associations in Andhra Pradesh" (jointly), *Indian Journal of Agricultural Economics*, Vol. 57, No. 3, July–September.

—— and P. Prudhvikar Reddy, (2005), "How Participatory is Participatory Irrigation Management: A Study of Water User Associations in Andhra Pradesh", *Economic and Political Weekly*, Vol. XL, No. 53, December 31.

—— and R.S. Deshpande (2006), "Sustainable Watershed Management: The GO-NGO Dichotomy", paper presented in Honour of Prof. A. Vaidyanathan, Institute for Social and Economic Change, Bangalore, April.

——, et al. (1997), "User Valuation of Renewable Natural Resources: A Study of Arid Zone", Project Report, Institute of Development Studies, Jaipur.

——, et al. (2001), "Watershed Development and Livelihood Security: An Assessment of Linkages and Impact in Andhra Pradesh", Project Report, Centre for Economic and Social Studies, Hyderabad.

——, M. Gopinath Reddy, S. Galab, John Soussan and Oliver Springate-Briganski (2004), "Participatory Watershed Development in India: Can it Sustain Rural Livelihoods?" *Development and Change*, Vol. 35, No. 2, April, 297–326.

, U. Hemantha Kumar and D. Mohan Rao (2005), "Watershed Management for Sustainable Agriculture: Need for an Institutional Approach", Mimeo, CESS, Hyderabad.

—— and Robert Jenkins (2003), "Development Politics or Politics of Development: A Case of Watershed Development in Andhra Pradesh", Unpublished Paper, Centre for Economic and Social Studies, Hyderabad.

Rennie, J.K. and N. Singh (1996), *Participatory Research for Sustainable Livelihoods*, International Institute for Sustainable Development, Winnipeg.

Runge, C. Ford (1981), "Common Property Externalities: Isolation, Assurance and Resource Degradation in a Traditional Grazing Context", *American Journal of Agricultural Economics*, Vol. 63, No. 4, November.

Runge, C. Ford (1986), "Common Property and Collective Action in

Economic Development", *World Development*, Vol. 15, No. 5, May.

Ruttan, V.W. and Y. Hayami (1984), "Towards a Theory of Induced Institutional Innovation", *Journal of Development Studies*, Vol. 20, No. 4, July.

Sarin, R. and J.G. Ryan (1983), "Economic Assessment of Improved Watershed Based Technology Options in On-farm Experiments", Economics Programme, Progress Report No. 46, ICRISAT, Patancheru.

Sastry, V.N. V.K. (2000), "Enabling Environment for Participatory Development in Andhra Pradesh", in SPWD proceedings of the Workshop on Role of Panchayat Raj Institutions in Natural Resources Management, Society for Promotion of Wastelands Development, New Delhi.

Scoones, I. (1998), "Sustainable Rural Livelihoods: A Framework for Analysis", IDS Working Paper 72, Institute of Development Studies, University of Sussex, U.K.

Seabright, P. (1996), "Accountability and Decentralisation in Government: An Incomplete Contract Model", *European Economic Review*, Vol. 40.

Sen, A.K. (1982), *Choice, Welfare and Measurement*, Basil Blackwell, Oxford.

——, (1995), "Rationality and Social Choice", *The American Economic Review*, Vol. 85, No. 1, March.

Sethi, R. and E. Somanathan (1996), "The Evolution of Social Norms in Common Property Resource Use", *American Economic Review*, 86(4): 766–788.

Shah, Amita (1998), "Watershed Development Programmes in India: Emerging Issues for Environment Perspectives", *Economic and Political Weekly*, 32(26), A66-79.

——, (2000), "Watershed Programmes: A Long Way to Go", *Economic and Political Weekly*, August-September 2.

Shankland, A. (2000), "Analysing Policy for Sustainable Livelihoods", IDS Research Report 49, Institute of Development Studies, Sussex, UK, p. 42.

Sharma, J. (1997), "Joint Forest Management: Some Fundamentals Reviewed", *The Indian Forester*, Vol. 123, No. 6, June.

Shiferaw, B., V. Ratna Reddy, S.P. Wani and G.D.N. Rao (2004),

"Watershed Management and Farmer Conservation Investments in the Semi-Arid Tropics of India: Analysis of Determinants of Resource Use Decisions and Land Productivity Benefits", Socio-economics and Policy Working Paper Series No. 16, International Crops Research Institute for the Semi-Arid Tropics (ICRISAT), Patancheru.

——, (2005), "Irrigation Investments, Shifting Cropping Patterns and Groundwater Depletion in Indian Semi-Arid Villages: The Effects of Alternative Water Pricing Regimes", Unpublished Paper, ICRISAT-Nairobi, Kenya.

——, and Nageswara Rao (2003), "Watershed Management and Farmer Conservation Investments in the Semi-Arid Tropics of India: Analysis of Determinants of Resource Use Decisions and Land Productivity Benefits", ICRISAT, Hyderabad

Singh, Katar (1991), "Determinants of People's Participation in Watershed Development and Management: An Exploratory Case Study", *Indian Journal of Agricultural Economics*, Vol. 46, No. 3, July-September, 278-86.

——, (1994), *Managing Common Pool Resources: Principles and Case Studies*, Oxford University Press, New Delhi.

Sitaram, Sasikala (2002), "Interface of Panchayati Raj Institutions and Community Based Organisations in Andhra Pradesh", Rural Poverty Reduction Project, Report submitted to Society for Elimination of Rural Poverty, Hyderabad, April.

Sivanna, N. and M. Gopinath Reddy (2005), "Panchayats and Watershed Development: An Assessment of Institutional Capacity", Project Report, Institute for Social and Economic Change, Bangalore.

Sjaastad, Espen and Daniel Bromley (1997), "Indigenous Land Rights in Sub-Saharan Africa: Appropriation, Security and Investment Demand", *World Development*, Vol. 25, No. 4, April.

Soussan, J. (2000), "Linking the Local to the Global: Can Sustainable Development Work in Practice?" in A. Granger and M. Purvis (eds.), *Sustainable Development: Geographical Perspectives*, Earthscan, London.

Soussan, J. and Arriens W. Lincklaen (2003), "Poverty and Water Security", *Asian Development Bank*, Manila

Sousson, J., P. Blaikie, O. Springate-Baginşki and M. Chadwick (2000),

"Understanding Livelihood Processes and Dynamics: Livelihood-Policy Relationships in South Asia", Working Paper 7, School of Geography, Leeds.

Stiglitz, Joseph E. (1986), "The New Development Economics", *World Development*, Vol. 14, No. 2, February.

——, (1989), "Rational Peasants, Efficient Institutions and a Theory of Rural Organisation: Methodological Remarks for Development Economics", in Pranab Bardhan (ed.).

Tang, Shui Yan (1992), *Institutions and Collective Action: Self-Governance in Irrigation*, ICS Press, Institute for Contemporary Studies, San Francisco, California.

Thilo, Hatzius (1994), "Reconsidering Agrarian Reform and Agricultural Production Co-operatives in Northern Coastal Peru: A Neo-institutional Perspective", *Quarterly Journal of International Agriculture*, Vol. 33, No. 1.

——, (1996), "Sustainability and Institutions: Catchwords or New Agenda for Ecologically Sound Development", Working Paper 48, Institute of Development Studies, University of Sussex, Brighton.

Toye, John (1995), "The New Institutional Economics and its Implications for Development Theory", in John Harriss, J. Hunter and C.M. Lewis (eds.).

Turton, C. (2000), "Enhancing Livelihoods through Participatory Watershed Development in India", Working Paper 131, Overseas Development Institute, London.

UNDP (2003), Human Development Report 2003, UNDP, New York.

Uphoff, Norman (1986), *Local Institutional Development: An Analytical Source Book with Cases*, Kumarian Press, Connecticut.

——, (1995), "Grassroots Organizations and NGOs in Rural Development: Opportunities with Diminishing States and Expanding Markets", in De Janvry et al. (eds.).

Vaidyanathan, A. (1991), "Integrated Watershed Development: Some Major Issues", Founders Day Lecture, Society for Promotion of Wasteland Development, New Delhi.

——, (1999), *Water Resource Management: Institutions and Irrigation Development in India*, Oxford University Press, New Delhi.

——, (2006), "Restructuring Watershed Development Programmes",

Economic and Political Weekly, Vol. 41, Nos. 27 and 28, July 8–15.

Varughese, G. and Ostrom, E. (2001), "The Contested Role of Heterogeneity in Collective Action: Some Evidence from Community Forestry in Nepal", *World Development*, 29(5), 747–765.

Wade, R. (1987), "The Management of Common Property Resources: Collective Action as an Alternative to Privatisation or State Regulation", *Cambridge Journal of Economics*, Vol. 11, 95–106.

Wade, Robert (1988), *Village Republics: Economic Conditions of Collective Action in South India*, Cambridge University Press, Cambridge.

Williamson, Oliver E. (1985), *The Economic Institutions of Capitalism*, The Free Press, New York.

Wolz, Alex (1995), "The Transformation of Institutions and Organisations in Agriculture Production in Slovakia", *Diskussion Schriften*, No. 45, Forschungsstelle für Internationale Agrar-und Wirtschaftsentwicklung e, V. Heidelberg.

World Bank (2006), Managing Watershed Externalities in India, Agriculture and Rural Development Sector Unit, South Asia Region, Discussion Paper Series, Report No. 1, April.

Index